Mary Polom
488 Dipping Hole
Wilbraham MA 01
413/596-3

D1596753

The Unfamiliar Abode

Islamic Law in the United States and Britain

KATHLEEN M. MOORE

2010

OXFORD
UNIVERSITY PRESS

Oxford University Press, Inc., publishes works that further
Oxford University's objective of excellence
in research, scholarship, and education.

Oxford   New York
Auckland   Cape Town   Dar es Salaam   Hong Kong   Karachi
Kuala Lumpur   Madrid   Melbourne   Mexico City   Nairobi
New Delhi   Shanghai   Taipei   Toronto

With offices in
Argentina   Austria   Brazil   Chile   Czech Republic   France   Greece
Guatemala   Hungary   Italy   Japan   Poland   Portugal   Singapore
South Korea   Switzerland   Thailand   Turkey   Ukraine   Vietnam

Copyright © 2010 by Oxford University Press, Inc.

Published by Oxford University Press, Inc.
198 Madison Avenue, New York, New York 10016

www.oup.com

Oxford is a registered trademark of Oxford University Press.

All rights reserved. No part of this publication may be reproduced,
stored in a retrieval system, or transmitted, in any form or by any means,
electronic, mechanical, photocopying, recording, or otherwise,
without the prior permission of Oxford University Press.

Library of Congress Cataloging-in-Publication Data
Moore, Kathleen M., 1959–
The unfamiliar abode: Islamic law in the United States and Britain / Kathleen M. Moore.
    p.   cm.
Includes bibliographical references and index.
ISBN 978-0-19-538781-0
1. Islamic law—United States. 2. Islamic law—Great Britain. 3. Muslims—United States.
4. Muslims—Great Britain. I. Title.
KBP69.U6M66 2009
340.5′90973—dc22   2009012883

9   8   7   6   5   4   3   2   1

Printed in the United States of America
on acid-free paper

To my son, Desmond

Acknowledgments

Two grants helped launch this study on Muslim communities in Britain and the United States. During 1997–98, the National Endowment for the Humanities, and in 2000, the University of Connecticut Chancellor's Fellowship supported my fieldwork in Britain. While writing this book on and off over the past 10 years, I have benefited from countless conversations with many individuals. I am indebted to Yvonne Y. Haddad, my mentor and longtime friend, who has provided insights, feedback, and encouragement in her inimitable style—direct, penetrating, and wise. I am grateful to Jane I. Smith, John L. Esposito, Christine L. Harrington, Susan Hirsch, Bill Maurer, and Eve Darian-Smith, for the ongoing conversations we've had on topics I've tried to touch on in this book. Each of the scholars just named exemplify what it means to be a valued colleague. And I can never express enough gratitude to the students who have helped along the way—Nadia Nader, Elliott Bazzano, Jazmin Puignau, Jenna Gray-Hildenbrand, Erik Love, Victoria Foreman Snow, and several others whom I, regrettably, have omitted. Thanks also go to the many people who graciously allowed me to interview them and learn something about their lived reality as Muslims in unfamiliar abodes. I must also mention my thanks for the enthusiastic support from Cynthia Read, senior editor of religion at Oxford University Press, and for the anonymous reviewers whose advice vastly improved the final version.

Fieldwork relies on networks of people, but writing is a solitary task. I am thankful for all the mothering angels who have shown up in the form of my loving friends to sustain me in the process of writing, most especially Teddie Foreman, Paul Foreman, Lucia Morales, Jerry Morales, Jean John, and again, Eve Darian-Smith. I thank them for inspiring me with their own capacity to work hard and to care.

I dedicate this book to my perfect son, Desmond, who is the best gift I have ever received, bar none. I thank him for his patience.

Contents

The Unfamiliar Abode

Introduction

*An Islamic Diasporic Framework in Britain and
the United States*

After the events of 9/11, the technologies for security in the midst of civil
uncertainties became abundant not only in the United States but around
the world. Terror reframed old debates about immigration, civil rights,
limits on state surveillance, the need to protect minorities from hate
crimes, and the due process rights of those detained by state security
forces in light of supposedly *new* security needs. All these debates were
propagated in (at times hyperbolic) discourses of nationalism that
extended various representations of "risk" beyond the boundaries of the
liberal state, to circulate in transnational media. In these circulations,
both America and Britain stood as signifiers of many diverse meanings,
not the least of which were of sites of multiculturalism, along with the
many global ties and interactions that a multicultural society involves.
However, the signification of multicultural can be volatile. The effort to
build a successful national consensus within the United States and
Britain in favor of a securitized state has relied on the capacity to morph
the ideal of multiculturalism as a source of strength that enriches us
(e.g., a "community of communities") into its opposite, namely, the fear
of local minorities linking across borders into a global majority.

The presence of Muslims in Europe and North America and the
discourse on citizenship in the context of globalization have become
more visible in the 21st century around the events of 9/11, with its "fractal
ripples"[1] well beyond Ground Zero. The everyday lives of Muslim
Americans and Muslim Britons have been affected considerably by the
heightened attention paid to them. Sharing some of the normative

ways in which nearly *all* ethnic and religious minorities with transnational ties have come to be constructed in the United States and Britain, Muslims are also living under exceptional circumstances. Many scholars have noted that for the past few decades, Muslim communities in the West have grappled with the problem of context and relevancy, having a sense of identity and linkage to the *ummah* or worldwide Muslim community that can be used to evoke new possibilities. The particular site for this struggle (the West) and the time period (the present) render the challenges facing Muslims today in some unique ways and yet, only a new phase in the systemic racialization of Islam. Muslims as political actors in the United States and Britain have become more visible in recent decades. Nevertheless, the social processes and problems encountered by Muslim groups and individuals have even deeper roots.

This book is about the emergence of an Islamic diasporic legality among British and American Muslim communities. Its chapters were developed, intermittently, between 1998 and 2008. Thus, the main arguments have gestated in the shadows of the bomb blasts—in the capitals of the United States and Europe, to be sure, but also in the bombing campaigns in Afghanistan and Iraq,[2] which rocked the American and British nations and have constructed the polarities of a politics of culture. I begin by exploring the recent calls by some individuals to reopen the process of (Islamic) legal interpretation for the purpose of adjusting it to the specificities of place, time, and the new realities presented by globalization and the resettlement of Muslims in non-Muslim societies. These calls reflect a concern over the maintenance of the religious authority and legitimacy of Islamic law in the lives of Muslims who permanently live in places once thought to be marginal to the core of the Muslim world. I describe what I call a diasporic jurisprudence within which interpretive communities seek to expand the possibilities for transnational knowledge production.

In a general sense, this book seeks to explain how the diaspora becomes the social problematic through which we see the interaction of people and the law. Law is implicated in the diaspora in the manner in which it works to heighten and nuance dichotomous categories. Law becomes the site where constructions of binary options take shape, where the clash-of-civilizations thesis finds material support, and where complex histories of internal dissent and alternative legal forms are sidelined. For example, in rights discourses, we find imagined categories of western women as emancipated bearers of liberal ideals such as equality, and of Muslim women as subjugated victims of cultural and religious practices. Law's considerable impact on cultural reproduction is nowhere more evident than in the discourse we find in diasporic communities of cultural specificity and difference. By juxtaposing the context-specific production of a diasporic legal consciousness in Anglo-American settings, I intend to provide insights into culturally inscribed understandings of law. The fundamental social construction we call *the law* becomes richer for our ability to see it in new contexts and from different angles. Awareness not only of the pluralism of law (in the different normative frameworks provided by Islam and western liberal legalism), but also of the particular sites of two nation states, provides a provocative comparison of the ways in which legal and popular discourses have represented "Muslim" and is particularly important in light of the "Enlightenment urge" to erase difference and privatize religion.[3] How various Muslims in the United States and Britain have had to learn to narrate themselves into the nation—negotiating a pragmatic political incorporation—can give new insights into our understanding of how both Britain and the United States (as social imaginaries) have sometimes been imbued with the ideal of cultural homogeneity, however much this contradicts reality. To put it another way, under exceptional circumstances in which the majority can feel possessive (and often defensive) about national identity, the inclusion of minorities in the nation requires disarming a coercive "othering" tendency. In this respect, how do Muslim subjects develop in relation to modern regulative institutions and within realms of social life that seem unrelated to state power?

Some Theoretical Considerations

In these pages three main theoretical issues are addressed in some depth. The first, about an emerging legality, highlights the connection between law and identity, as it analyzes the social relations at the heart of the political and legal debates in and around Muslim communities in the United States and Britain. Here my interest lies in understanding the exceptional circumstances under which Muslims develop lexical strategies to "normalize" their presence in Britain and the United States, not in terms of the dominant institutions of society, but internally, in a consciously "Islamic" idiom.[4] The second issue is that of the dialogic process of appropriating certain discourses, and it entails the examination of significant moments in the construction of normative claims *through* law. Only particular kinds of subjects, gendered and racialized in specific ways, have access to and can appropriate dominant concepts linked with fluid notions like citizens' rights or a sense of "Americanness" or "Britishness." I draw insights about the dialogic, contested dimensions of social life and the constitutive role of law to study how Muslims construct for themselves a general public space by means of normative claims. Constitutive theory about law shows us that legal conventions contribute to the cultural materials that facilitate our capacities as meaning-making subjects. It also shows us that when we look at adjudicated incidents and complaints involving Muslims, we can see how profoundly formative the power of law is as a constitutive element.[5]

And in a reciprocal sense, the third topic I address is about a growing repertoire of tools used to *resist* assimilation into a secular-liberal discourse of rights.
The cultural concept of "the West" can be seen as a significant part of this repertoire, wherein "the West" has been, at least in part, portrayed as the locus of age-old
prejudices against Islam and tendentious discourses about the underdeveloped
conditions of Muslims, the place where no other religion is held to account when
one of its followers commits violence.[6] In other words, I elaborate on the discourses
that produce not only a "Muslim" spiritual space but also "America" and "Britain,"
because "a particular kind of nation-state comes into being, as does a particular
kind of national subject," when we speak in dichotomous terms.[7] I want to bring
together the discourses of engagement not solely between "the East" and "the
West"—between institutions of the (secular, western, liberal) state and Muslim
subjects—but also *within* particular communities that do not necessarily have territorial boundaries. The dividing lines between a series of binary tropes—for
instance, "the East" and "the West," "modern" and "premodern," "fundamentalist"
and "moderate"—are not only context-specific, but are constantly shifting and
charged with political value judgments. This book illustrates how popular and legal
discourses *take* meaning from these shifting dualisms, in order to *make* meaning
using particular categories and events. It provides a detailed exploration of the
sometimes subtle ways through which the law is invoked, not invoked, ignored, and
resisted.

A few general observations are in order when we ask about the nature of a
diasporic legality and how law, context, and identity converge. The first point is to
start with an explanation of what I earlier called a consciously "Islamic" idiom, by
which I designate the lexical strategies used to normalize Muslims living in the
West. Briefly, this implies a discursive approach aimed at navigating the comprehensive world of officialdom (the bureaucratic security state) on one front while on
another front, focused on maintaining the *bona fides* to speak to, and on behalf of,
fellow Muslims, avoiding in the meantime the trap of being stereotyped as divisive
or extremist. To be sure, the normalizing effect of an Islamic idiom operated *prior*
to the crises through which a distinct Muslim public identity became increasingly
salient (e.g., the Rushdie affair and terrorist attacks on American and European
civilians) to dispel accounts of cultural incompatibility and counter the forces of
social isolation. But it has been more intensely policed since the late 1990s. The
idiom to which I refer consists of material signs—minarets, *hijabs* (women's head
scarves), burqas (outer garments worn by some Islamic women over usual clothing), beards—as well as of concepts and principles represented in public speeches,
popular culture, scripture, and legal opinions. Examples of uses of a consciously
Islamic idiom then would range from the assertion of a right to dress in a "religiously prescribed" way (discussed in chapter 5), to the use of scriptural references

to call for community cohesion (elaborated in chapter 2), and to debates about the Islamicity of law evoked by the shari'a debate in Britain (chapter 4). This trend is also demonstrated in the various meetings of religious leaders in the West to address the questions faced by Muslims in secular society. The pronunciation of this idiom requires the speaker to choose vocabulary very carefully, to engage in practices of dissent from established norms and from immanent strategies of racialization that are based on centuries of white Christian domination, without losing standing as a credible interlocutor. This effort is problematical, as the idiom has been formed and channeled through the constraints placed upon Muslim participation in the public sphere. Moreover, it is an idiom that is potentially provocative, as it seeks to transform living space into a different cultural idiom.[8]

To understand the framework for this consciously Islamic idiom, it is useful to consider a distinction that is often made between *shari'a* (Islamic law) and *fiqh* (jurisprudence). The former is widely considered a set of first principles, extracted from revelation, from which the rules for human relations are established. The latter is seen as a human invention, the product of the application of reason to discern God's will in circumstances not explicitly addressed with indisputable clarity in the two Islamic textual sources, the Qur'an and the Sunnah (the actions and practices of the Prophet Muhammad, which serve as a normative model). Both serve as a basis for guidance on how to live as a Muslim. The former, being derived from the word of God, should remain immutable, but the latter is subject to change to fit varying circumstances. However, in actual fact, as Abdullahi An-Na'im points out, shari'a and jurisprudence are both the products of human attempts to grasp the sacred sources in a particular historical context. *Any* understanding of shari'a is the product of human reasoning, and whether a specific proposition is said to be shari'a or fiqh, it is open to the same ideological bias or influence by its proponents' economic interests or social concerns. To illustrate, An-Na'im offers this: The "protection of religion" is an objective of shari'a, but this neither makes sense nor has any practical utility without first having a clear definition of *religion*, which is contingent on a given context. Does religion include the "nontheistic traditions" of Buddhism and atheism? Can a Muslim profess another religion or belief?[9]

Awareness of this distinction, which exists in the discursive domain, then, begs the question, what is utterable in an Islamic idiom? The answer to this question is important in determining precisely where the boundaries around an Islamic field of reference lie. While many acknowledge the existence of contending interpretations and a diversity of readings of the Qur'an "that can be attributed principally to the greater or lesser role the human intellect is allowed to play,"[10] the fear also exists that the West will denature Islamic principles through its unyielding demand for the privatization of faith, to the point that they remain Islamic in name only. Tariq Ramadan, somewhat optimistically, argues that Muslims have the means to enter debates about governance and citizenship "on an equal footing" with the western interlocutors, fully prepared for the "confrontation of ideas and ideals."[11] There is, he argues, a "veritable silent revolution" of Muslim youth and intelligentsia actively looking for ways to bring into accord their faith and their participation in their secularized societies. In time, this revolution will exert considerable influence over a global Islam.[12]

Yet, in the closing decade of the 20th century, several media spectacles drew diasporic Muslims into public engagement with the civic political processes, on antagonistic terms not of their choosing. Treated as inferior by "an oppositional hegemonic bloc [that] includes intellectual elites as well as 'real' violent racists,"[13] Muslims were denied the discursive or structural legitimacy to test the limits of the liberal commitment to equal treatment under the law embodied in universal citizenship. To understand how this works, it is necessary to keep in mind that, for instance, Britain has a compensatory set of multicultural policies that simultaneously recognizes difference and preserves social distance. Because of the official view that racism can affect only conventionally conceived racial minorities, Muslims *as Muslims* have been denied race protection under British law. This supports the view that Muslims voluntarily choose their religious identity, and thus cannot properly be considered a racial minority. Yet the idea that only biological determinants (i.e., skin color) make race an involuntary category ignores the manner in which Muslims can be subject to practices of cultural racism in the dominant law and society in Britain and the United States.[14] Cultural racism operates on the presumptions that cultural demarcations (manifested as outward appearances, such as religious practices, attire, and accent) are immutable and inherent, and are understood as a sign of inferiority. Thus, the Muslim citizen can be racially "othered" in the course of self-identification and public claims making. Being at this disadvantage, Muslims are often compelled to act as virtuous citizens, reproducing the dominant ways of being citizens rather than contesting the racial and orientalist foundations of citizenship in Britain and the United States.[15] As I will show in chapter 5, where I discuss shari'a councils, to be a "good" Muslim, a moderate and virtuous citizen of the modern secular state, entails the embodiment of a particular set of civic virtues, and this expectation has a disciplinary effect on a consciously (and differentiated) Islamic idiom.

The second point to take into account relates to the geopolitical realities of contemporary diaspora (and to the title of this book). Muslims in the United States and Britain have had to engage contingently with core elements of Islamic jurisprudence to make a home in these two contexts. Within an Islamic frame of reference, is there a justification for Muslim settlement in non-Muslim polities? The comprehensive doctrines of Islam are set out in traditional genres of theology and jurisprudence, which provide the underpinnings for a terminology of universalism and a discipline ("the path that leads to the spring") that unites the individual's quest for virtue with the social goods of justice and solidarity.[16] From the perspective of traditional Islamic doctrine, then, can one seek for virtue and the common good (*al-maslaha*) without living in the Muslim world? To put it another way, are there prohibitions on submitting to the authority of non-Muslim sovereigns? Or is there a basis for affirming citizenship in a non-Muslim pluralistic liberal democracy?[17]

In the first centuries of Islam, distinctions between so-called Islamic regions and countries and those of non-Islamic territory formed fundamental spatial categories for social and political relations. In the general conception of the world, *dar al-harb*, the "abode of war," was a category held separate from *dar al-Islam*, the "abode of peace" (alternatively understood as the "domain of Islam," or the place in which the ruling authority is Islamic). For the *ulama* (the religious and legal scholars), this opposition defined a clear binary vision of the geopolitical reality of their time.[18] Numerous definitions of these two spatial categories, as well as commandments and prohibitions for Muslims living within them, were formulated in the fiqh of the four principal Sunni schools of law. Disagreements that emerged in terms of the criteria required to define each abode gave rise to refinements and exceptions, producing even more categories of "abodes" and a number of interpretations of how Muslims should conduct themselves within those "worlds." For instance, one might live in *dar al-ahd*, the "abode of treaty," or in *dar al-amn*, the "abode of security," in which believers are safe and have the opportunity spaces that allow a Muslim identity to flourish. Nevertheless, apart from the definitional problems and regardless of how refined the content of these concepts, the binary format essential to the old geographical representation is based on concepts that are no longer relevant or adequate to explain contemporary circumstances. To continue to think in this way allows people to avoid questions about the processes of othering and the vicissitudes of today's world, in which populations are in constant movement and in which global formations of finance and politics are shifting. Several voices have called for new appellations within an Islamic frame of reference that would encompass the current situation. For instance, as Tariq Ramadan puts it, western Muslims' "paths to faithfulness" must be based "on a double dialectical approach, encompassing both the contextualized study of the texts and the study of the context in light of the texts."[19] Beginning from this approach, I consider the double function that legal consciousness in the western "abode" plays, insofar as it is an element in constructing a Muslim living space. From the elaboration of a way of thinking that is justified through scriptural references to the marking of Muslims as suspect citizens, I will offer several examples of how Muslim women and men are living in what I provisionally call the "unfamiliar abode." I argue that this abode is experienced as unfamiliar ground first because of the lack of any fixed meaning to the liberal abstractions of universal citizenship. In other words, the logic of the dominant system in the United States and Britain lies in its appearance of being open, rational, and pluralistic, yet these attributes may in fact prove illusory when Muslims find themselves to be marginalized and, as Sherene Razack puts it, "evicted from the universal."[20] To say the least, the treatment of Muslims in law and society is unpredictable on the grounds that the particular manifestation of cultural difference in question is a threat to the nation. I also argue that the term *unfamiliar abode* reflects a paradox of globalization—namely, that it causes familiar points of reference to fade away as it stirs "passionate affirmations of identity" in a creative vehicular language and place. In this way, the unfamiliar abode to which I allude offers novel, perhaps even surprising, consequences for the development of a Muslim living space in these two liberal secular democracies. I explore this concept further at the end of this book.

Jurisprudence as Mediation

To arrive at a better understanding of what this assertion of law's relevance may have to do with how Muslims live in contemporary United States and Britain, I propose to follow several steps. First, the interpretive strategies offered by cultural studies dovetail in this project with comparative studies in law and society and in Islamic legal studies. Literary and discursive analyses provide tools to help our understanding of how the uncertainty spawned by assimilation and globalization can produce new forms of thinking about the legitimacy of law and what it means to be cultural mediators between worlds mutually constructed as totalizing entities. I begin with an overview of the exceptional circumstances that Muslims in the United States and Britain now face, locating this project within the particular time, place, and politics that have marked certain affiliative practices as a security risk for the common weal. As I explore the significant relationship between religion and place, and the importance of public space for the construction of law, I remain primarily interested in the subjectivities that grew out of particular kinds of "assemblages," which include loosely strung abstractions of Islam, secular neoliberalism with its valorization of the (somewhat deceptive) concept of choice, and the diaspora—all of them produced by the regimes of security and global economic exchange that characterized the turn of the 21st century. I argue that, as we have witnessed the debunking of the myth of homogeneity and monoculturalism, we have also seen a more or less widespread recognition of Islamic legal norms as important, and, for better or worse, a connected effort to understand and respond to the social facts about the people who look to these norms for guidance. The new millennium has brought with it new forms of surveillance as well as an intensified effort to curtail immigration from South Asia, the Middle East, and Africa. Census and other official categories have continued to delimit boundaries around indigenous Muslims, immigrants, and their offspring. Efforts to count the number of Muslim residents in the United States and Britain continue, even despite the conceptual difficulties raised by what constitutes a community and "who counts" as a Muslim. This problem leads to discussions about what qualities or characteristics individuals must have in order to qualify as "Muslims."

As many politicians, commentators, and myriad others would have it, these regulatory measures were necessitated by the terrors of 9/11 and 7/7.[21] The desire to reduce, monitor, and police risk from external threats is often justified by a number of security concerns. Yet this book demonstrates that this desire is not an entirely *new* reality; rather, it is the continuity of disciplinary and governmental practices that have a long history in relation to ideas of difference and, specifically, of the Islamic Other in the West. In the public imagination, all other variants of belonging through which many migrant subjects historically were viewed—ethnicity, tribalism, race, national origins, and so forth—have been pushed off the table as (already always) not being as salient as religion. So what results is a rearticulated Muslim subject, a racial formation of all Muslims (regardless of class, gender, and ethnicity/ race variations) as likely terrorists, fanatical and dangerous, made barbaric by their allegiance to a religion that is constructed as different as possible from the civilized, cosmopolitan "westerner" and the secular American and British nations. Following the work of scholars such as Inderpal Grewal, I describe this as an archetypal "other," even if from an old history, recuperating in new ways an old category of the Oriental to reproduce the notion of a people without history.[22]

The current processes of globalization implicate new forms of identity and connection as well as disjuncture.[23] The discursive practices of formulating a diasporic jurisprudence confront the threat of erasure encountered in globalization, particularly in migration. The impetus to synthesize universal principles and adapt them to changing social and cultural environments posits a knowledge base that is both deeply classical and radically new, with multiple points of reference. The meaning of the term *diasporic jurisprudence* is fully developed in the book but by way of introduction, I will provide a brief description here. In my view, the marriage of *diasporic* and *jurisprudence* juxtaposes two words that are almost at odds with one another, practically constituting a social field that is somewhat normative and that creates an amorphous pattern of human mobility against which the geographical and territorial certainties of nation-states are becoming less determinate. Chapter 2 demonstrates that the postmodern sense of *diaspora* is fluid and open-ended, deploying aesthetic representations of identity fabricated from a mélange of cultural practices and molded by (sometimes resisting, at other times acquiescing to) specific relations of power. In contrast the word *jurisprudence* denotes stability, fixity of tradition, and a closed system of meaning, closely tied to a classical written text. What holds these two oppositional words together generates a productive tension. In their reciprocity they exemplify the self-consciousness of migration and settlement, of *adding on*, rather than substituting, sites of production of normative claims. With the *diaspora* as the decisive modifier, *jurisprudence* suggests ways in which legal symbols and practices can be appropriated and contested in the processes of transnational relocation.

In this book, I offer an argument about the nature of diasporic legality, which highlights the connection between law and context. This connection in turn reflects the tension between the religious duties and obligations of Muslims living outside Muslim "majoritarian" states and the responsibilities and prerogatives of liberal democratic citizenship in their new societies of settlement. Here I want to note briefly that when I refer to jurisprudence and legality, I flag two legal concepts that require definition. As I have alluded to already, by *jurisprudence* I mean the positivist reference to a written canon of interpretive decisions, which also refers to the body of knowledge of positivist legal rulings. This use of the term *jurisprudence* is different from my use of the term *legality*, which denotes a concern with the legitimacy of law and is ultimately rooted in the individual's belief in and acceptance of the legal order. Legal consciousness—the way that people conceive of the "normal" way of doing things, or the habitual patterns of talk and action—has become an important topic in sociolegal research because it represents the intersection of law as an institutional force and the individual as knowing agent.[24] How do we account for the complexity of the relationship between systems of legal meaning and decisions that individuals and social groups make about their lives? How do certain norms and public images become internalized? As others have shown, "legality is an emergent feature of social relations rather than an external apparatus acting upon social life."[25] How this intersubjective emergence of a diasporic legality affects individuals' choices and perceptions is at the heart of this project and informs the shape and substance of a self-consciously "Islamic" idiom. As will be explicated in the pages of this book, the creation of such a legality represents an effort to reinscribe a particular sense of community and to shelter it from life in so-called post-faith societies prone to bouts of secular fundamentalism.[26] At the same time, calls to reconsider Islamic juridical concepts of *fiqh al-aqalliyyat* ("minorityness" or jurisprudence of minority) have been influenced by resources, including legal discourses accessible through dominant media channels, and are creative responses to the challenges of the present in ways that produce a particular kind of knowledge.[27]

It is now widely argued that a significant proportion of Muslims in Britain and the United States are neither particularly "observant" nor concerned with the interpretation of primary Islamic sources in western contexts. In this study, I try to avoid the reductionist tendencies to treat communities as bounded and discrete, and to overdetermine the behaviors of Muslim subjects. Cultural forms and practices within Islam vary widely, and of course, some people who come from predominantly Muslim countries, or whose ancestors do, may not wish to affiliate themselves with *any* faith tradition at all.[28] However, this disclaimer aside, the argument that unfolds in this book posits that efforts to create an Islamic *diasporic* jurisprudence are in some measure reactions to the perceived threat of an encroaching secularization these nonobservant Muslims seem to exemplify. Referred to as "casualties" of Westernization, these nonobservant Muslims are the very symbol of the faithless (and effacing) secular society against which many Muslim activists and intellectuals struggle in order to define the terms of their existence in a non-Muslim world.[29] What I am calling an Islamic *diasporic* jurisprudence is an area that concerns key issues raised by Muslim settlement in non-Muslim societies, the creation of which represents an effort to preserve a particular sense of community and to protect offspring from secularizing pressures. On many occasions, the practice of fiqh has been promoted as providing a means for sacred expression that is at once personal and communal, making Islam relevant to unique contexts. In some locations, it has been lauded as "a lively and dynamic system of strategies and tools that can address and be applied to differing contexts and situations Muslims experience within the non-Muslim world."[30] In the negotiation of individual and collective identification, the confluence of cultural information derived from myriad variables (sexual, ideological, economic, generational, ethnic/racial, as well as legal and religious, etc.), provides the "hyphenated" subject fluid new forms of transnational governmentality. Diasporic subjects can move from one subjective position to another, sometimes affiliating with the collectivity but also keeping outside it at times, coexisting with contradictory and diverse subject formations. A distinctive set of beliefs about social and legal norms emerges, as the product of the legal instruments at hand and the evolution of cultural information that is instantiated in some Muslims and makes them the people they are.[31]

Of course, legal pluralism is not new in Islamic history. Historically, as Islamic civilizations expanded, Muslims carried their own legal systems into places of new settlement and, with them, their own law-enforcing institutions and practices.[32] Sectarian differences, accretions of local customary laws, and western colonialism have also shaped the variegated character of Islam, as it has adapted to its environments, producing localized, culturally specific manifestations of Islam on every continent. As the more theoretical aspects of Islamic law grew, embodied in the corpus of works on legal methodology and jurisprudence, the authority of legal opinions formulated in diverse social and historical settings made its mark on the abstractions about Muslims' duties and obligations. The individual interpretations of the *mufti* (the opinion giver), situated to handle the more mundane, everyday problems of daily life, also had a significant impact on the development of legal theory.[33] The work of the mufti gave a more practical aspect to the diverse body of Islamic law and continually adjusted law to changing circumstances while stimulating the development of Islamic law from below, "in response to the specific needs of particular Muslim communities."[34] The weight of the historical record demonstrates that environments change juridical concepts and legal forms. By the same token, the legal claims—and claimants—brought to them also affect environments. This process calls for an increased understanding of the context and the role of the individual interpreter in altering the dominant rationale of law.

Yet to date, little attention has been given to the specific relations of law—religious and civil—in shaping British and American Muslims' experiences and identities in the contemporary era, when global migration to an unprecedented degree has juxtaposed people from different cultural and religious backgrounds and traditions.[35] Broadly speaking, the point of this book is to begin to fill this gap in the literature, to examine the intersubjective framework that provides a normative structure through which we can see people and law existing in relation to each other. While stressing that neither Muslim identities nor the production of authoritative knowledge are monolithic, because significant distinctions and disagreements exist among Muslim communities, I attempt to redress an imbalance in the literature by making visible the context-specific production of diasporic legal cultures within British and American Muslim communities. I argue that where, to some degree, Muslims have experienced discrimination and exclusion at the hands of the dominant society, identification with an imagined global community (the Muslim *ummah*) has become stronger. Yet cultural forms and practices are still locally expressed, even while being connected to global systems of meaning. Or as Sally Engle Merry puts it, "they are constructed and transformed over historical time through the activities of individuals as well as through larger social processes."[36] Thus, I take into account the social and cultural forces that produce movement politics and action at the level of the group, when these groups are tied globally through a range of organizations and media that further suggest that the dispersion of Muslims should be seen as a diaspora.[37] Although Britain and the United States are not completely similar demographically and juridically, I juxtapose situations in these countries because they can provide insights into how a locally situated legal consciousness takes shape within global movements of people.

Who "Counts"?

How many Muslims live in the United States and Britain? The answer to that question is not as easy as it might seem at first glance when talking about the United States, primarily because the U.S. census does not collect information on religious affiliation. However, several different sources have estimated the size of the U.S. Muslim population. While estimates range widely because of differences in methodologies and of disagreement about who "counts" as a Muslim, the often-cited consensus among scholars has been that there are about 6 million Muslims in the United States, and the community is growing rapidly.[38] Nevertheless, since 2001 other studies, by government agencies and research institutions, have ratcheted down that figure. The 2001 American Religious Identification Survey (ARIS), conducted on behalf of the U.S. Census Bureau, reported 1.1 million Muslims in the United States.[39] Another study, conducted by the director of the General Social Survey at the National Opinion Research Center at University of Chicago, put the figure between 1.9 million and 2.8 million.[40] In 2006 the Pew Forum on Religion and Public Life conducted a survey of Muslim Americans, basing its polling on an estimate of 1.4 million Muslims in the United States (or about 0.6% of the total population). In sum, academic information widely used by mass media prior to 9/11 reported that Muslims constituted roughly 3 percent of the total U.S. population, but since 9/11, survey-based estimates derived from government statistics provided by the Census Bureau and Immigration and Naturalization Service (now named the Immigration and Customs Enforcement, or ICE), have deflated the estimated size to be no greater than 1 percent of the population in the United States.[41] One of the intractable research issues is that census taking sets up artificial boundaries, and while the social processes of Muslim community building might realistically be discussed without precise numbers, any attempt to count the population requires some agreement on what constitutes membership in the group. It may be that family background is thought to be most relevant in the case of determining who is Muslim, but if that is the case, then religion is viewed as having an ascriptive characteristic. Or, it could be that outward appearances and behaviors become measures of faith. At any rate, census taking is a crucial way the state and civil society exercise authority by imposing (falsely) stable categories. The methodologies used by the census bureau and independent researchers require critical examination.

Statistics are collected differently on the other side of the Atlantic. Britain has been gathering data on religious identification since 2001, when the U.K. census reported a population of 1.6 million Muslims, or approximately 2.7 percent of its total population. In fact, it was the response to the clamor of Muslim protests over the Rushdie novel *The Satanic Verses* that led to the eventual creation of a Muslim umbrella organization to promote unity on Muslim affairs in the United Kingdom. Established in 1997, the Muslim Council of Britain (MCB) is composed of over 400 local, regional, and national organizations, with the purpose of representing British Muslims in various public bodies. The MCB lobbied for the inclusion of the Religion Question in the 2001 Census of the Population, leading to a more precise estimation of the demography of the British Muslim population.

Why write a book on a population of such small size? The answer is multifaceted. First, there has been a great deal of interest in Muslims' experiences in the United States and Britain as a racialized category, particularly in light of the hegemonic turn to align the term *Muslim* with the ominous global enemy, Terror. An argument in this book is that minorities do not come pre-formed. Rather, they are produced under specific circumstances and are perennially "weak claimants" to the nation's entitlements.[42] Moreover, as transnational subjects with ties to a global community of co-religionists, Muslims' connectivities are portrayed as a security risk for the state. And above all, a renewed sense of Islamic identity, in conjunction with heightened concerns about national security, have at the same time made the Islamic Other more visible *and* constructed new "Americans" and "Britons" as those who stand in solidarity with victims of religious bloodshed domestically (e.g., 9/11, 7/7) or overseas (e.g., on the battlefront in Afghanistan and Iraq). Thus, an Islamic diasporic legality is contingent upon each of these factors and more.

British Muslims

Muslims in Britain are evolving infrastructures and approaches that synthesize or introduce a variety of influences from within and outside the Muslim world.[43] Observers have noted that the rapid development of Muslim organizations in Europe in general has largely been motivated by the new and growing need to rear children in a non-Muslim society.[44] The desire to ensure the reproduction of religious traditions, regardless of the degree to which these traditions have been transformed through migration, and the will to direct the trajectory of Islamic values and practices among the younger generations have motivated the mobilization of Muslim groups in Europe. The agendas of Muslim organizations have included the construction of new mosques, the creation of Islamic institutions, the freedom to exercise religious practices, and the granting of official recognition and political representation for Muslims as Muslims. These projects have increasingly displayed an assertiveness about placing demands for entitlements, for integrating Islamophobia into the policy discourse on racial equality to counteract the coupling of Islam and Muslims with violence and terrorism in the public imagination, and for specific legal protections against religious discrimination. It has been, as Tariq Modood notes, "a politics of catching up with racial equality and feminist achievements."[45]

Another primary area of concern for Muslim organizations has been the field of public law. Legal institutions are often called on to resolve disputes between people with widely varying interests and cultural logics. This situation has raised specific sets of concerns for Muslims: To what degree does the legal system of the

non-Muslim polity accommodate/allow for practices and arrangements constituted by Islamic legal provisions? What level of accommodation would be reasonable between "the law of the land" and the "supplemental jurisprudence" offered by
shari'a? Can Muslims in diaspora residing in Britain hope to reform shari'a by
democratizing *ijtihad* (independent interpretation of Islamic law) without interference or discrimination from the British public and the state? I hope to demonstrate
that the emergence of calls for an Islamic diasporic jurisprudence is a political
project that navigates the terrain between two seemingly disparate and, some would
argue, incommensurate world traditions: Islam and western secularism. The disjuncture between these two traditions, between images of the Islamic radical and
the western celebration of secular "neutrality" vis-à-vis religion, is discursively constructed through law (both Islamic and western varieties) and is made to appear to
be impossible to resolve. My argument requires a fair amount of deconstruction of
the presumed "essences" of both Islam and western secularism, a stripping away of
the claims to authenticity that depend on crude axiomatic oppositions between
"us" and "not us." A reductive set of binary oppositions about the two categories—
Islam and western secularism—mentioned above reflects a kind of cultural determinism that finds receptive audiences for the most part because it confirms the
expectations of its readers. To wit, the argument goes, the habits, ideas, and customs
fundamental to the invention of each tradition determined the social, political, and
economic forms and were the source of their unique strengths and weaknesses. Of
course one of the crucial blind spots of this argument is the totalizing presumption
of homogeneity, without cognizance of the relation between the self and the Other
in the mode of thinking that made it possible even to conceive of the "collective" as
a distinctive entity. It would be outside the scope of this book to go into all of the
exclusions through which European thought has silenced the role of non-European
actors in its narrative of self-becoming, in its historical self-understanding, which
has depended very much on the dialectic of Europe and its colonized others.[46]
However, what we *can* observe in the growth of Muslim organizations and mobilization in western societies are voices emerging from the interstices between these
totalizing conceptions, in relative proximity to the prevailing norms of both the
western and Islamic "hegemonic" modes of understanding, to narrate themselves
into the state and the nation.

The communities of Muslims in Britain form a highly differentiated and heterogeneous population.[47] About three-quarters of the roughly 1.6 million Muslims
in Britain are South Asians, largely the result of postwar commonwealth immigration from India, Pakistan, Bangladesh, and East Africa.[48] Many came from rural
backgrounds with little formal education, lured in the 1950s and 1960s by prospects
of employment or displaced by processes of decolonization. Many settled in the
geographic and industrial center of Britain, in manufacturing and textiles cities,

such as Bradford and Birmingham. Other recent arrivals have since contributed to the diversity of the population, adding Arabs, Afghanis, Somalis, Bosnians, and other Eastern European immigrants to Britain's Muslim communities. During the 1970s the number of Muslim organizations began to grow steadily, including mosques, Qur'anic schools, local and national associations designed for fund raising, liaising with the government's "multiculturalism" industry, and lobbying for religious accommodation in public spheres.[49] However, Muslims really only gained the attention of the encompassing society in Britain in the 1980s, when they weighed in on questions of religious practice by requesting the provision of halal foods in public institutions (e.g., prisons, schools, hospitals). They also participated in public debates on the reform of religious education in the national curricula of primary and secondary education and demanded state-subsidized schools. By the close of the 1980s, a broad spectrum of Muslims were mobilized to protest Salman Rushdie's novel *The Satanic Verses*. The heated debates generated by the Rushdie affair about the historic Islamic prohibitions against apostasy and the extreme punishments that it entailed called attention to the religious dimension of South Asians' lived experience in Britain. Racism negatively affected many Muslims of "Asian" origin (e.g., Pakistanis, Bangladeshis) not only along color lines, but also in terms of the scruples of their culture, which were increasingly perceived in British society and the law as having an ascriptive characteristic as immutable as skin color.

Given the variety of Muslims in Britain along lines of national origins, local customs, linguistic divisions, sectarian affiliations, and migration histories, it is impossible to generalize solely on the basis of religion. Rather, as Fred Halliday notes in his study of Yemeni Muslims in Britain, what is sorely needed is a better understanding of how religion interacts with other sociological variables under diasporic conditions—race/ethnicity, culture, gender, and politics.[50] By studying contemporary Muslim communities in Britain, a "political sociology" of settlement may emerge to help us understand and assess the constitutive effects of law on debates regarding politics, religion, ethics, and community among Muslims in diaspora. One determining feature is the British common/statutory law that shapes the trajectories of antiracism debates and praxis such that Muslim Britons increasingly seek inclusion under the umbrella of protections and rights afforded universally to citizen subjects. Another is the fact that for some Muslims in Britain, Islamic law is superior to western law because of its divine origins and because of its connection to a world community (the ummah) united by a common belief system that stands out as an alternative to western values.

Antidiscrimination legislation such as race relations and human rights laws have offered protections against discrimination on the basis of gender, race, and ethnicity in Britain. However, there are significant limits to the law. For instance, an important ruling of the British House of Lords in 1983, *Mandla v. Dowell-Lee*, held that Sikhs were legally protected against discrimination under the 1976 Race Relations Act, and were thus recognized as an "ethnic group." The judgment allowed a Sikh boy to carry religious symbols in school. The House of Lords argued that Sikhs are not racially distinguishable from other Asians but added seven criteria to broaden the definition of "ethnic minority," including a common religion (according to which Sikhs were defined as an ethnic group). Under the 1976 Race Relations Act, Jews, Sikhs, Gypsies, Rastafarians, and others were categorized as ethnic minorities, but so far, Muslims, Hindus, and Afro-Caribbeans have been excluded.[51] A 1988 case, *Nyazi v. Rymans Ltd.*, specifically excluded Muslims from this legal protection. The case concerned an employer's refusal to allow an employee time off to celebrate the Islamic holiday Ed il Fitr. The House of Lords ruled that Muslims do *not* constitute an ethnic group because their regional and linguistic origins are much more diverse than Sikhs and Jews. Muslims, who were denied protection under race relations laws, became embittered by the consequences of this ruling. Some complained that the law did not protect them from antireligious sentiment when, in a subsequent case, the courts found that an employer had discriminated "only indirectly" when he refused to employ Muslims because he considered them "extremist." According to the law, the employer had indirectly discriminated against Asians, a protected category based on ethnicity, because a large percentage of Muslims in Britain are of Asian origin.[52]

In January 1998 an Industrial Tribunal in Luton, Britain, held that a 23-year-old Bangladeshi Muslim woman had been discriminated against on the basis of her sex and race in violation of Britain's race relations and equal opportunities laws. The tribunal ruled that her employer, Isuzu Bedfordshire Company (IBC), had tolerated a culture of antireligious and racist comments on the shop floor at IBC, and had fired the complainant because she wore the hijab at work once she returned from her pilgrimage to Mecca. Although the tribunal acknowledged that the allegations against the employer were of religious discrimination, it held that the act of wearing the hijab, although *understood* as a religious act, was related to the Muslim woman's "race" and sex. The tribunal ruled that the case was analogous to the *Mandla v. Dowell-Lee* (1983) case because Bangladeshis, like Sikhs, are "a nation whose nationhood and religion are one and the same thing." Hence, in this tribunal's interpretation of the law, religion becomes not a matter of choice but rather an ascriptive and defining characteristic identified with "race," which is understood as nationality (Bangladeshi). This interpretation implies a cultural determinism that sees factors of religion, race, and nationality as being more important in determining who the individual is than the power of thought, agency, socialization, or political and economic conditions.

Not all Muslims necessarily saw this ruling as a step forward. The tribunal's ruling extended legal protections only for some Muslims, specifically for those from

Pakistan or Bangladesh, because the populations of those nation-states are under-stood as homogeneously "Muslim" and because in Pakistan and Bangladesh the national constitutions define religion as an important component of national iden-tity. However, according to this ruling, Muslims of other nationalities are not pro-tected under British law. Sarah Joseph, a "white" English convert to Islam and founding editor of *Emel*, a British magazine that celebrates Muslim life, pointed out what she saw as the inherent irony of this ruling. Because the law protects only a narrow class of Muslim subjects, she protested in an editorial letter in *The Muslim News* on December 25, 1998, by stating that "Islam is my religious faith: it is not my race, my nationality or my ethnicity. It transcends all that. However, because I chose to be a Muslim I have become a 'foreigner' in my own land." Until employment equality regulations included religious discrimination in 2003, it was not the right of all Muslims to expect accommodation in the workplace, or official protection from personal offenses; judicial policy was to protect only those from recently migrated ethnic groups in Britain, in which Muslims are a significant number.[53]

Recent high-profile cases regarding religious clothing in Britain illustrate what Sherene Razack calls the "eviction" of Muslims from the political community, in cases in which the Muslim woman is constructed as an individual not yet deserving full citizenship, including the right to practice her faith as she sees fit. The cases represent instances of the secular state saving Muslim women from the more con-servative elements within their patriarchal communities. *Begum v. Head Teacher and Governors of Denbigh High School*[54] concerned the wearing of the *jilbab* (long robe covering face and hands) in school. A Muslim female secondary school student attended a school that was predominantly Muslim and that had adopted the *shalwar khameez* (a long tunic and pants) as the school uniform, which had been developed in consultation with leaders at three local mosques. The student claimed the uniform did not comply with the requirements of her religion as she understood them, and the school refused to permit her to attend in the jilbab. In essence this case concerned the exclusion of a student from school because she adopted a form of veiling that was different from her school's uniform. Would the courts leave the decision whether to accommodate differences internal to Muslim communities to institutions such as schools? The student was unsuccessful in her suit against the school at the High Court but won her appeal, and the school took recourse to the House of Lords. The House of Lords reversed the decision of the U.K. Court of Appeals and ruled that the exclusion of Sabina Begum for her unwill-ingness to comply with school uniform dress code was not a violation of Article 9 of the European Convention on Human Rights. Some members of the House of Lords noted in their opinions that the school had wished to avoid clothes that were perceived by some Muslims as signifying adherence to an extremist version of Islam, and had acted to protect schoolgirls from extremist pressures. Within this conceptual framework, we can see a particular form of governmentality at work, one in which the school and the state together function to save the imperiled Muslim female by keeping (premodern) Muslim communities in line, pre-empting the threat of radical Islam in schools.[55]

Somewhat ironically, though the ruling in the *Begum* case allowed schools to prohibit the form of Islamic attire associated with extremism, similar arguments do not seem to prevail in courtroom environments. The British judicial administration has opted in favor of accommodating the attire in courtrooms. In 2007 the Judicial Studies Board's Equal Treatment Advisory in Britain issued guidelines to the courts advising that, in deference to diversity, Muslim women should be permitted to wear the face-concealing *niqab* when appearing in court, that it should never be assumed that it is inappropriate for a Muslim woman to give evidence in court wearing full veil. However, the guidelines continued, judges should determine the acceptability of the attire on a case-by-case basis, and what is paramount are "the interests of justice."[56] Judges were told that Muslim female lawyers should be allowed to cover. This follows the adjournment of a trial in Stoke-on-Trent after a lawyer from a Coventry-based law firm was dismissed for her refusal to remove her veil.[57]

Another example concerns Muslim female employees wearing the face veil. In *Azmi v. Kirlees Metropolitan Borough Council*, the employment appeal tribunal found in favor of the employer who rejected the concealing form of dress.[58] Mrs. Azmi had been employed as a bilingual support worker in a school in Dewsbury, in the West Yorkshire urban area, near the cities of Bradford and Leeds. She was hired to assist children aged 10 and 11 at Headfield Church of England (Controlled) Junior School with a predominantly Muslim enrollment (92%). The school's headmaster directed Azmi not to wear the face veil when working with children because obscuring the face and mouth would deny to the pupils the nonverbal signals required for optimum communication. (However, she was permitted to cover her face in open areas when walking around the campus, provided she was not communicating with children). Wearing the face veil in the workplace, a letter from the local educational authority stated, had an adverse impact on educational aims, but the hijab, the head scarf which left the face uncovered, was permitted and in fact was worn by other employees at this school. Azmi took medical leave due to stress and filed a grievance claiming discrimination on the basis of religious belief. On appeal, the employment appeal tribunal applied the employment equal treatment framework promulgated by the European Union Council Directive 2000/78/EC to determine whether discrimination on religious grounds had put Azmi at a disadvantage, and found that the prohibition of the face veil was justified by a legitimate state objective—optimum communication.

In contemporary Britain, questions of religious identity, belonging, and citizenship in a multicultural society continue to dominate social, political, and academic thought. Perceptions of Muslims in Britain continue to rely on the construction of the Muslim Other as disloyal to the state and in conflict with democratic principles of individual choice and equality. The veil and headscarf stand in as potent symbols of "premodern" repression and extremism. Growing concerns of homegrown terrorism make law and society uncomfortable with Islam, and the image of the imperiled Muslim woman in need of rescue from dangerous ideas has been produced through various discursive practices that can be understood in relation to the locus of power in which they are embedded.[59] In later chapters, I offer further examples of how Muslim women stand in as markers of their communities as "insufficiently modern."[60]

American Muslims

Although present continuously in the United States since the 1870s, the bulk of the American Muslim population has taken shape over the past 40 years or so. Due to the liberalization of immigration laws and the large-scale displacement of people created by the decolonization of the so-called Third World, the number of Muslim immigrants entering the United States has more than doubled since the mid-1960s. Add to that the growing number of conversions by African Americans and others, and we can see that the presence of Islam in America is diverse in terms of ethnicity, socioeconomic backgrounds, levels of education, regions of settlement, sectarian affiliations, and intergenerational differences.[61]

It was not so much the publication of Rushdie's novel *The Satanic Verses* that catalyzed, as in Britain, Muslim collective action in the United States, as it was the Oklahoma City bombing of the Murrah Federal Building in 1995. In the days and weeks following the Oklahoma City bombing, the subsequent downing of TWA flight 800 in July 1996, and ultimately, the terrorist strikes of 9/11, the number of reported incidents of discrimination and harassment against Muslims grew rapidly.[62] The Council on American Islamic Relations (CAIR) was founded in 1995 as an advocacy group with the objective of monitoring reported instances of discrimination and abuse against Muslim individuals and organizations, and of assessing opportunities for American Muslims to take remedial action (e.g., litigation, filing complaints with the Equal Employment Opportunity Commission [EEOC], press conferences, and letter-writing campaigns).[63] In the United States, Muslims were partially protected by the provisions of federal antidiscrimination law (e.g., Title VII of the 1964 Civil Rights Act) prior to 9/11, but their experiences with legal protections were uneven. Since 9/11 the stereotyping of Muslims as terrorists became especially pronounced, resulting in a reported increase in backlash violence. The FBI reported that between 2000 and 2001, anti-Muslim hate crimes increased by 1,600 percent, and during the same period, several local law enforcement agencies also reported significant increases in crime against Muslims and Muslim- or Arab-owned property. Similarly, in monitoring workplace discrimination, the EEOC documented such a high volume of complaints of backlash discrimination from individuals perceived to be Muslim, Arab, South Asian, Middle Eastern, or Sikh that the agency had to create a separate category just to handle the workload of "9/11-related" cases.[64]

An overview of Muslim American history is provided in the next chapter. What is important to mention at this point is how different understandings of the legal conventions and rights of the Anglo-American traditions (as well as their limitations) become articulated and mobilized within Muslim communities, which inevitably impinge on the development of legal consciousness. Encounters with Anglo-American common law and with conventional political avenues of mobilization have had important assimilative effects for the development of a Muslim diasporic positionality. By and large neither in the United States nor in Britain have Muslims sought consciously to change Anglo-American law or its legal institutions through their activities or to excuse themselves from their authority. Rather, many Muslim organizations have sought to secure their inclusion under religious liberty and equal treatment protections. Nevertheless, their actions have subtly changed the terrain in which these institutions are rooted. Positivist law plays a significant part in directing social practices, in consciously articulating ideologies and embedded meanings that legitimate hegemonic power relations. Legal conventions contribute to the cultural materials that facilitate our capacity as meaning-making subjects, and when we look at adjudicated incidents and complaints that involve Muslims we can see the degree to which the constitutive power of the law is profoundly formative.

A case in point is the 1998 dispute in Gainesville, Florida, where the subject of controversy was a middle school's dress code. The school administrators in question repeatedly disciplined a student, Nafis Abdullah, for violating the public school's dress code by wearing his shirt untucked. However, Abdullah's parents called district officials to explain that their son required an exemption from the code for religious reasons. His long, tunic-like shirts, which fall to the knees, are, in their words, customary Muslim clothing designed to cover the lower torso. School district officials were unmoved by their appeal even when the Abdullahs framed their complaint as a legal one. They mobilized their rights by contacting the American Civil Liberties Union (ACLU) and the Council on American Islamic Relations, to frame their complaint as legally "actionable." Commenting on the dispute, an ACLU representative said, "*Common sense* says this is a free country . . . and if a student has a good reason like his religion for dressing a certain way, you should respect that."[65]

Making this appear to be a matter of "common sense" naturalizes the logic that underlies the social order and the desired outcome. The common sense category is hegemonic in the sense that it structures our daily practices and how we interpret our lived experiences. This appeal to "common sense" supports the Adbullahs' position and dictates that the exemption from an otherwise valid dress code be allowed, yet without making specific reference to case law. The unspoken authority of judicial constructions of legal norms (e.g., defining religious liberty) has been internalized, and this mobilization of moral reasoning, strongly influenced by legal logic, is an example of situated knowledge that has constituted the Adbullahs' actions. This reasoning incorporates the justice norms of formal equality and leaves the disputants rooted in the "common sense" category of a certain kind of positivist law.

Contestation over such issues as dress codes or job discrimination against Muslim women wearing headscarves, or Newark, New Jersey, policemen wearing beards, or claims for legal protection against hate crimes or blasphemy, has a constitutive effect on the Muslim claimant.[66] Proffered legal protections from discriminatory treatment have shaped conceptions and expectations about law. When a person makes legal arguments, allows others to make them for him or her, or criticizes certain actions as unlawful, how does that person understand authority? People respond to and resist certain constructions of rights, and in doing so are simultaneously affected by and progressively transform them. Law constitutes interests, but it sometimes also works against them.

Whatever form an Islamic diasporic legality may take in Britain and the United States will reflect to some extent the logic of Anglo-American legal conventions regarding race relations and civil rights. "Rights in action" play a role in constituting persons as social actors whose identities are transformed through the mobilization of some particular rights discourse. However, the intent of this book is to shift away from an emphasis on positivist law and from the fixed categories of regulation and identity found there. Instead of looking only at the political aspirations and litigation activities of Muslim organizations and individuals, I strive to look at something more fluid, namely, at the diasporic mediation that tries to keep open the connection between law and context. The point is to examine views of legal authority and meaning in places where a variety of normative structures exist within a single polity. I pay attention to the dynamics of interlegality, or interactions between systems of symbolic and cultural meanings, in different contexts in response to questions posed by the existence of minorities. This approach entails examining varying degrees of an ambivalent desire, both to affirm separateness from the official law of the state and to transcend that separateness to join in the universalizing discourses of the law.

Organization of the Book

My focus on legal pluralism places this work at the intersection of two significant bodies of literature. The first consists of scholarly works on cultural studies, which offer a rich vein of materials that provide such analytical concepts as "disjunctive temporality" as well as theoretical insights into the processes of migration and settlement.[67] I combine this with scholarship from the second group of works, which consists of works from the law and society movement on the constitutive role of law. The purpose of this strategy is to gain some perspective on how legal consciousness is formed, or constituted, by the broad effects of ideologies that are embedded in power relations. More evocatively, the notion of legal pluralism means that knowledge producers are not entirely monopolized by the state. An increase of attention to the discourse of decentered subjectivities helps to instantiate the existence and circulation of a society of different legal systems. Insights from the intersection of these literatures help in analyzing developments in interpretations of Islamic jurisprudence in the West, where in particular young people are exhorted to engage in ijtihad. My intent is to consider the constitutive effects of legal pluralism, hegemonic constructions of the nation, and the articulation of a new legality upon the communities of interpretation and challenge.

The chapters are organized to alternate between the British and American contexts. The book is based in part on fieldwork conducted in Britain from 1996 to 1998 and in 2006 among Muslim Britons, and from 2006 to 2008 in Los Angeles, New York, and Chicago among Muslim Americans. Fieldwork involved face-to-face and telephone interviews, as well as informal conversations. In my research, I have also made substantial use of archival materials, including stories in the mass media, legal documents, and court cases.

Chapter 1 offers an overview of the exceptional circumstances that Muslims face in the United States after September 11, 2001. In the contemporary United States, can Muslims draw on religious authorities living in other, very different societies and on the normative ideas espoused by those authorities, or is it a challenge that cannot be tolerated by distinctively American dogmas of what constitutes a good society? The concept of pluralism, as fact and theory, is discussed in light of what the Muslim American experience has to tell us about the limits of tolerance. The situation of Muslims in the United States gives rise to both an internal struggle about what it means to be pluralistic and to an outward struggle to negotiate rights and liberties in a climate of fear that has intensified since 9/11. This chapter is a further elaboration of an article published in the *Annals of the American Academy of Political and Social Sciences* (2007),[68] adding to the analysis an in-depth look at how the American Dream takes shape in Islamic finance. It looks at the challenges facing Muslims in the United States, where they simultaneously seek to maintain ties with the worldwide Muslim community (ummah) and also pursue a uniquely "American" set of political and legal concerns. The chapter defines the exceptional circumstances under which the discursive construction of pluralism and Muslim American identity occur. These circumstances are characterized by the siege mentality that saturates much of the attention focused so intently on Muslims in the United States since the terrorist attacks on U.S. soil. The agency found in the slippage in the fragmented and mobile subject of "Muslim" identity is illustrated when Muslims are narrated, and narrate themselves, into the multicultural nation and state. The implications of the post-9/11 backlash for the pursuit of justice and the vicissitudes of American pluralism are discussed.

Chapter 2 provides a deconstruction of a British call for the formulation of an Islamic diasporic jurisprudence, in which juridical activity is proposed as a mirror. It begins with a review of theoretical works on diaspora and the legal sociology of jurisprudence. I explain and discuss my view of what a "diasporic jurisprudence" is, and use this concept to examine the text of a speech given by a Muslim intellectual-activist before an assembly of Muslim British college students in London in December 1995. I defer my discussion of the term *diasporic jurisprudence* until this chapter, but in a nutshell my view of it is the following. In the vein of cultural studies, I argue that "culture" is neither an autonomous nor an externally determined field, but a site of social struggle and differences. Thus, as alluded to earlier, when we bring together the analytical concepts "diaspora" and "jurisprudence," we are juxtaposing two words that reciprocally constitute a particular social field in which symbols and scruples can be appropriated and contested. Although a bit of an oil-and-water combination, these two concepts (diaspora and jurisprudence) hold as if suspended in a colloid, sustained by opportunity spaces allowing them to assert claims for rights and forms of justice. This summary does not by any means exhaust the elements that are active and resourceful in constructing a diasporic jurisprudence as an affiliative practice but suggests the ideas that I develop in detail in this chapter.

The semiotics of sacred texts, and specifically the Qur'an, as a signifier of verity is the topic of chapter 3. Here I examine the cultural logic of symbols and public service, beginning with the small but significant symbolic decision of the first American Muslim elected to Congress to substitute the Qur'an for the more commonly used Bible for his swearing-in ceremony. U.S. Representative Keith Ellison (D-Minn.) was elected to Congress in November 2006, in an election that marked a momentous event in American history. Not only was the first Muslim elected to Congress, but the first two Buddhists also were. When Ellison announced his choice of the Qur'an for his re-enactment of the oath of office, a media panic ensued in which the category of "Muslim" was inextricably tied with terrorism. Conservative talk show hosts decried this choice for its lack of Americanness, while major metropolitan newspapers published op-ed pieces that celebrated the diversity of America. The story is filled with contemporary depictions of America as a Christian nation and the "clash of civilizations." As political theorist Bill Connolly well notes, "the McCarthyism of our day, if it arrives, will connect internal state security to an extraordinary version of the Judaeo-Christian tradition."[69] Chapter 3 analyzes the narrative representations of America against the backdrop of the threat to national identity represented by Ellison's choice of the Qur'an. It then proceeds to look at the use of a sacred text in the swearing in of witnesses in courtroom trials, another controversy involving the use of the Qur'an to ensure verbal truth telling. Every system of meaning has mechanisms for interpreting the veracity of truth claims and qualifications for public trust. The reliance on a sacred text in a ceremonial oath to confirm the trustworthiness of a public servant is examined in this case, where the dominant text (the Bible) is displaced by a rival (the Qur'an). The election of a Muslim congressman for the first time perhaps unexpectedly engendered in mainstream society not more ease with an advancing diversity in America, as much as *unease* with a sense of whiteness under siege in the world at large.

Chapter 4 returns to the British context. In March 2008, Britain's Christian Research organization disseminated a study that made the following projection: By 2020, the number of Catholics attending Sunday mass will have been surpassed by the number of Muslims worshiping in mosques in Britain. This study came out in the middle of growing tensions about the place of Muslims in British society and fanned some alarmist flames about the changing face of Britain. This backlash was not far off the heels of a lecture given at the Royal Courts of Justice, in February 2008, by Dr. Rowan Williams, the archbishop of Canterbury and the head of the worldwide Anglican Communion, which also ruffled British feathers. He suggested that British Muslims be allowed to live freely under the shari'a law, signaling that there is something more than just the official British legal system alone. This speech not only highlights the significance of legal pluralism; it also raises the question of what it means to be a Muslim by conviction and free choice. This chapter discusses how some Muslim intellectuals have dealt with the question of the religious neutrality of the liberal state. It examines the question raised by official recognition of a shari'a council in Britain: To what extent should religious identity and practice be accommodated under a liberal legal framework? The chapter explores the related questions of power and representation at this significant site, where the diaspora intersects with the national spaces that it continually negotiates.

Muslim engagement with civil law and shari'a must be read within the broader context of the social and political climate, without sliding into representations of cultural essentialism and homogeneity that tend to reproduce binary oppositions. While I further examine how Britain continues to seek an inclusive dialogue on the question of shari'a with Muslim women who, many have argued, frequently rely on shari'a councils, in chapter 5 I return my attention to the American context. This chapter places Muslim women in the U.S. legal landscape and discusses tensions between women's rights and secular notions of neoliberalism. How does a state committed to egalitarian principles accommodate a religious legal system widely believed to be patriarchal and oppressive of women? Here is a good example of where the clash-of-civilizations thesis purports that the values of a secular society are at odds with Islamic beliefs (never mind the discomfiture between other religions and women's rights). Chapter 5 examines the problem of anti-Muslim discrimination as it affects women, and then considers instances of divorce and child custody in which Islamic provisions have been evaluated in U.S. courts of law. Finally, the chapter discusses the development of an Islamic feminism in relation to cultural testimony offered at trial in a California court of law. Notions of reworking the feminist subject outside of the terms of an "epistemological given" are taken up by Islamic feminists who call for a certain kind of Qur'anic hermeneutics.

The epilogue summarizes the insights gleaned from juxtaposing circumstances and discursive projects in the United States and Britain. I review how deeply rooted the images of the Muslim Other are in the unfamiliar abode, specifically in the institutionalized practices of governance. I highlight how the formulation of a new diasporic legality takes on the internal logic of Anglo-American legal conventions while at the same time resisting them. This argument has one foot planted in each debate: from a Muslim vantage point, over what kinds of space the United States and Britain are; from the dominant American and British vantage point, over the status of their own countries as the nations and pluralist societies they are or may become. The emphasis is on how a language to normalize Muslim presence in the United States and Britain shows the intersection of the processes of globalization with local practices of legal interpretation and gives us a deeper understanding of the inner struggle to be pluralists under exceptional circumstances.

1

Muslims in the United States

Pluralism under Exceptional Circumstances

Many accounts of transnational religious movements begin with a story about unprecedented mobility and communications on a global scale.[1] However, just as important are the efforts of community leaders and political actors to stake out a distinctive *local* space for expressions of religious life, where people make sense of themselves as having a collective identity.[2] Challenges facing Muslims in the United States, where some simultaneously seek to maintain ties with the worldwide *ummah* (Muslim community) while also developing a uniquely "American" religious experience, give rise to significant adaptations of rituals and convictions in a reflexive project of identity construction. While networks of goods, information, and people *regularly* span the political boundaries of nation-states, the growing salience of "Muslim" identity as public identity is the by-product of local exigencies. Variations in ideology, theology, and degree of religiosity are highly contingent on pressures toward conformity exerted on individuals, in one instance, by a central tenet of Islamism,[3] which highlights an external authority—the global Muslim *ummah*—and in another instance by the internal dynamics of the adopted homeland. These variations highlight the strain of preserving the authority of religion while also adapting to local social and political demands in a modern society that embraces pluralism (if not secularism) as a defining feature. Can Muslims in the contemporary United States make legitimate references to authorities living in other, very different societies and to the normative ideas those authorities espouse?[4] Or is this too much of a strain on the limits of liberalism?

Asking these questions helps to examine the ideological function of pluralism by defining pluralism as a specific phenomenon, by situating its value and effectiveness, and by outlining the interdependence of identity construction and difference, as illustrated by the experience of Muslims in a pluralistic society.

In the United States, Muslim leaders have sought to develop a version of Islam and Muslim identity in accordance with local norms and values, the vicissitudes of which this chapter explores. The effort to both preserve and adapt is played out on at least two levels: First, on the level of internal struggles within Muslim communities to be "pluralist"; and second, on the level of tensions between Muslims and state officials or government policies, which tend to consider pluralism to be an exclusively political concern. Here we consider the specific conditions of pluralism in the United States, as they influence Muslim Americans. For Muslims in the United States today, experiences of hostility, misperception, and exclusion from the dominant society and state are pervasive and endemic. Intolerance toward "Muslim" as a definite category during the 1980s and 1990s was somewhat random and amorphous and only became more concrete through the methods of state surveillance and social stigmatization, particularly after 9/11. With this development, some have argued that, on the basis of the sheer magnitude of its vilification in the United States, Muslim identity has undergone a "racialization" process, becoming a stigmatized racial group with an ascriptive and naturalized distinctiveness.[5] The emergence of "religion" as an ascriptive identity marker and perhaps the most salient source of identity for this particular social group is variable, and I argue here, highly contingent on the formative role played by the national context. With this in mind, I offer first a consideration of the theoretical construct of pluralism and the ideological work being done; and second, a discussion of the tensions between pluralism and Muslim identity in the United States.

What Is Pluralism?

A particular set of social processes emanates from the demand of modernity that we embrace diversity while maintaining a common life. This demand can be understood as pluralism, that is, as a normative ideology of inclusion and tolerance. According to this view, to be a pluralist means being someone who "prizes cultural diversity along several dimensions and is ready to join others in militant action, when necessary, to support pluralism against counterdrives to Unitarianism."[6] This understanding of pluralism goes beyond using the word *pluralism* as a mere descriptor of social conditions—the existence of people of diverse backgrounds living in proximity to each other—to using it prescriptively to promote a desired outcome.

Sociological theories of modernity illustrate the importance of pluralism as the defining feature of modern societies. Modernity *pluralizes*, writes Peter Berger, in the sense that individuals experience their identity through the prism of *several* parallel institutions instead of just one or two. Whereas in the premodern age, the traditional community provided only a few "plausibility structures" (e.g., family, religious texts), in the modern age, an individual can choose from multiple sources of knowledge and norms to construct an individuated identity. This turn toward the individual as arbiter of meaning was made possible by the onset of modernity. The modern subject entertains thoughts not only of what he or she wants to *do* but also what he or she wants to *be*. This ontological struggle is possible only if multiple "plausibility structures" exist to provide alternative sources of meaning. Under such conditions, a person is free to create and recreate identity, to individuate, and to rationalize, and therefore is required to reflect on what it means to be. The capacity for reflexive identity construction—a trademark of modernity—is premised on certain moral imperatives: individual freedom, human rights, and autonomy.[7]

Pluralism, according to Berger and Thomas Luckmann, is a necessary condition for modernity to even exist. By bringing competing ideologies and totalizing world views into proximity, pluralism becomes an accelerator of social change. It encourages skepticism and innovation and is thus inherently subversive of the status quo. It destabilizes the political and moral concepts upon which the traditional definition of reality is based. Berger and Luckmann assert that modern societies are fundamentally pluralistic because they have a "shared core universe, taken for granted as such, and different partial universes coexisting in a state of mutual accommodation."[8] The degree of accommodation in any given society depends on that society's ability to replace conflict between discrepant ideologies with tolerance or even cooperation. "The pluralistic situation changes not only the social position of the traditional definition of reality, but also the way in which these are held in the consciousness of individuals."[9] What was once extraordinary and untouchable becomes just another version of truth among the myriad alternatives available to the public.

Yet here we need to foreground an assumption that requires explanation. The view that nation-state and society converge (as implied by the concept of the "American" society) is powerful ideology in the United States and in U.S. scholarship, and produces a consensus on the homogeneity of the U.S. national context. Conventional social science overlaps with folk understandings of the "American" nation, by assuming that nation-states normally contain whole societies, diverse though they may be. Reflecting what Waldinger and Fitzgerald have described as the widespread legitimacy that the "container model" of society enjoys, the ideology of pluralism necessarily obscures coercive efforts to create and maintain a "nation-state society." It excludes the foreign element through control of external borders, and it distinguishes between full-fledged members and ambiguous residents of the territory via institutionalization of membership rules leading to citizenship and legal residence. Waldinger and Fitzgerald argue that this is "why the appearance of foreigners and their foreign attachments are viewed as anomalies expected to disappear."[10] The steady flow of new foreigners generates official efforts to secure the society it encloses, to bind all people to one nation-state. Also, the potentially disruptive effect of international migration provokes possessive feelings about the definition of national identity, thus mobilizing attempts in law and society to reinforce the boundaries of the national community. The collision between conceptualizations of nation-state and society as coterminous and of Americans as fundamentally pluralistic articulates an aspect that is of interest; namely, the project of de-privileging the status of universalism.

This perspective equips us with a foundation for theoretical inquiry about the relationship of pluralism to modernity. What we need to add to this is an examination of the problem of modernity, characterized as it is by secularism and its relationship to religion. Scores of scholars have theorized on the disappearance of religion with the rise of modernity. For instance, Stuart Hall, in his edited volume *Modernity: An Introduction to Modern Societies*, sets out the defining traits of modern societies, which are presumed to be predicated on the dominance of secular forms of power and authority, and on the concomitant decline of tradition and the religious world view typical of traditional societies.[11] The presupposition is that religiosity exists in inverse relation to modernity and that the absence of religion is not simply an artifact of modernization—it is its essential characteristic.

Yet, as we know, modern history has not confirmed the expectations of many 19th- and 20th-century scholars with respect to the disappearance of religion. Religion not only survived, it has prospered, to the extent that taking religious affiliation as a basis for civil legal relations is now commonplace. So much so, in fact, that, as Jon Butler points out, when President George W. Bush claimed in an interview with a Middle Eastern news agency that God spoke to him about invading Iraq, "neither supporters nor critics initially found the claim implausible, although the White House later denied its accuracy."[12] In the early 21st century, then, a religious world view is commonly presumed to exist at the center of political power.[13] Modernity has not necessitated the abandonment of religion, which is no longer a taboo subject in the public sphere but is instead a yardstick for measuring the legitimacy of candidates for elected office. And *pluralism* is a term that does more than describe a demographic reality at this momentous and breathtaking time in American history. Perhaps no idea has mattered more, even in what by most standards should have emerged as the most secular nation on earth. By opening the door to change and novelty, pluralism in America today does significant ideological work, possibly challenging the assumed permanence and fixity of secularism and modernity.

In suggesting that such categories are unstable, we need to take one step further in explaining what we mean exactly by *pluralism*—is it a strictly cultural phenomenon (e.g., language, folk ways, and customs), or a synonym for diversity (i.e., an ethnic pluralism)? Are we interested in legal pluralism, or the acknowledgement of law's plural nature, that the law of "the people" is not fully represented by the system of state law? Or as an alternative, is it instructive to look back at James Madison's essay on factions? Famously he defines factions as "a number of citizens, whether amounting to a majority or minority of the whole, who are united and actuated by some common impulse of passion, or of interest, adverse to the rights of other citizens or to the permanent and aggregate interests of the community."[14] Doesn't this amount to interest group pluralism? Also of particular note here is the conceptual use of religious pluralism as a culture. As early as 1867, the Catholic Bishop Thompson called the Pacific Coast the "theological equator"—a space where Latin and Greek orthodoxy met, "where monotheism in its various forms collided, and deism and polytheism came together."[15] In this sense, religious demography mirrors the global cosmopolitanism introduced by migratory patterns.

What Are the Exceptional Circumstances?

Where do Muslims in the United States stand in relation to the discursive construction of pluralism, understood either as a simple description of a demographic reality (myriad coexisting beliefs and ideologies) or as a normative creed (prizing cultural diversity)? Living in a pluralistic society proves to be a source of contention for Muslim Americans, who find themselves in a difficult social space after the terrorist attacks of September 11, 2001. Their experience in the United States, particularly after 9/11, shows us a form of *pluralism under exceptional circumstances*, exceptional in a couple of respects. First, the exceptionalism of the Muslim American experience with pluralism stems from the response of the government and the public at large to the problem of terrorism and national security, a response that after 9/11 has sharply tilted toward "guilt by association" and has scapegoated Muslims residing in the United States. The scapegoating began prior to 9/11, and the terrorist attacks of 2001 were merely the dramatic tipping point that justified disparate treatment of Muslims by the media, society, and the government. The question is, how have Muslims made sense of their position in American society, given the contradictory claims of pluralism as an ideology (espousing tolerance and inclusion) and given what many are calling the "9/11 backlash"? Will these developments further the political marginalization of Muslims in the United States?

Second, the Muslim encounter with pluralism in America is of an exceptional nature because as an ideology, Islam represents, like modernity, a universalistic world view. How can a world view that is considered to be totalizing and universal accommodate another world view of a similar conception? These questions raise both the clash-of-civilizations thesis and the often repeated rhetorical question, "Why do they hate us"? Recall that George W. Bush's answer to this last query was that "they" hate us for our freedoms. If this is truly the case—and here the anger and analysis underlying the question conflates terrorists with Muslims writ large—then how can modernity, with its moral imperatives of liberty and tolerance, accommodate an essentially "illiberal" (hostile to liberty) world view? On a related note, some critics of Islam use the media (talk radio, cable television, and blogs) to keep alive the perception that Muslims in the United States do not speak out frequently or forcefully enough to condemn terrorist acts and religious extremism in the Islamic world and elsewhere. How Muslims deal with this pressure will reveal through a particular lens something about the phenomenon of pluralism, and will be critical to the successful political integration of Muslim Americans.

The terrorist attacks on U.S. soil dramatically increased the visibility of Islam in the media and in private and public conversations among Americans. Up to that point, many non-Muslim Americans had little interest or knowledge of Islam, aside from occasional news about Islamic extremist attacks overseas. After 9/11, a broad new group of commentators sought to speak about Islam and Muslims, and there emerged many news, talk radio, and cable TV programs on the subject. Anti-Muslim sentiments increased in the American public at large and were reflected in these media outlets and policymaking circles. Widespread and routine stereotypes in the media and in the conversations of non-Muslims may be connected to the increase in reported workplace discrimination and verbal and physical attacks on Muslims in public places.[16]

With public scrutiny so intently focused on Muslims in America since September 11, 2001, questions about who Muslims are and the size of the Muslim population in the United States continue to defy easy answers. Researchers have disputed who counts as a Muslim, and demographers have long faced difficulties in counting religious populations of any stripe. Definitive figures are hard to come by because, ostensibly, due to the separation of church and state, the U.S. Census Bureau is prevented from collecting data on individuals' religious affiliation. (However, this concern has not prevented the federal government from collecting information in the American Religious Identification Survey [ARIS], mentioned earlier, which published the low estimate of 1.1 million Muslims in 2001.) Houses of worship and religious organizations generally base their estimates on membership lists, an approach that can yield numbers that are both under- and overinclusive. In the case of Islam, if we base estimates simply on membership lists of mosques and Islamic centers, we run the risk of overlooking individuals who identify themselves as Muslim but either attend mosque only on important religious holidays, or not at all.

If we take another approach and choose to count as Muslim those people who appear to have "Muslim-sounding" names (e.g., listed in telephone directories), then we risk including many who do not consider themselves to be Muslim adherents (who may be of another faith or of no faith at all) and ignoring those whose names may not be "Muslim-sounding."

Polling organizations and Muslim researchers and interest groups in the United States have grappled with how to come up with better ways to get at this issue. Estimates of the Muslim population at the beginning of the 21st century range from a low of about 2 million to 7 million, and the considerable discrepancy between these figures suggests that much work remains to be done to craft a reliable methodology. What should *not* be overlooked in this quandary, however, are the public perceptions associated with the growing U.S. Muslim population. For instance, are Muslims of sufficient number to influence election outcomes or important policy discussions?[17] Will the Muslim population change the face of America in significant ways? The downside of pluralism is the risk of change. Secret grand juries investigating Islamic charities for possible ties to global terrorism reflects the generalized fear that America is being Islamized.[18] The contemporary crisis, which has categorized Muslims as *the* public enemy, promises to be the birth pangs of a new era for Muslims in the United States.

Historical Background

Muslims have been in the United States for more than a century, yet they have lived largely at the margins of political history. Dispersed throughout, Muslim inhabitants concentrate on the East and West coasts and in the upper Midwest, and are one of the fastest growing minorities in the nation's largest cities. Muslims today comprise a vibrant mosaic of ethnic, sectarian, and socioeconomic diversity. Representing an array of origins, the Muslim population hales from more than 80 different countries and multiple sectarian orientations and socioeconomic backgrounds. Muslim Americans represent every philosophical, theological, and political strain in Islam. While widely perceived as a "foreign" population, less than half of Muslims today are actual newcomers to the United States—most are native-born. This means that many Muslims are second- or third-generation Americans, and it is estimated that fully one-third of the population is African American. Whether as immigrants, as part of the African American experience, or as converts from racially and culturally varied backgrounds, Muslims comprise a substantial and growing segment of American society. Muslims in the United States are a major new group and a significant part of an increasingly diverse U.S. population.

Demographics

Recorded history of Muslims in the Americas dates as early as the pre-Columbian period, with slight evidence of Muslim presence in the New World. The influx of Islam during the 18th and 19th centuries, via the slave trade across the Atlantic, has more substantial documentation as many American contemporaries of enslaved Muslims recorded their experiences. In the period following the Civil War up to the end of World War II, immigrants from a wide range of ethnic and national groups came to the United States, bringing with them not only their economic aspirations but their cultural distinctiveness. Many newcomers from the Middle East in this period were Arab Christian, and much of what was written about this community provided little detail on the fledgling Muslim minority in their midst. It was not until the 1950s and the advent of the Cold War that a Muslim presence in the United States became discernible. Beginning in the middle of the 20th century the United States opened its doors to immigrants from "third world" countries and, in unprecedented numbers, foreign students from Africa and Asia received financial support to study in American universities. Muslim peoples from around the world became the beneficiaries of this turn of events, which altered the Muslim experience in the United States. Muslims from several nations around the world have come to call the United States home in growing number since the 1960s; today, Muslim inhabitants of the United States are foreign-born at a ratio of two to one.

Although the numbers are only approximate, the consensus among researchers of Muslim American ethnic diversity holds that the largest three groups of Muslims in the United States are Arab, South Asian, and African American, followed by several smaller ethnic groups—Turks, Iranians, Bosnians, Malays, Indonesians, Africans, and so on. Including recent immigrants, their children, and "indigenous" African Americans, the Muslim population defies easy categorization. Generally, the vast majority of Muslim Americans of every generation wants to be integrated at some level, and is most successfully integrated into the American mainstream economically. Muslim Americans are by no means among the "worst off" in society in terms of the most common socioeconomic indicators, including economic activity, rates of incarceration, and levels of education attained. By all accounts they are "middle class and mostly mainstream."[19] Often employed in the professions, Muslim Americans by and large enjoy high standards of living, although a recent study indicates a downturn in Muslim wages and salaries, which, in turn, may negatively impact philanthropy. The study, conducted in 2006, covers 20 states where 85 percent of Arab and Muslim residents live, and found the earnings of Arab and Muslim men aged 21 to 54 dropped by an average of 10 percent after 9/11. The adverse earnings effects, while only temporary, were even more pronounced in areas with higher than average instances of hate crimes motivated by religious or national origins.[20]

Educational attainment of Muslim Americans is above average in the United States. Well over half have earned college or postgraduate degrees (compared to about 27% of the general population). Appreciably, the Muslim American populace is youthful and the young generation is considerably influenced by, as well as influencing, national cultural trends (e.g., music, comedy, film, television, and journalism). Moreover, Muslim youth participate actively in several Muslim organizations, including student associations, and have intensified outreach efforts to train the next generation's leaders. This demographic transformation, with American-born Muslims struggling to balance religious teachings with the secular values of mainstream America, often provokes intergenerational tensions arising from different approaches to questions of cultural accommodation, social and political integration, gender issues, and religious practices. While the immigrant generation might be more closely aligned with the homeland and familiar cultural customs and languages, the political involvement and engagement with the mainstream on the part of second- and third-generation Muslim Americans is increasing. This trend is demonstrated by the rising number of registered voters, civil servants, and candidates for public office.

Appreciably, the lure of the American Dream has played out in the various communities of Muslim Americans. As Bill Maurer notes, homeownership has been central to middle-class identity in the United States at least since the end of World War II, and what is implicit in the American Dream is the notion that citizenship and property go hand in hand. Since the payment of interest is proscribed by Islamic law, owning "a piece of the rock" has necessitated the development of an alternative mortgage product, an Islamic mortgage, which contributes to the economic and cultural citizenship of Muslim Americans.[21] Britain has also experienced a recent phenomenal growth in the Islamic financial market including Islamic, or halal, mortgages. Shari'a-compliant banking has reached a niche that has been underserved, and in the current tightening of global finance, represents itself as a viable option.

Above all what is intriguing about this is how it signals the underlying principles and performances of the 21st-century global economy, in which various and disparate practices make up neoliberal political rationalities. According to Maurer, Islamic banking and finance consciously and critically recreate the forms and formats of financial activity by writing new kinds of contracts and developing new products and transactions.[22] The commodification of Islamic law as the frame of reference guiding these financial products takes place within the development of alternative mortgages (marketed as "riba [interest]-free") and is itself a product not only of Islamic legal expertise (providing fatwas to legitimize financial arrangements), but also, significantly, of government partnerships. The government-sponsored enterprises Freddie Mac (created by the 1970 Emergency Home Finance Act) and Fannie Mae, which buy and sell conventional mortgages, gave rise to the secondary mortgage market. Early in 2001, both agencies signaled their interest in the Islamic home financing industry by purchasing Islamic mortgage alternatives. The market for shari'a-compliant financial services has expanded since the involvement of the federally sponsored agencies.[23]

These developments have meant at least two outcomes worth noting. First, in the expansion of Islamic financial services, Islamic legal tenets appear "as a volumetric substance (one can have more or less of it) and as a quality of action (one can 'do something Muslim') that is additive to the other aspects of one's existence and identity."[24] For example, one mortgage product can be more shari'a-compliant than another, making mortgage consumption a nuanced performance of Muslim subjectivity. Moreover, the approval of financial products is not the sole prerogative of Islamic jurists, who declare whether or not something is halal. Now it is also the purview of U.S. bureaucracy, which weighs whether a financial product is sound in a legal sense. Are there contracts that will reassure borrowers that they are dealing with a legitimate business? At this level we see the impact of legal positivism, since the loan is deemed halal not simply by word or reputation but also by the form in which the Islamic scholars deliver their opinions to endorse these loans. The finance companies have crafted fatwas in written forms that parallel official civil law documents, which endorse the transaction as shari'a-compliant. For instance, the Ethical Advisory Board of SHAPE Financial Corporation endorsed as "shari'a compliant" the Profit Sharing Insured Deposit product offered by that financial institution which is in compliance with federal law as well as shari'a.[25] In other words, the extent to which a Muslim seeking a mortgage loan can believe the deal is in accordance with shari'a depends not only on a religious frame of reference but also on popular understandings of how the law works. This understanding hinges on disclosure documents, deeds, forms with seals and places for signatures, and other accoutrements of a bureaucracy, which make a mortgage look valid.[26] Therefore, it is not just that property ownership confers cultural citizenship, signifying the American Dream. More important, it is in *how* property is acquired—in the securitized transaction—that we can see the profound impact of the deep frames of law on Muslim Americans' contemporary legal consciousness and on the praxis of shari'a in the United States. Since the expansion of the home finance industry, several other financial services have been added to a growing Muslim lifestyle market, such as shari'a-compliant credit cards, auto financing, personal banking, and investments.

Inderpal Grewal offers some interesting insights about how culture and neoliberalism combine in this context. Neoliberalism, she notes, consists not only of the privatization of welfare but also of the "segmentation of consumer markets producing a multiplicity of lifestyles."[27] Just one example that she provides is in relation to feminist empowerment. Once only marginal to technologies of marketization, feminism became a mainstream niche by the close of the 20th century, with consumption patterns and pleasure becoming inextricably linked to the promise of what it means to be a woman. These patterns also tied in with the affirmation of feminist subjectivity (the conversion of feminist concerns into lucrative marketing can be seen in health clubs and exercise products, book clubs and talk radio programming, self-esteem, new age movements, and magazines and other media). A feminist "lifestyle" emerged as an identifiable market niche, a by-product of the struggles waged around new social movements and a specific rights discourse of the 1970s, 1980s, and 1990s. Thus, Grewal argues persuasively that, while loosely connected through the technologies of consumer culture, market niches correspond to rights-based identity movements. Something analogous is currently happening in the formation of the Muslim lifestyle market with the recent growth of a specifically halal niche in everything from financial services to women's clothing, toys, magazines, food, music videos, and even bumper stickers ("Allah Bless America," and "Born Right the First Time: I Follow Islam"), providing modalities though which a religious affiliation/lifestyle can be imagined in the American context, in ways that promote practices of self-regulation.

Levels of Integration

Identity is always fluid, and in the case of Muslim Americans, the intersection of identity and religiosity at this moment in history yields a particular framework for understanding some common values that may facilitate political integration. The substance of Muslim identity—who "counts" as a Muslim, and what Islam stands for—is something that has to be worked out internally, in the periodicals and conversations of Muslims in the United States. However, convictions and behaviors ascribed to Muslims by others (whether accurate or not) will shape to some degree how that identity becomes relevant in the political sphere, where non-Muslims' perceptions of Muslims have an impact on Muslim American engagement and institutional capacity building. These perceptions frustrate Muslim Americans' efforts to be civically engaged.

During the 1970s and 1980s, the Muslim communities in the United States enjoyed a degree of anonymity that allowed them to concentrate on economic advancement and pursuit of the American Dream. Several largely ethnically based organizations were founded at the local and national levels during this period, representing primarily "Arab" interests, as opposed to Islamic interests *per se*. Many of these interests sought to address the negative portrayal of Arabs in the media and to counteract the media effect by giving accurate information to an American public that was seen as unduly supportive of the Israeli perspective.[28] But none of these organizations was truly representative of the Muslim population in all its diversity, either in terms of spanning the various ethnic, theological, or ideological differences or in terms of bridging the divide between immigrant and indigenous African American Muslim communities. Most organizations existed at the local level and, rather than define themselves as advocacy groups, were community oriented, focusing on providing services and building schools, mosques, and Islamic centers to meet the needs of the growing Muslim population.

However, beginning in the 1990s, these community organizations were superseded by new groups established to advocate their interests under the umbrella of a specifically Muslim identity. This shift in identity and interest-group politics, and the appearance of a new generation of activists mobilizing involvement of American Muslims *qua* Muslims, was spurred on by the Arab-Israeli wars in 1967, 1973, and 1982, and by the civil war in Lebanon, which had a profound effect on the identities and allegiances of immigrants coming to the United States from the Middle East in the 1980s. The impact of these conflicts led to the beginning of an important shift in identity. Slowly, in some segments of society, people began to replace a secular Arab nationalist identity with some form of an Islamic identity, intended to foster strength and unity in the face of the division and defeat imposed by their enemies. What developed was a modern discourse of political opposition discussing issues of social injustice and ethical life. Many U.S. immigrants arriving from the Arab world in the 1980s and 1990s were then able to relate to the world view of those immigrants from South Asia who identified themselves with the Islamist group Jamaati Islami (Islamic Group) active in Bangladesh, India, and Pakistan.[29] Today, for many second- and third-generation (American-born) youth facing vilification by the dominant society and marginalization from the immigrant community, such variant forms of Islamic identity offered a powerful means to assert a positive and distinct sense of identity.

The growth of Islamic activism and identity in the United States, then, has been to some degree the legacy of the Arab-Israeli wars of the 20th century, as newcomers sought refuge from the persecution they suffered at the hands of their governments for their affiliation with such Islamist movements as the Muslim Brotherhood and Hizb at-Tahrir. Frequently, prominent Islamist activists from overseas were invited to address participants at conventions of American Muslim organizations. Abu Al'a Mawdudi, then leader of the Jamaati Islami group of South Asia, often lectured throughout the United States, suggesting that Muslims be isolationist in order to resist the allure of a consumer culture and the social problems of America. This guidance inhibited desires to integrate by calling on Muslims to restrict their social interactions with non-Muslim individuals and institutions in American society. Reluctance to participate in the public domain can still be seen in a very small number of groups because of the condemnation of such activity as un-Islamic.

The second watershed event that incited Muslim interest group politics in the United States, and tipped identity construction toward a religious (as opposed to ethnic-group) orientation, was passage of the 1996 Antiterrorism and Effective Death Penalty Act. During the presidency of Bill Clinton, a shift in policy toward Muslim nations was discernible when Secretary of State Madeleine Albright decided that the Islamic world was composed of many rogue states. In 1995, the media frame associating terrorism generically with Islam had become so deeply embedded that it seemed only common sense to conclude that the bombing of the Murrah Federal Building in Oklahoma City had been the handiwork of Islamic terrorists. Following on the heels of the 1995 bombing, Clinton signed into law the sweeping 1996 act of Congress that held certain groups (none of which the Oklahoma City bomber, Timothy McVeigh, was associated with) to blame for the problem of terrorism and that contributed to the way in which public officials subsequently handled the "war on terror" after September 11, 2001. The antiterrorism law effectively gave congressional approval to the U.S. State Department's definition of who counts as a terrorist, by adopting the executive branch's suspicion of Arabs and Muslims as potential terrorists and by defining several Muslim countries as rogue states. Perhaps more than any other single piece of legislation, this counterterrorism law crystallized the impression that Islam and Muslims were the new enemy of the United States in the post–Cold War world. This law was the necessary precursor to the government policies after 9/11 that, in the name of national security, have selectively profiled and constrained the rights of Muslims in the United States.

Combined with the ascendancy of such media pundits as Steve Emerson[30] and Daniel Pipes,[31] who were only the most prominent of Islam's critics in the United States, the impact of such official pronouncements was monumental. Muslims soon realized that the turn toward hostility against them and their faith could be irreversible, and many began to respond. A survey of Muslim Americans in 2001 before September 11 demonstrated that more than 70 percent of mosque leaders in the United States supported the idea that Muslims should participate in the political process.[32]

Political History

A major challenge to understanding the political history of Muslim Americans is in appreciating the wide spectrum of the many communities that are considered Muslim. Demographers have approximated that Muslim residents in the United States are foreign born in a ratio of two to one. About half of those born in the United

States are African American (roughly 20% of the total U.S. Muslim population). There are differences in belief and practice between Sunnis and Shi'as—two major sectarian groupings—and also a range of variation within both affiliations. Moreover, there is a growing number of Sufis who teach mysticism and include many Euro-American converts. Large numbers of native-born Americans of African, Hispanic, and European backgrounds have converted to Islam or "reverted" (returned) to the faith. Thus the population can be generally divided between "indigenous" Muslims and the foreign born. Finally, there are the offspring born to immigrants and converts. Each of these sources accounts for a considerable share of the total U.S. Muslim population and each constitutes an important facet of the political history of Muslim Americans.

The political history of African American Muslims has been exceptional. Interrupted by slavery, African American Muslim history restarts its thread in the early 20th century, with the creation of Islamic organizations as alternatives to the racially segregated churches associated with slavery and Jim Crow. African American Islamic communities began to appear in the 1910s. The Moorish Science Temple (1913), the Universal Islamic Society (1926), and the Nation of Islam (NOI) (1930) developed from small communities of black Muslims in the midwestern and eastern United States. Many of these groups created self-help philosophies emphasizing the value of sustaining economic investment and seeking self-sufficiency. Islamic practices of prayer, modest dress, and fasting, as well as abstinence from the "slave behaviors" of eating pork and drinking alcohol, were maintained and used to propagate the idea that Islam is the true religion for black people (who were, so it was argued, by nature Muslims). These communities grew out of the pan-African movements of the turn of the 20th century. Many proclaimed an esoteric and sometimes racist theology (for instance, that white men are devils).

In spite of major doctrinal divergence from the orthodox or mainstream beliefs and practices of Islam, by the middle of the 20th century these African American Muslim communities had grown rapidly. Their popularity was based on their particularistic expression of Black Nationalism. In 1964, Malcolm X became the first prominent leader of the NOI to repudiate the separatist and racist teachings of the NOI's leader Elijah Muhammad in favor of a broader vision. It was Elijah Muhammad's son, Warith Deen Mohammed, who assumed the leadership of the NOI upon his father's death in 1975. With classical training in Arabic and Islamic sciences, Mohammed moved away from the teachings of his father to align the NOI with a mainstream Sunni understanding of Islam. Mohammed's organization changed its name to the American Society of Muslims, and is often referred to simply as the ministry of Warith Deen Mohammed. When Warith Deen Mohammed stepped down as leader of this organization, he remained active until his death in 2008 with an organization dedicated to interfaith relations called "The Ministry Cares." While

Mohammed forged closer ties with mainstream organizations and with Muslims outside the United States, Minister Louis Farrakhan split from the group in 1977 to revive the doctrines and practices of the former NOI leader Elijah Muhammad. Minister Farrakhan continues to lead a small number of members of the NOI.

The pioneering efforts made by African American Muslims to secure political and legal rights have made a significant contribution to the political history of Muslim Americans. In particular, their struggle in the prisoners' rights movement of the 1960s and 1970s secured for inmates the rights to pray, receive services of imams and Muslim newsletters, eat halal (Islamically slaughtered and prepared) foods, and wear religious insignia and clothing. These courtroom victories opened the way for other Muslims to make broader claims on American society in further arenas, such as employment discrimination, protection from hate crimes, and zoning restrictions on the construction of mosques.

African American Muslims have had other significant "firsts" in public affairs. In 1991, Imam Siraj Wahaj became the first Muslim invited to give the invocation prayer at the opening of the U.S. Congress. In 2006, U.S. Representative Keith Ellison (D-Minn.) became the first Muslim elected to U.S. Congress, and this was followed shortly thereafter by the election of the second Muslim congressman, U.S. Representative Andre Carson (D-Ind). The first Muslim American judges, male and female, are also African American. Judge Adam Shakoor has served as Detroit's first Muslim deputy mayor. The first female Muslim judge is Sheila Abdus-Salaam, a justice on the Supreme Court of New York State.

The history of immigration is also highly variegated. Federal courts in the early 1900s denied citizenship to several Muslims because of the practice of polygamy, repudiated under American law even when those aspiring toward citizenship neither practiced nor even supported plural marriage. Nativists in the same period targeted Muslims, along with Catholics and Jews, who were seen as a threat to jobs and as a source of cultural defilement. Public anxiety over cultural pollution was used to justify the early 20th-century legislation of immigration quotas that affirmed many of the societal prejudices about the supposedly innate characteristics of those from the Muslim world (wicked, autocratic, unclean, and oversexed), among other ethnic and religious minorities.

Yet for the most part, Muslims remained disengaged from the political process. With a few notable exceptions, Muslim participation in the American legal and political systems in any sustained way began really only a decade or two before the fateful 9/11 attacks. Representation of a collective voice in the policy arena was not apparent until the 1980s, when a handful of national nongovernmental organizations (NGOs) were formed. The most prominent are the American-Arab Anti-Discrimination Committee (established in 1980); the Islamic Society of North America (founded in 1982) and its affiliated organizations, including the Muslim Student Association, the

Islamic Medical Association, the American Muslim Engineers and Scientists, and the American Muslims Social Scientists; and Warith Deen Mohammed's national ministry. Two local organizations established in the 1980s became major national NGOs in the 1990s: the Muslim Public Affairs Council (MPAC), founded in southern California in 1988, and the American Muslim Alliance/American Muslim Taskforce, founded in northern California in 1989. Subsequently several national organizations were founded in Washington, D.C. (see table 1.1). These Muslim NGOs represent a variety of missions, and in general aim to produce leaders in media and politics and to articulate policy concerns regarding American domestic and foreign policy.

It would be difficult to characterize Muslim Americans as predominately conservative or liberal. While a large percentage express a preference for a larger government providing more public services, many are not consistently liberal in their views. A solid majority believe that government should do more to protect morality in society. The 9/11 terrorist attacks cast a long shadow over Muslim Americans, and many worry about government surveillance, job discrimination, and street harassment. In the 2000 presidential election, most voters identifying themselves as Muslims supported George Bush by a wide margin, yet in 2004 their preference changed to John Kerry. Anxiety and fear about personal liberty in the war on terror is a likely cause of this realignment, since many Muslims felt the brunt of profiling and discrimination at the hand of government surveillance and security agencies along several fronts after 9/11, as well as because of extralegal acts by individuals and groups. According to a nationwide survey of Muslims conducted by the Pew Research Center, a majority (53%) say that it has become more difficult to be a Muslim in the United States since the 9/11 attacks, and many also believe that the government singles out Muslims for special monitoring and surveillance. Muslim Americans have been mobilized by the backlash against terror and the all too common tendency to conflate terrorists with Muslims writ large.[33]

Still, overall Muslim Americans have positive attitudes about living in the United States and are middle class and highly educated. The Muslim population is youthful, and the young generation participates in several Muslim organizations that have intensified outreach efforts to train the next generation's leaders. The vast majority of Muslims believe that they should be engaged in American political life and civic affairs, and do not see a conflict between being a devout Muslim and living in a modern society. Besides voting in elections, political and civic engagement includes contributing time and money to voluntary associations, participating in interfaith activities, supporting political candidates, calling or writing the media or an elected official about an issue, attending a rally or convention on behalf of a cause or political candidate, or being active in a political party in some other way. Increasing participation by Muslim Americans in local school boards, city councils, interfaith alliances, and electoral politics has been evident. A nationwide survey of

TABLE 1.1. Major American Muslim Nongovernmental Organizations

Name	Date Founded
American Muslim Alliance/American Muslim Taskforce on Civil Rights and Elections	1989
Council on American Islamic Relations (CAIR)	1994
Institute for Social Policy Understanding (ISPU)	2002
Islamic Society of North America (ISNA)	1982
Muslim Alliance in North America (MANA)	2005
Muslim Public Affairs Council (MPAC)	1988
Muslim Student Association (MSA)	1963
Muslim Women Lawyers for Human Rights (KARAMAH)	1993
National Association of Muslim Lawyers (NAML)	2000
South Asian Americans Leading Together (SAALT)	2000

Muslim Americans in 2004 reported a very high rate of political participation compared to the general population. For instance, 61 percent of Muslim Americans voted in the 2000 elections, compared to slightly more than 50 percent of the general voting-age population. For the first time in 2000, both the Democrat and Republican nominating conventions opened with Muslim prayers among other rituals of the party gatherings.

Flying while Muslim

One example of the coordinated efforts of Muslim American advocacy groups stems from the current standing of Muslims as *the* public enemy. In November 2006, six imams (prayer leaders) were taken off a U.S. Airways passenger jet after other passengers observed three of the six praying in the terminal prior to boarding the aircraft. A nervous passenger passed a scribbled note to airlines personnel, bringing attention to the imams who allegedly were heard chanting "Allah, Allah . . ." and criticizing the American war effort in Iraq. This incident tells us that in the minds of many Americans, Islam remains so suspect that even simple religious observances such as sunset prayers take on sinister interpretations. On a positive note, the incident merited repeated mainstream media coverage—on several TV news programs ranging from CNN's *Paula Zahn Now* to PBS's *News Hour*. And Muslim American organizations, presenting a fairly clear case of injustice, were able to gain some degree of vindication in the press. The incident raised questions about the power of law enforcement to override civil liberties in the name of national security, and in 2009 a federal judge ruled that the six imams could sue the government for discrimination and false arrest (in the absence of probable cause).

Muslims' Internal Struggles with Pluralism

What do Muslims in the United States make of the ideological claims of inclusion and tolerance promoted by the normative usage of the term *pluralism*? How are Muslim thinkers situating Islam and Muslims in relation to the phenomenon of American pluralism? As a novel element in a pluralistic society, are Muslims poised to change the face of American society, or will pluralism demand a reformation and a "modernized" Islam? In this section, I briefly consider the attention given within Muslim circles to the idea of pluralism and the tensions underlying the relationship of pluralism and identity in contemporary Muslim America.

The new social and political circumstances that Muslims find themselves in as a minority population in the West create an urgent need to reexamine the religious and legal guidelines for living a contemporary "Islamic" lifestyle in a non-Muslim setting. A reappraisal of what is legally valid is currently being undertaken by several Muslim scholars.[34] This is a process of discerning what is essential to Islam, and hence immutable, versus what is contingent upon historical context and open to reinterpretation. When the concept of pluralism is addressed, it is often rooted in discussions about Islamic traditions and scripture. For some, pluralism entails the rethinking of applications of Islamic law to fit changing circumstances in such a way that the legitimacy and relevance of Islamic law is restored. For others, the successful intersection of pluralism (inclusion and tolerance) and Islam lies in the universalization of core ethical teachings. Husain Kasim's *Legitimizing Modernity in Islam*, for instance, contests the thesis of the "clash of civilizations" and suggests a "Muslim modus vivendi" in western modernity that would promote an Islamic ethical discourse grounded in rationality yet drawing on universal metaphysical truths.

Sulayman Nyang, professor at Howard University, provides a fairly dismal view of the status of pluralism. With the expansion of globalization comes the growing realization among Muslims that all religions, ideologies, and belief systems have to live under one roof. The days of isolation, he writes, are gone forever. What had once been taken for granted in the Islamic tradition becomes an occasion for self-consciousness and introspection; namely, the presence of the Other. Historically, coexistence with *ahl al-kitaab* (people of the Book, or in other words, Jews and Christians) was an important scriptural ideal in Muslim societies, though far from flawless in its implementation. In addition, the concept of "no compulsion in religion" also provides a basis for peaceful coexistence and tolerance in an age of unprecedented migration and communication.[35]

Yet aside from the scriptural supports for pluralistic attitudes and the inherently pluralistic nature of the religion, Nyang goes on to characterize a range of viewpoints on the phenomenon of American pluralism, based on lived experience. He divides the population into three categories: grasshoppers, who are what he calls "cultural" Muslims, who align themselves with secular humanists; oysters, who enjoy middle-class wealth but seek to isolate themselves from the secularism of American society and find that the separation of church and state impedes their personal faith; and owls, who strike a balance between grasshoppers and oysters. Grasshoppers hope to blend into the sea of faces and names that constitute America the nation of immigrants, in the process shedding anything distinctive. Oysters plan on sheltering their spiritual lives from plain view and avoid perilous encounters with the depraved. Owls, in contrast, consider themselves to be individually equipped with a moral compass sufficient to guide their encounters with cultural Muslims and nonbelievers alike. Nyang considers them to be most sensitive to the demands of pluralism and capable of engaging in dialogue.[36]

In addition, Nyang argues that the same tolerance shown internally between categories of Muslims—from grasshopper to oyster, for instance—must be extended to the Other from whom one differs fundamentally.[37] This is a call to extend one's spiritual embrace to include all humans and is the moral imperative of the 21st century. Qualifying this position, however, Nyang outlines ways in which American society limits opportunities for meaningful pluralism. He points to the excessive individualism and consumerism of American society, which strain the conditions and opportunities for public policies that are not devoid of moral or spiritual content.[38]

According to Nyang, the way in which the vicissitudes of American pluralism effect a change upon Muslims in the United States is in terms of internal pluralism that underlies the dynamics operating among categories of Muslims, elevating those he calls "owls" to the position of interlocutors. To individuate one's spiritual life, to establish a foundation in faith and scriptural vision for dialogue within Muslim constituencies, prepares one to represent Islam outwardly to the Other. Alliances with other faith communities in pursuit of political change—namely, to oppose the pernicious effects of secularism—is a new and transformative reality that can result in an idiosyncratic expression of American Islam.

Another orientation is typified by the broad-based Sufi interpretations, represented (among many others) by Qumar al-Huda of Boston College and by Feisal Abdul Rauf in New York City. In general, this orientation asserts the commonalities among various faiths at the metaphysical level, superseding the specificities of textual proscriptions associated with Islamic law. For example, Sufi Shaykh Kabir Helminski of the Mevlevi Order of Muslims has written that God has not granted a spiritual monopoly to any one religion, and that the Qur'an in fact encourages competition among people of faith to promote virtue and cooperation. Islam is uniquely situated to reconcile the various religions because it is inherently tolerant and respectful of all faiths. This type of religious pluralism prohibits the humanist rejection of the signs of God and encourages prosperity in spiritual terms within the context of American pluralism.[39]

A very important aspect of the Muslim experience with pluralism in the United States can be characterized as the pursuit of justice. Justice, of course, raises many of the concerns alluded to in the beginning of this paper regarding the civil liberties restrictions inherent in antiterrorism laws and the vilifying of Muslims by associating them with terror. It raises questions about equal treatment and due process. But the insistence that Islam itself is inherently pluralistic (open and tolerant to all believers) begs the question of relationships between men and women. The full inclusion of women has been at the forefront of Muslim American dialogue about justice concerns. Author Asra Nomani and Virginia Commonwealth University professor Amina Wadud are just two of the many vocal critics of the failure of Islam to recognize the equality of women. Wadud promotes an alternative exegesis of the Qur'an that provides the basis for a feminist theology. This exegesis supplies the crucial platform for identity development, which delineates the interdependence of the notions of "difference" and identity. She rejects both neotraditionalism, as a conservative and reactionary force that disenfranchises women, and secularism, as a pro-western force, ignorant of the important role of Islamic spirituality as a basis for women's identity. No discussion of pluralism can proceed, she argues, without empowering women's voices and recognizing that Islam is a dynamic process of engagement and creation in accord with the cosmic order.[40]

Finally, the growing Muslim youth movement is an important venue for debates about the fact and theory of pluralism. The current generation of Muslim American youth under the age of 35 interacts with non-Muslims in classrooms, playing fields, shopping malls, and the workplace. Still, most often these everyday encounters have nothing to do with matters of faith. The religious dimension of the younger generation of Muslim Americans has largely been silent. However, with the significant demographic transformation of the United States and with the marginalization of many as the reviled Other in the war on terror, a Muslim youth leadership is beginning to emerge and to promote a philosophy of deliberate and positive engagement with people of different backgrounds. The salience of a religious identity has come to the fore in the consciousness of many individuals. Religion is playing a more important role among alienated youth in inner cities, and Islam is one among the various faith communities to which young urbanites are drawn. The emerging hip-hop youth culture draws together African Americans, Latinos, and Muslims in unexpected ways. Young Muslims experience what it means to be in proximity with multiple traditions and world views, and absorb alternative norms and values to an extent never encountered by their elders. Eboo Patel, founder and director of a Chicago-based nonprofit organization called the Interfaith Youth

Core, discusses the challenges that diversity presents for today's faith communities and emphasizes that Muslims have a lot to learn from the civil rights struggles of African Americans.[41]

The new historical reality for Muslims is that they now find themselves living as minorities in an established, advanced industrial society that is non-Muslim. Muslims of all backgrounds—from a wide range of sects and theological schools of thought, as well as ethnic or national origins—are living together on a permanent basis in the crucible of American society. The relationship between pluralism and Muslim identity in the United States is an idiosyncratic one, moving in contradictory directions. One path follows the internal struggle over the meaning of pluralism, both as a religious ideal and as a social reality. The other divergent path stems from the relations between the Muslim American communities on the one hand and, on the other, government policies and public perceptions of Muslims in light of the war on terror and related events in the Muslim world. This latter path colors Muslims' perceptions of the ideological role played by pluralism—is modernity truly committed to tolerance? The exceptionalism of the Muslim American experience illustrates the desirability, and perhaps even the inevitability, of rethinking what it means to speak of pluralism in America.

2

Jurisprudence as Mirror

Some Reflections from the Muslim Diaspora

Individuals maintain cross-cutting ties on various levels, sometimes with international or nonterritorially based communities and organizations. In the postcolonial situation, what appears to be "local" is actually not, since ethnic or religious groups that may constitute a relatively isolated minority within a nation-state must be understood as part of a transnational network. While Muslims in Britain and the United States might be minorities vis-à-vis the state and society, they are also a part of a transnational ummah with a transnational set of universal laws.

This chapter examines the emergence of an Islamic diasporic jurisprudence in Britain. This is a juridical activity that seeks to destabilize the Old World as the key referent in the production of religious-legal knowledge while simultaneously trying to avoid the wholesale adoption of British legal conventions. It is about the construction of Islamic thought and a concrete consideration of the realities on the ground. What key cultural values, codes, and rules are internalized and contested in the process? To set the basis for this argument, I take account not just of the ideas reflected in this emergent jurisprudence but of their combination, particularly, culturally specific discourses that reveal patterns of adaptation and critique. I argue that the emergence of an Islamic diasporic jurisprudence is an interactive and contingent process, one that reaches its limits discursively, within the confines of an Islamic sphere of reference and debate.

In their ethnographic account of cultural dialogues in *Debating Muslims*,[1] Michael Fischer and Mehdi Abedi suggest that the simple, binary juxtapositions of East and West, past and future, nationalism and cosmopolitanism, generate new and complex hybridized spaces that turn on contested notions of authenticity and contingency.[2] Hybridized spaces themselves bracket a conceptual geography that is multiply positioned and in flux; they are at times fertile, at other times sterile, but always "hard to image, hard to project into a future that gives the present significance."[3] My interest is in exploring how the law provides powerful discourses to navigate such spaces and how these shape ideas about community and the future. Representations of identity and belonging are always provisional; how do people in diasporic spaces imagine community and envision the future, and what role does the law play in these meditations? Here I identify some of the main characteristics of the interpretive regime, or regimes, under which a legal discourse on Muslim settlement in the West is used. Seemingly remote from political and moral dimensions of social life, the interpretive regimes may in fact have enormous political and moral consequences, enhanced by the fact that they imagine the Muslim subject to be re-centered discursively, no longer being positioned marginally vis-à-vis the Muslim world and the West. In the diasporic renegotiation of identities and space, jurisprudence plays a determining role in constituting a particular sense of community and common purpose.

My analysis brings together two words that are almost at odds with each other: the modifier *diasporic* and the noun *jurisprudence*. This conjunction juxtaposes "text" and its mediation in the politics of the diaspora—an emergent transnational social space. The juxtaposition of these words generates a productive and defining tension. With the *diaspora* as modifier, these words (diasporic + jurisprudence) suggest ways and places in which symbolic interactions can be analyzed for what they generate and what they inhibit. The diasporic subject both appropriates and contests legal practices and discourses while relocating. The following section outlines the bipolar dimensions of the term *diasporic jurisprudence*: one evoking fluidity and versatility, and the other, fixity and tradition. The fundamental assumptions of each are in tension and, when juxtaposed, they produce an ambiguity that opens the possibility for various interpretations. Does the modifier *diasporic* enrich the abstraction *jurisprudence* in a creative manner, or does it point to an absence in the latter? An examination of this tension, and of the ambiguity of its meanings, shows how local politics and transnational processes interact in constructing the constitutive power of this idiom.

To elucidate this process, I focus on the specific example of Muslims in Britain and the production of an Islamic diasporic jurisprudence. I will try to show that this concept opens up avenues for understanding the creation of diasporic identities and legality in culturally specific ways, which can help us see more clearly the constitutive effect that the articulation of a "new" jurisprudence has on the community of interpretation and challenge. First, I review recent cultural studies and postcolonial literature on the diaspora and explain my understanding of what diasporic jurisprudence is. Next, I show how current trends in interpretation draw on, and reinscribe, Islamic legal conventions on minorityness. I closely examine an example of a call to create a "new" and creative Islamic jurisprudence in the diaspora. This call presents a political metaphor for the community— jurisprudence-as-mirror—and summons/invents a collective consciousness that partially deactivates the western colonialist legacy by establishing alternative practices and values.[4]

Literature on Diasporas

Before beginning with this analysis, however, some conceptual key points need to be defined. First, what is meant by the term *diasporic*? Certainly the use of the term has increased with attention given to globalization and transnationalism. By reading the pages of such journals as *Public Culture, Diaspora, Cultural Studies, Social Text, Global Networks*, and the *Journal of Ethnic and Migration Studies*, one can find accounts of the diaspora that range from postcolonial analyses of the causes and effects of massive "non-white" dispersions of decolonized subjects to cultural critiques of diasporic writings as a newly emerging literary genre or to feminist critiques of the ways gender and sexuality are deployed in diasporic social formations.[5] Indeed, just taking a feminist inquiry of diaspora for the moment, we can see that the etymological roots of the word itself underscore the idea of masculinity and that the usage of *diaspora* has disseminated and reinforced patriarchal images of kinship. In the pages of the journal *Diaspora*, Stefan Helmreich suggests that the word comes from the combination of the Greek roots meaning "dispersion" and "to sow or scatter." He argues that the word appears in its first usage in the Greek translation of the Book of Deuteronomy: "Thou shalt be removed into [a diaspora] all kingdoms of the earth" (Deut. 28:25 [King James version]).[6] Helmreich writes that the original meaning of *diaspora*, found in the Old Testament, suggests scattered seeds. In Jewish, Christian, and Islamic cosmology, he continues, seeds are "metaphorical for the male 'substance' that is traced in genealogical histories. The word 'sperm' is etymologically connected to diaspora."[7] The derivation of each term is traceable to the same Greek stem, which designates sowing or scattering; thus *diaspora*, in this literal sense, makes patriarchy legible, as it lies at the very root of kinship systems generated through male lineage.

If we take seriously the possibility that diaspora is inextricably tied to the genealogy of patrilineal order, does this necessarily mean that women's subjectivities are devalued or excluded in diasporic accounts? Or is it possible to imagine diasporas in ways for which maleness is not "essential"? Is there a differently gendered vision? Can diasporas offer women possibilities for actively reworking gender relations? As important as these questions are, I can only begin to lay the groundwork for a feminist analysis of gender in diasporic communities and forewarn that as a concept, diaspora, as any concept, continues to bear meanings derived from its past. In other words, it carries traces of its masculinist properties constructed in its prior usage. What has made this masculinist bias in the diaspora invisible is the fact that until very recently the concept has received only limited attention and has not been applied beyond its defined limits. The gendered quality of diasporic conventions and identity are just beginning to be analyzed and will open up an important avenue for our understanding of the diaspora itself.[8] Recent literature has appropriated the term, expanded its usage, studied the conditions which give rise to diasporas and their associated cultural politics, and challenged the series of simple binary oppositions that positions diasporic communities as weak reflections of the originary nation. The next section reviews some of this literature.

Decentering Diasporas

Since antiquity, the word *diaspora* has been applied first to Jewish, and later to Greek and Armenian exilic social formations.[9] It was from these three "classical" diasporas that scholars later determined the essentials of diaspora. These archetypes were precipitated by a catastrophic event that propelled a "people" into exile. According to this literature, to conform to the ideal type, a community's experience had to include several of the following features: (1) coerced departure, or the forced uprooting and resettlement of large numbers of people; (2) a protonationalism, that is, a specific kind of social relationship in which the community retains a clearly defined ethnic or minority identity already formed or acquired at home, prior to expulsion/departure; (3) a distinctive body of collective memory and/or traditions related to the community's site of origin—its location, history, and achievements—which serves as the foundational element of identity; (4) the belief that they are not, and perhaps cannot be, fully accepted by their host society, which leads members of the community to police their communal boundaries and fosters feelings of alienation and/or superiority; and (5) the continued involvement with matters in the home country (the originary site), by providing financial and intellectual resources for the support of communal institutions and struggles there, or by maintaining the myth of return.[10] This restrictive list illustrates the asymmetrical relationship between the home country and the diasporic community through which the home country is refracted. According to this model, one means of assuring the privileged position of home vis-à-vis the diaspora is found in the requirement that diasporas do *not* emerge out of the experience of transnational migration as an effect of dislocation. This requirement dictates that the exiled people have to have held an already established, separate existence as a homogeneous social and cultural formation in the country from which they emigrate.[11] This paradigm secures claims of authenticity and closure around hegemonic constructions of the shared descent of a particular folk or people (i.e., nation), and dispersed peoples are expected to situate themselves within the bounded narratives of identity and difference that emanates from the center. This hegemony precludes alternative visions and is not a fitting description of contemporary migration experiences.

More recently, the word *diaspora* has undergone substantial reworking in the semantic domain. Particularly for scholars of cultural studies, the meaning of *diaspora* has come to represent something radically different from the sum of its paradigmatic elements. Significantly, it is no longer deployed for specific and limited purposes, providing a narrow and static definition of community that reinforces the authority of the originary position held by the home country. Moreover, the mere act of dispersion no longer defines the diaspora, and the term is rather used to refer to a particular kind of constitutive activity within and among dispersed communities. Not all dispersed persons see themselves as members of a diaspora, but those who do often demonstrate strong attachments to the homeland in imaginative constructions of identity and futurity.[12] The paradox, however, is that this attachment to a home country or region, to a fixed and stable point of origin and a coherent group identity, becomes decentered by the multidirectional flows of globalization, as diasporic subjects evade the focus of (imagined) centralizing structures (e.g., the nation-state) and inhabit what is in between or interstitial.[13] In its growing complexity, diaspora contests its binary position vis-à-vis the home country and is characterized increasingly by a triadic relationship among (1) the home country whence diasporans or their forebears came, (2) the place of settlement, and (3) another locale, elsewhere in the diaspora, wherever similarly situated members of the collective group can be found.[14]

The emergence in the literature of contested notions of the diaspora—ranging from traditional definitions concerned with boundaries and roots in a geographically defined homeland to postmodern treatments based on fluidity, movement, and destabilization of homogenizing boundaries—attests to the growing salience of diasporic formulations in global society. Pnina Werbner notes how diasporas are at one and the same time "ethno-parochial" and "cosmopolitan" in their reach, being both local and global.[15] The challenge is how to articulate the diasporan subject without reproducing the essentialized notions of place and identity that the diaspora is supposed to transgress. Some suggest it might be more useful to cite diasporic stances, projects, idioms, and practices, rather than refer to *a* or *the* diaspora as a discrete unit.[16]

What differs most significantly here from the ideal type of diaspora is that the "diasporic" features of dispersed communities emerge precisely *as* an effect of dislocation, or in other words as the result of the trauma of migration and the inescapable pluralities involved in the movement between "home" and abodes of settlement. What is often argued to be the constitutive experience of diaspora in the modern world involves being "in the West but not of it."[17]

Diaspora is the contingent *process* of translation and negotiation that goes on in situations where quite loosely related populations, who once were possessed of many different subject positions and strikingly dissimilar identity markers in their home countries, now find that the dominant culture in their adopted societies regard them as one culturally cohesive or social group. The constructed sense of unity—and unification—in diaspora has its own critical and dynamic relationship to the racial structures of power in Britain. Diasporan formations are particularly adaptive *and* critical. This way of understanding diaspora as a process recognizes agency of the diasporan subject and contest in places where multiple cultural logics compete for hegemony at the same time as it underscores constraints on that agency.

Dispersed communities become "diasporic" in the gaze of the societies of settlement, for when resituating a diasporic identification, as Paul Gilroy writes, "it ain't where you're from, it's where you're at."[18] It is in the "where you're at" that an artificial "oneness" becomes, in a provisional sense, "the truth" as diasporans retell the past in the very process of being forged into one people, with stable and continuous frames of reference and meaning, despite the shifting vicissitudes underlying their actual history. The process of becoming "one people" involves an inner expropriation of cultural identity as diasporan subjects actively produce creative self-representations that offer a way of imposing an imaginary coherence on the experience of migration. This reflects some of the technique for subject-making called ethnogenesis—when minority groups foster a sense of common identity by forming panethnic coalitions to address a common political problem. Under diasporic conditions, we see strategic patterning expressed through a diasporic aesthetic and its formations in the postcolonial experience. Syncretic artistic forms combine elements from the master-codes of places of origin and settlement. A representative example of this in Britain is "bhangra" music, a popular hip-hop style of dance music played largely by Asian bands. This art form combines the traditional music of the Punjab region of Northern India with western styles of reggae and pop. Sung in Urdu (the language of Pakistan) and English, such music is performed by bands with such names as Naseeb (meaning "destiny"), Bi-Polar, Asian Dub Foundation, and Fun∧da∧mental. Popular disc jockeys adopt such stage names as "Apache Indian," reflecting the juxtaposition of East and West, of the cowboy frontier of the Wild West (in the United States) and the geographical space of the Indian subcontinent.[19] Such aesthetic renditions of past and future are elastic sites of cultural and social critique that encapsulate British South Asian identity formation. Certainly, the diasporic abode entails more than just cultural displacement and reproduction. It also entails acts of creativity and imagination, deploying symbolic resources that yield a sense of diaspora that is self-consciously constructed.

A diasporic consciousness has become the focus of analytical attention in recent years and is described variously as being marked by a dual or paradoxical nature. Steven Vertovec writes that a diasporic consciousness "is constituted negatively by experiences of discrimination and exclusion, and positively by identification with a historical heritage (e.g., 'Indian civilization') or with contemporary world or political forces (e.g., 'Islam')."[20] Competing sources of identity formation—religion, ethnicity, gender, aesthetics, class, regional location, etc.—offer momentary anchors for political attachment. For instance, we can see Muslim subjects move in and out of different interpretive communities, at one place engaged in a politics of recognition, at another in human rights discourse, at yet another in a campaign to counteract extremism, and in a fourth space passionately involved in a juridical dialogue with Islamist activists overseas. While the concept of diaspora is celebrated currently in certain postmodernist analyses because of its reworking around such concepts as fragmentation and contingency, at the same time diasporan subjects practice what sociologists Smadar Lavie and Ted Swedenburg refer to as "provisional closures . . . in order to enact agency toward dismantling the Eurocenter, or to enable identity politics beyond the reactive mode."[21] Gayatri Spivak notably calls this "strategic essentialism," a practice in which the subaltern subject reproduces identity from within hegemonic frames of knowledge, taking up some of the essentialist stereotypes of oneself as a resource for resistance, representation, and engagement. However, this kind of essentialism is not to be mistaken as permanent or natural; it is only a contingency needed to make meaning legible in the semiosis of language.

What is meant by *diaspora* has been described most concisely and compactly, perhaps, by specialist in comparative religion Roger Ballard, when he proposes that it is a condition best captured in the phrase of the Indian subcontinent, *desh pardesh*, which translates as being "at home abroad," or "home from home."[22] This condition is about simultaneously being British *and* something else, *not* a condition of perennial marginality but of acquiring a different sense of historicity within one's present location. The diasporan subject attempts to recall, comment on, and supplement earlier conditions of existence in synchronizing the identity politics of one's place of origin with that of one's place of settlement, a process that is transformative both of the subject and of her locality. The transformation reconfigures the imperatives of an earlier "elsewhere" in an active and critical relationship with the semantics of one's present home, all within the dynamic of a reciprocal displacement. Both a constructed past and an imagined future shape how one bridges the homeland and the new land.

In its current postmodern iteration, diaspora signifies spaces of displacement where signs are assembled, rehistoricized and reread. Place preoccupies, yet previous conflations of geographic space and social identity are undone. Significantly, if the nation-state is imagined as a collective body with an identifiable center and genealogy, the diaspora seeks to destabilize the idea of that center and to frame a new location for the expression of particular sets of values and sensibilities. Diasporas renegotiate the relationship between people and places disentangled from nation-states, whether "home" or "host," at times evoking and at others eliding nostalgia to fabricate a power base. Diasporas are normative as they endeavor to create patterns of belonging that contain points of temporary attachment, eliciting a counter-strategy to the techniques used by the territorially bound nation-state to secure and regulate the population.[23] Aihwa Ong theorizes this in her use of the term *flexible citizenship*, a formulation in which diasporic ideas about multiple identities are framed in relation to transnational movement.[24]

Still others emphasize the materialist dimension by analyzing the political economy of diasporas when attempting to understand the global social relations of migration.[25] In the current moment of late global capitalism, neoliberal forces have physically dispersed peoples and in effect deterritorialized the older Westphalian system of nation-states. The increasing and more pervasive penetration of capital around the globe has carried with it particular contradictions and dislocations. In contrast to the conception of nation-states as sovereign territories secured by geographic boundaries, diasporas have been conceptualized as a potent rival to the nation-state. Emblematic of optimistic cultural/material fusions, a diasporic community is, in its ideal form, "an example, for both the homeland's and hostland's nation-states, of the possibility of living, even thriving in the regimes of multiplicity which are increasingly the global condition, and a proper version of which diasporas may help to construct, given half a chance."[26] From this perspective, diaspora is a heightened awareness of the paradoxes of multiple belonging, a situation that increasingly faces *all* modern citizen-subjects in the transnational era. The experience entails a process of creating social fields that cross national boundaries and become the means of transnational existence in a world that remains filled with disjuncture and difference. New sources for normativity beyond those embedded in the home country become meaningful.

Religion in Diaspora

Recent thought on diaspora is helpful, and can be extended further in a way that moves us closer to the subject of a diasporic legality. There is a particular kind of investigation that diasporic conditions stimulate, in which emphasis shifts from

"*What* shall I believe in?" to "*How* shall I believe it?" Elizabeth McAlister demonstrates this in her account of the actively transnational religious culture of Vodou and Haitian Catholicism. According to McAlister, Haitians in New York perceive themselves as defined against Haiti as an essential location of its own, and festivals and rituals play a major role in constructing that perception.[27] Religious expression, production and performance manifest themselves in culturally specific ways and become formative as Haitian transnationals move in circular migration, back and forth between New York City and Haiti with great frequency. Certainly earlier immigrants from Europe maintained home ties and continued involvement in nationalist struggles, too, but McAlister suggests that in comparison these were only pale counterparts to the contemporary patterns of Haitian labor migration. Migrants in the Americas as a whole have been yo-yoing because of job insecurity, particularly in low-wage marginal sectors of the economy and in seasonal occupations (e.g., farm labor). As a result, we see not only the political formation of an immigrant underclass with all its social and political implications; we also learn from McAlister's study that religious sites of pilgrimage in the United States become inflected with meanings that span the home and host countries. Haitians concurrently worship and undertake pilgrimages *nan djaspora* ("in the diaspora") while continuing religious activities in Haiti where they return during periods of illness or unemployment, or on business and vacation trips. This means that religious sites in the United States—shrines, churches, and the rituals enshrouding them—are added to the Haitian religious continuum, multiplying rather than supplanting spiritual sites in the homeland. Instead of substituting U.S. locations for Haitian ones, they add the diasporic locations to the expanding "religioscape" of transnational Haitian religious culture.[28] This places originary sites of Haitian culture in complex relation to an expanding, polyvalent social organization of a moral geography that encompasses the diaspora.

This contributes a particularly useful insight about studying religion as it is lived and experienced, inflected as it is with strategies of racial alterity in diaspora. It shows that *how* Haitian migrants practice their religion in diaspora stresses their distinct identity and understandings of pilgrimage, relocation, migration, and displacement. It shows how they elaborate their social identities in the cultural politics (and temporalities) of both their countries of origin and settlement. *How* they believe holds them apart from their co-religionists who remain in Haiti, where the effects of colonization had already syncretized some of the African deities within a specific kind of Creole Catholicism. Once they are in the United States, however, Haitians respond to a different set of social relations. Their practices form a strategy through which Haitian migrants distance themselves from the African American population, calling on representations of themselves that not only elaborate their identity as something other than "black" but also further racialize social location. Discovering that the dominant society has associated them with African Americans because of their phenotype, Haitian migrants respond by contesting their "racialized" identity through cultural markers. By developing Francophile identities, stressing their French and Creole language and style of dress, and attending Roman Catholic churches, schools, and pilgrimages, Haitians consciously display their distinctive language, culture, and religion. However, this strategy, with its performative element of Catholicism, comes at a price. Part of the price is paid by the spiritual world of Vodou with its roots in African spirituality, which, although subtly intertwined within Haitian practices of Catholicism, is downplayed as Haitians try to define themselves against the racialized backdrop of U.S. society. Like many immigrants to the United States, Haitians discovered that to achieve in their new setting, they would have to differentiate themselves from "blackness" and assimilate to the ideal of "whiteness." McAlister regards this transformative act— burying the African roots of religious practice—as a conscious (re)constitution of the self vis-à-vis American racial classifications.

Nonetheless, what appears to be attenuated culturally continues to reside deeply embedded in religious practice, because rather than extract and discard the Vodou ethos, if that were even possible, Haitian migrants have become adept at religious "code-switching" in the face of pressures to repress their African-based spirituality in favor of the Catholic sacraments and spirit world of the saints. For instance, McAlister writes, in many Catholic prayer services and sacraments some of the Voudou spirits gain counterparts in the Catholic roster of saints, and the Catholic ritual language is filled with coded signs that are meaningful in the logic of Vodou. The one ritual practice is performed through the codes of the "other." This is a fine illustration that, as Stuart Hall notes, the diasporic identity is not about essences, or *what* diasporic subjects believe, but about positioning, or in other words *how* they will believe it in context, from a particular place and time. Hall mentions that a politics of representation always mediates cultural identity, "which has no absolute guarantee in an unproblematic, transcendental 'law of origin.'"[29]

The Haitian experience provides an example of how heteronormative sites of religious knowledge production are worked into the diasporic landscape within a frame of reference decidedly shaped by place and time. It also illustrates how it is not just the practices of the state that produce racialized subjects, but also the strategies of non-state actors in their autonomous projects of self-invention and difference. A particular discourse of racial alterity gets internalized by individuals and guides conduct. Specifically, Haitians' link to the American nation as well as their struggles with the nation's biopolitics of racial hierarchy show us something about how the organized practices (mentalities and techniques) through which subjects are governed gets developed.

Supplemental Reflections

In another transnational context, the existence of heteronormative sites of knowledge production similarly has been determinative of an emerging consciousness. As
we can see from the Haitian experience, the postmodern condition of fragmented,
postcolonial, and spatialized identities allows an opening for innovation at the level
of daily practice. Not only religious but also juridical practices provide affirmations
that underscore narratives of connection and separation. The diasporan existence
of some Muslim immigrants in Britain provides a clear demonstration of this.
Muslims in Britain confront and rework different hegemonic constructions of
identity developed in their home countries and their societies of settlement. Law is
one field that mediates this process by defining the boundaries of possible action
and the range of alternative aspirations—and by providing political, cultural, and
spiritual metaphors that can serve as the basis around which to enact provisional
closure.

While the meaning of diaspora remains important in regard to formations of
legality, this section turns to a brief account of the second concept central to my
analysis: jurisprudence. By examining jurisprudence I intend to explore the intersection of law and the social environment, which produces what others have called
a "double consciousness" about the law. Jurisprudence is not generated by or on
behalf of the affluent middle class alone, but also develops from the downside of
social relations, from the standpoints of those who are relatively disadvantaged and
who struggle practically and theoretically with their need to use the law without
being contained by it. Jurisprudence, then, has to be socially grounded in order for
it to be meaningful. "It has to make sense of some experiences of life to find its
grip."[30] It needs to (at least partially) capture the nuances of the realities that are
embedded in people's lives if it is not to be completely jettisoned by extra-legal
forms of resistance such as non-cooperation, avoidance, and foot-dragging. This
delineates the defining characteristics of a range of *outsider* jurisprudences, from
perspectives held by women and by many minority communities including African
Americans, Asian Americans, Hispanics, and other legal subjects.

At the same time, though, jurisprudence is neither particularly nuanced nor
responsive to human consequences because it is about fixed notions of law. It carries the past forward as an authoritative source of substantive societal norms. It
exudes the false impression of permanence and duration. Liberal legalism holds
that jurisprudence is positivistic and *non-normative* in the sense that it is impartial
and based on reason, and that it is exclusively a juridical activity that is the domain
of certain institutions of government rather than being generated in any sense by
its subjects. Its proponents seek to ensure the viability of law and to maintain law's

authority. As such, jurisprudence is a rigid theorizing about the principles contained in the law, reinforcing orthodoxy, and hence an ineluctable tension arises between the two (seemingly contradictory) terms I seek to join here: *diasporic*, which denotes fluidity and openness, with an open-ended and contingent politics, and *jurisprudence*, which speaks of the essence and stability of legal principles in fairly resolute terms. Here I suggest that the concept of diasporic jurisprudence is something similar to what Peter Fitzpatrick has identified as a *supplemental* jurisprudence—an alternative to the conventional understanding of jurisprudence as under-determined, which seeks to add something to the corpus of law. It extends the *idea* of jurisprudence—what it regulates independent of its authors' intentions—to an examination of its social meanings, at its enclosure within discourses of migration, diaspora, and Muslim life in the West, which define spatial and power relationships between those in countries of origin and those in receiving societies. What is open to contestation in the diaspora are representations of jurisprudence as something fixed, as something original or natural. This is important to note if we are to think of jurisprudences (in plural form) as texts that are not sealed or closed totalities. At a minimum a supplemental jurisprudence "would keep open the connections between 'law' and 'context' and avoid the protective and premature closure around law which jurisprudence seeks to effect."[31] In doing so, such jurisprudences may bring to the surface otherwise suppressed or marginalized voices, thereby challenging the more settled underpinnings both of jurisprudence (as something stable, fixed, and complete) and the law it encases.

Borrowing from this analysis of supplemental jurisprudences, we can argue that the call for a new Islamic diasporic jurisprudence this essay is concerned with simply means to *supplement*—that is, complement—a pre-existing law, to which the conditions and necessities of diaspora are to be brought. In other words, we can view this as a benign call to improve what already exists *naturally* by making sure everything needed to make the pre-existing law contemporary and relevant is "on board." This perspective, which posits the law as underdetermined, maintains the authority of law. The law is regarded as having existed for all time, coterminous with God the Creator. Yet the supplement adds on to, or enriches, what is taken to be natural or divinely given.[32] The diasporan subject seeks to contemporize the law (and lawgivers) and its fixed regulatory categories. However, in this view, the essence of law remains unassailable. If we could just smoothly blend into the law those necessary things that it lacks, we would have "supplemented," in the sense of "completed," the law.

But there is at least one other way to understand what the call to supplement jurisprudence means, which is destabilizing. Drawing from the argument of Jacques Derrida, supplements are inherently dangerous. They are critical appendages to the law, which will constantly remain outside because they are never fully assimilable.

Being allegedly secondary—as in coming after the original—supplements are potentially disruptive. Supplementarity is a clandestine project; the supplement can be subversive since it is never entirely clear (is "undecidable") whether it adds on to, or replaces, something. Is it an accretion or substitution? Further, a supplement upsets the equilibrium—and *closure*—achieved through tradition. It provokes anxiety because it indicates a desire—a desire to attenuate the blindness of law—but in fact, a supplement only accentuates the law's shortcomings. In a nutshell, the call to formulate a new diasporic jurisprudence might be received *not* as a call to complete the law but for the radical transformation of what already exists.[33]

The point in calling what I am looking at a diasporic jurisprudence is to highlight the transformation-through-relocation that occurs in law, and in the perspectives of persons who perform the interpretation of law in various locations. Persistent transformative conditions in diaspora make possible the translation of the incomprehensible (i.e., seemingly culture-bound ways of thinking) into legible forms for political ends. This translation involves an attempt at a "restorative genealogy" that retrieves/invents a collective consciousness and partially deactivates the western colonialist legacy by establishing alternative practices and values.[34] The diasporic dimension brings the subjectivities of displaced people to the interpretation of law and influences the configuration of regulatory regimes.[35] Islamic jurisprudence is indicated here as *the text* through which the changing self-conceptions of the interpretive community are signified. This interpretive turn vis-à-vis a text helps this community to navigate the new and complex spaces of Muslim settlement in the West and occasions a specific form of legality. Extending the metaphor of a mirror analyzed in the following pages, I argue that an Islamic diasporic jurisprudence is a reflective surface that provides linkages and constitutes a sense of belonging and common purpose. It speaks of "a time not yet lived" and of a history, "at once a familiar path to the future and a conceptual lineage," that will form the basis of (an imagined) intactness and serve as an important resource for resistance and identity.[36]

This new jurisprudence of the diaspora is foregrounded by a pre-existing law and a premodern set of juridical debates about Muslim minorities, which establish themselves as tradition. Yet this process is not, as some would have it, an oversimplified "reverting to type" since, regardless of any infinite desire to return to lost origins, there can be no final and absolute return to the past (imagined or otherwise).[37] At the very least, as Tariq Ramadan points out, colonialism and the 20th-century creation of "protectorates" caused major changes in Muslim countries, which introduced a foreign and westernized legal system into the governing structures of much of the Muslim world.[38] This would belie any claim to see an Islamic law as an unadulterated and closed system of meaning. The discursive practices of formulating a diasporic jurisprudence are a modification of prior meanings in relation to the social, political, and economic conditions in which Muslims currently find themselves through a particular kind of self-consciousness brought on by diaspora. The corpus of Islamic law that addresses the status of Muslims who reside in non-Muslim societies, referred to earlier, as well as the Islamist rhetoric about historical prohibitions against customary accretions, pejoratively labeled as *bida* (innovation),[39] represent just two (albeit empowering and authoritative) dimensions of the structures of social life, law, and jurisprudence that might configure contemporary orientations toward social action and interpretation.

The next section presents an overview of the struggle to appropriate and elaborate the immense network of meaning in law and religion. The section does *not* focus on the struggle around the meaning of Islam. Instead, it concentrates on the struggle for control over symbolic space and identity and on the historical antecedents for minority status under various interpretations of Islamic law. Only once we have identified these dimensions and what is at stake in the very representation of the social world can we begin to appreciate the significance of an emergent Islamic diasporic jurisprudence. We can then discern the subtle but important ways in which culturally specific discourses constitute the diasporic community.

Muslims in Britain

To speak of a diasporic community—*any* diasporic community—is to give the false sense of cohesion, and to run the risk of emphasizing too much the unity that is forged under the gaze of the receiving society. Any attempt to look at a diasporic community, such as Muslims in the West, as a homogenous entity is illusory. Yet monolithic images of Islam as the principal threat in world affairs certainly have taken hold of western public opinion in recent years and affected the conditions under which Muslims currently reside in Britain. The impact of America's 9/11 on European conceptualizations of Muslim identity, the growing feeling of hostility toward Muslim populations, and the increasing visibility of extreme right movements and political parties all have presaged a decidedly negative turn in public discourses and policies.[40] As Aziz al-Azmeh trenchantly puts it, there is a view of European Muslims that "takes them for a cliché"—as a collectivity that is unreconstructed and unreconstructable, determined to be antimodern and irrationally obsessed with prayer, fasting, and modesty, and whose presence in Europe is a mere accident rather than the legacy of colonial experience and globalization.[41] Alarm over a likely connection between what is happening abroad and the presence of Muslim immigrant communities in Europe provides fertile soil for stereotypes of a locally homogeneous (and dangerous) Muslim population in Britain.

This is a view that has gained considerable momentum in the opening decade of the 21st century. However, the beginnings of this trend to manufacture "otherness" can be traced earlier and can be attributed to the hegemonic discourses of state-sponsored multiculturalist policies that have structured local ethnic (and also religious) mobilization as a means of representation and empowerment. Muslims in Britain were already gaining prominence as a new social movement in the 1990s, yet they were said to be internally differentiated in important and complex ways with respect to national origins, ethnicities, local or linguistic divisions, devotional orientations, settlement histories, intergenerational differences, and socioeconomic backgrounds. However, within just a few years, recognition of the salience of these demographic variables yielded to alarmism and a degree of conflation of Muslims, in general terms, as sharing the same innate characteristics and making unified social and political demands upon the broader society. The countervailing pressures of media representations of Muslims as a grave security risk, coupled with the powerful discourses of multiculturalism, accelerated the homogenizing shift from a hyphenated (largely ethnic) to a singular Muslim identity.

While it is true that the category of *Muslim* has been crafted out of heretofore divergent groups in Britain—South Asian, Middle Eastern, African, and so forth— and that inaccurate representations are often made about the views and intentions of this general population based on the actions of a few extremists, it is also overly simplistic to lay the blame entirely on a reactionary and xenophobic Europe. Rather, the speed and intensity with which ideological and material elements traverse national boundaries in this era of globalized economies creates new levels of uncertainty in the social order. One such uncertainty relates to census concerns: how many persons of this or that kind reside within the territory? Or to put it another way, how many of "them" are now among "us"?[42] Uncertainties exacerbate the desire to control, and regimes of control fuel even greater fears within the public. Census taking is a concrete way the state imposes (falsely) stable categories and, as mentioned earlier, the British census included a question on religious affiliation for the first time in 2001. The rationale for such data collection was based on the argument that government agencies would need to demonstrate their compliance with the law under legislation that addressed educational, employment, and other social inequities reflecting discrimination on the basis of religion. British and European Union legislation remedying xenophobia and religious discrimination would be more apt to provide adequate solutions if governments had comprehensive information on the assemblages in question. Resistance to inclusion of a religious affiliation question came from sectors that were uncomfortable with seeing Britain as anything but a secular society. The desire to count persons on the basis of creed required a shift in self-perceptions on the part of members of the dominant society as well as minorities.[43]

The census question incorporates the religion category into governmental statistics—which actors drove this process? While many Muslim organizations in Britain campaigned for the inclusion of this question—often referred to as the largest minority religious group—some leaders were dissatisfied with the government's focus on race and ethnicity alone as statistical markers for resource allocation in the public sector. Opponents said that they felt they would be more defined by their religion than by other demographic information. The census question might exaggerate the salience of religion as the operative identity and promote it as a powerful signifier. Others feared that it would result in increased surveillance of and discrimination against those identified as Muslim. Confirmation of the size of the Muslim population (roughly 3% of the total British population) and of the age structure (Muslims have the youngest demographic profile, with more than 60 percent under the age of 30) inflamed xenophobic sentiments, reflected in what has been said by politicians and some sections of the media about Europe's heritage.

For instance in October 2006, Cabinet Minister Jack Straw's comments to British Muslim women sparked controversy in the media. When meeting with constituents who were covered with face veils, the leader of the House of Commons asked them if they would mind removing the veils. He said he did not want to "be prescriptive," but he believed covering people's faces could hinder community relations. Prime Minister Tony Blair, a strong proponent of secularization in the public sphere, supported Straw, calling the full-face veil a "mark of separation" that makes non-Muslims uncomfortable. Straw represents a district where 25 to 30 percent of the constituents are Muslim.[44]

At the same time, many internationalist organizations encouraged British Muslims to think of themselves as marginal subjects as well. From the perspective of many Muslim jurists and scholars in so-called majoritarian[45] Muslim countries, Muslims in Britain were understood to be simply part of a larger category of worldwide minority Muslim communities, estimated to be as much as one-third of the global Muslim population.[46] The status and welfare of Muslims in diaspora have become a growing concern for such majoritarian institutions based in Saudi Arabia as the Muslim World League and the Organization of Islamic Conference (OIC). These two organizations have set up the Islamic Fiqh (jurisprudence) Council, the OIC Fiqh Academy, and the International Shari'a Research Academy that have commissioned the further study and development of *fiqh al-darurah* (jurisprudence of necessity) and fiqh al-aqalliyah (jurisprudence of minority). Both terms designate classical Islamic legal conventions that deal with questions faced by Muslims residing in what has historically been classified the dar al-harb (abode of war/unbelief) or the place where Islam is neither the dominant religion nor the religion of the government. This institutionalization of the juridical articulation of minority status places Saudi Arabia in the position to dominate the development of a "genuine" and singular Islamic response to minoritization, which in effect denies agency and heavily regulates "bottom up" movements in politics. It points to ways of thinking in which dominant cultural speakers continue to perceive themselves as the epistemic and moral center of the struggles over the meaning of Islam. Yet these high-level pronouncements from majoritarian institutions show little understanding of what it means to live in Britain. They efface the perspectives and political concerns of many Muslims in diaspora who may be doubly marginalized by their experience of migration and by their entry into the specific social relations of their new setting. Through the agency of international organizations, which pronounce universal truths and classicist edicts for Muslims living outside the Muslim fold, the local realities and particularisms for Muslims in Britain are elided. Islamic legal conventions collapse into a series of twofold oppositions, arranging the world in dichotomous terms into either familiar or hostile domains.

A counterhegemonic trend started in the 1980s, with various meetings of religious leaders in the West to address challenges facing Muslims. The institutionalization of this dynamic can be seen with the establishment of the Fiqh Council of North America (1986) and the European Council for Fatwa and Research (1997). The purpose of these bodies is to provide shari'a-based guidance to Muslims living as minority members in what are seen as predominantly secular societies. The latter council was created at the initiative of the Federation of Islamic Organizations in Europe and is currently presided over by the Egyptian-born jurist Yusuf Abdullah al-Qaradawi. A controversial figure in the West, al-Qaradawi has been denied a visa to enter the United States since 1999 and has been denied entry to Britain since 2008 (because in a 2004 visit to London he defended suicide attacks against Israel as "martyrdom in the name of God").

Questions about minority status are nothing new in Islamic jurisprudence. Indeed, as Yvonne Haddad points out, minority consciousness today has been influenced by "the development of a genre of literature advocating a political Islam, one that taps into powerful imagery of the struggle of the early believers under the leadership of the Prophet Muhammad to establish a righteous and just state in a hostile environment."[47] Attempts to formulate juridical positions on the issue of minorities began early in Islamic history, addressing three basic questions: Under what conditions are Muslims permitted to live in non-Muslim territory? Are Muslims accorded a special status, as exceptions to the rule, for which conventional duties do not apply? And what are the obligations of Muslims in non-Muslim territory vis-à-vis the host society and Islamic law? Most scholarship on legal developments in the early period of Islamic civilizations tends to assume that the discourse on minority status operated in a monolithic manner, yet answers to these questions left themselves open to various interpretations. These questions were raised by Muslim settlement in non-Muslim territory in the second century of Islamic civilizations (eighth century CE). By the sixth century of Islamic civilizations (12th century CE), the Maliki school, one of the major Sunni schools of jurisprudence, emerged as being fairly resolute in its opposition to such residence.[48] According to this line of thought, Muslims were obligated to return to an Islamic polity: "A Muslim should never reside in a non-Muslim territory, primarily because he or she will be subject to non-Muslim law."[49] Two other major schools of Sunni jurisprudence, the Hanafi and the Shafii, said in essence that if Muslims can practice their religion in non-Muslim territory and do not fear the loss of their religion, return to an Islamic society is not necessary. In fact, it was recognized that some Islamic polities were Islamic in name only and in practice were oppressive and unjust, so under certain circumstances residence in a non-Muslim territory would even be preferable. Moreover, the Hanafi school of jurisprudence by the sixth century of Islamic civilizations (12th century CE) maintained that if a locality has a Muslim judge and applies Islamic laws, then it can be considered part of dar al-Islam even if the government and society are not predominantly Muslim.[50] Nevertheless, this position does not apply generally even within the Hanafi tradition since there has been no consensus among Muslim jurists as to the degree to which religious freedom must be permitted before a location can be considered a part of dar al-Islam.

In more recent times, since the 1960s, works of popular activists such as Pakistan's Abu al-Mawdudi and Egypt's Sayyid Qutb have been referred to as advocating the *hijra* (emigration) of devout, ideologically committed Muslims who oppose their governments to more congenial sites, where they may "enhance their Islamic consciousness" and prepare for their eventual return to their home countries to cleanse their governments from corruption and replace "what they consider to be un-Islamic nationalist and socialist governments."[51] According to this perspective, permanent minority status is incompatible with Islam. However, others insist that relocation and permanent settlement is legitimate provided efforts are made to Islamize the society in which one lives. For example, the late Dr. Zaki Badawi, imam of the London Central Mosque in Regents Park and founding director of the Muslim College in West London,[52] justified Muslim settlement in the non-Muslim West by saying that it is clear that Muslims can be expected to obey the laws of the local ruler and still be considered "good" Muslims. He draws this conclusion from a 15th-century CE *fatwa* (religious/legal opinion) issued by a mufti of Morocco to whom Muslims in Spain remained loyal after the Christian conquest of Granada. The fatwa stated that Muslims should obey the public law of the land and keep their religious observances private.

For Dr. Tariq Ramadan, author of *To Be a European Muslim*, the prerequisites for an area to fall within the abode of Islam are based in the concept of security.[53] He suggests that an environment that guarantees freedom of conscience and worship and that protects the physical safety of Muslims in their conduct of religion is not a hostile space. Accordingly, the guarantee of five fundamental rights would make any society a positive living space for Muslims: "The right to practice Islam, the right to knowledge, the right to establish organizations, the right to autonomous representation, and the right to appeal to law."[54]

Contemporary global movement has exceeded the historical legal frame of reference. What remains significant for our understanding of the contemporary era is the constitutive effect of particular discourses, because these discourses—whether considered pre-modern or something else—have become the organizing frame for an alternative model for Muslim living in the West. As it seeks to supplement the existing canon of law, the articulation of a diasporic jurisprudence encapsulates the process of minoritization as it happens in various sites. It displays the development of a uniquely minoritarian legal consciousness, shaped by contemporary challenges and solutions that are also traceable to certain historical relations. The content of that diasporic jurisprudence is varied, as there is no uniform Muslim understanding of law and jurisprudence. Moreover, the form diasporic jurisprudence takes depends not only on the initiatives Muslims take, but also on the response, structures and historical relations of the receiving society. It is about the interaction between legal and social norms within a prescribed public space. Legal systems provide a structure for interpretive activity since the law influences ways of thinking and acting, and people create a pattern of demands and desires within the possibilities (and impossibilities) allowed by the law. Indeed, people involved in the diasporic process are putting together a range of conceptual tools and normative logic offered in contrasting ways by different discursive frameworks. Rather than offer assertions about specific content, my effort is to outline the contours that this call for a new jurisprudence takes, and to analyze how the emergence of such jurisprudence takes shape discursively, in culturally specific ways. Identities are multiple and complex, and the more constituents' circumstances diverge the less likely it is that any single identity or legal consciousness will be suitable or shared across a broad range of sects and groups.

The practice of fiqh enables Muslims to continuously make Islam relevant, and represents a moment of critical negation. At the heart of current discourse regarding Islam in Europe lie summons from Muslim scholars and associations to bring the old up to date. Their entreaty is for their autonomous creation of a diasporic jurisprudence, to formulate a fiqh for a Muslim community that (implicitly) critiques the originary forms of Islamic jurisprudence. For instance, in Britain in 2004 the Association of Muslim Social Scientists (AMSS), in conjunction with the Muslim College and Q-News Media, convened its fifth annual conference on the subject of "Fiqh Today: Muslims as Minorities." The conference call identified a "minority fiqh project," which is at once an intellectual and spiritual challenge to compensate for the inadequacies of mainline thought, to "draw on the classical heritage and corpus" while at the same time negating it via supplementation. As one conference participant queried, can minority fiqh play a creative role in helping Muslims deal with the differing ethos of "the West" by applying shari'a in the present social milieu?[55]

In the following section, I begin to unpack the meaning of a quote that contains a call for the creation of a diasporic jurisprudence, which foregrounds the meeting date of this conference by nearly a decade. This excerpt uses the metaphor of a mirror to describe jurisprudence. Understanding how this call and the mirror image are freighted with cultural meanings about community, difference, and change is key to my analysis of Muslim life as it exists in the fragments of colonial empire. By bringing to light the logic that informs the choice of a mirror as metaphor for an Islamic diasporic jurisprudence, it becomes possible to outline the specific characteristics of the relationship between emerging ideas about reality in the articulation of a new jurisprudence and the image that the interpretive community has of itself and its place in the world. This outline can clarify the constitutive effect that the articulation of a new jurisprudence has upon the community of interpretation and challenge.

The Islamic Basis for Creative Jurisprudence

In 1995, Dr. Azzam al-Tamimi, founding director of London-based human rights organization Liberty for the Muslim World,[56] delivered an address to the annual meeting of the Muslim Student Association of the United Kingdom and Northern Ireland (held in Birmingham on December 23–26).[57] The Arabic-language magazine *Al-Mujtama* published the address the following month. The following is an excerpt from that speech:

> While some of the problems of coexistence and engagement that
> Muslims face in the West are the product of western society itself, others
> are the product of the Islamist vision, with cultural concepts that
> developed in and for an environment other than this [western] one, and
> under circumstances different from the present circumstances of Europe.
> The Islamist intellectual output bears some responsibility for this
> situation because its vision was generally fashioned to deal with the
> realities of the home countries, where Muslims constitute the
> overwhelming majority of the population. Were Islamists aware that
> their works are being advocated and used by the minority populations in
> the West, they would have been disturbed and would condemn such an
> application—including what they have written about the West,

describing the role of western imperialism and its conspiracy, blowing
reveille in order to wake up the local Muslim community from its sleep
and in order to expose the traitors in their midst, who have been content
to serve as the means to further the imperialists' aims in Muslim
countries.... [In comparison,] we Muslims in Europe are in need of new
ideas, indeed, of a creative jurisprudence that takes into account the
present circumstances. *Jurisprudence is the mirror that reflects the
conditions of time and place to realize the greatest good and impede
corruption.* (emphasis added)[58]

These words are a narrative of displacement. According to this account, Muslims in
the West are displaced because of the dominance within their communities of the
Islamist vision, which is at least partially responsible for creating problems through
the displacement, or silence, of diasporan realities. By foregrounding the mirror
image of this displacement, this statement attempts to contest the dominant (Islamist) vision by calling for a *creative* jurisprudence that takes into account the new
realities experienced by those in the West, who inhabit the margins of social as well
as geographical boundaries. Jurisprudence is contextual and intersubjective, and
here a call is made to transcend familiar paradigms of history and legal doctrine.
Tamimi suggests that what is appropriate in Muslim countries, where the immediate postcolonial concerns are focused on political resistance to the legacy of western
imperialism, is not particularly relevant for Muslims who live, ironically, in what
was once the very provenance of western imperial power, the center of western
consumer capitalism. The political economy of globalization—the transnational
flow of migration, information and capital with new speed; the global spread of
neoliberalism with its emphasis on deregulation and privatization; and secularization based on scientific rationality as the dominant determiner of truth and justice—has much to do with displacement. The sense of hopelessness borne of the
urbanization and of increasing income and wealth disparities only exacerbates the
growing impoverishment that accompanies globalization. Jurisprudence is portrayed here as playing an important part in knitting together the displaced fragments of community.

Besides being contextual, jurisprudence is also intersubjective. The discursive
practices of formulating the new jurisprudence being called for confront the cultural disjunctures Muslims encounter in the diaspora. The first sense in which
Muslim diasporans are confronted by disjuncture stems from the problem of myo-
pia. Because Tamimi characterizes the Islamists' vision as being "fashioned to deal
with the realities of the home countries," the Islamists fail to see, that is, they are
unaware of how their writings are being advocated and used by Muslims in western
contexts. At the same time, diasporic Muslims become, in a sense, extralegal because

their circumstances transcend classification. At a time when Muslims in Europe were becoming increasingly visible in the traumatic upheavals of ethnic conflict (e.g., Bosnia, Kosovo), Muslims as diasporans were invisible from the Islamists' point of view in the 1990s. Diasporic Muslims were outside the field of the Islamists' vision and, consequently, were outside the law as it was because their conditions were not reflected in the law. For example, as Arjun Appadurai argues, it is possible at the end of the 20th century to see identities changing among Bosnian Muslims, "as they find themselves pushed away from a secular, Europeanist idea of themselves into a more fundamentalist picture."[59] Pressures come not only from Serbian threats to their survival but from Islamists in Saudi Arabia, Egypt, and Iran who have suggested that Bosnian Muslims are "paying the price" for their neglect of their Islamic identity under communist rule. This extralegal status of being an "outlaw" effaces diasporic Muslims, whom Tamimi calls to redefine the terms of the debate about minorityness. Muslims in Britain are exhorted to form "a creative jurisprudence that takes into account the present circumstances." By means of circulating ideas and interpretations of an Islamic jurisprudence *outside* of certain Islamist conventions, these diasporans can produce new textual works, thereby adding on sites of production of normative claims. Innovations in one field (Islamic law) can be brought in line with changing conditions in society. The interpretive community—the "we Muslims in the West"—is both the mediator between two axes represented by Islamic law and British society and the entity that is different (i.e., wholly "other") from either one. The community fashions life practices in the dialogic relationship between the two axes. Hence there exists the (suppressed) possibility that the dominant framework of knowledge in each axis can be displaced and its authority subverted.

Another related sense in which this excerpt speaks of disjuncture stems from the dualism informing both classical and modern social thought. The excerpt itself capitalizes on the binary sense of "them" versus "us," which in this case defines the seemingly natural and essentialist opposition between those who reside in the domain of Islam, where shari'a is sovereign, and those who are exterior to this domain by virtue of their residence in non-Muslim territory. This is a foundational effect of the conventional juridical categories into which classical Islamic jurisprudence has divided the world. This conventional view is based on the inseparability of identity from place: dar al-Islam (the abode of Islam) and dar al-harb (the abode of unbelief). The normative term in this pair is *the abode of Islam*, while the putatively *non*-normative or *a*moral term, in the sense that it designates culturally deficient "others," is the *abode of unbelief*. This inherited dualism and the limits it places on vision—for instance, not recognizing the potentialities for Muslim life outside of dar al-Islam—present an essentializing paradox. The author of the excerpt subtly bases his assertion of "outsiderhood," and hence, his freedom to declare his dissent from this inherited system of classification. His very presence in the West (dar al-harb), betokens his simultaneous attempt to move beyond the system's oppositional binaries. He would like to bring jurisprudence out of the historicity of these preceptive categories, which are linked to specific material conditions and social relations, and inscribe jurisprudence in a different context of situated or localized knowledge. By means of his very practice, Tamimi brings to attention and questions both the inner conditions of the forms and categories upon which Islamic jurisprudence is founded and their corresponding forms of exclusion.

Although trying to transcend binaries, Tamimi's attempt marks a paradoxical situation because he slips back into making distinctions that are taken in his account as prediscursively "real." Distinguishing Muslims in Europe from Muslims elsewhere, the discursive logic of Tamimi's argument about difference operates in a manner that conceals its very role in the production and reproduction of such differences. The argument in effect is complicit in the construction of sharp contrasts between Europe and its "other" cultures. Accordingly, the Islamist vision may have its place in the Muslim majoritarian countries. However, this move separates the author and his readers, the interpretive community, from the social relations and politics of the home countries, where the dominant perception is that the "role of western imperialism and its conspiracy" must be resisted. He construes Islamists as being subjects of the legacy of colonial-imperial domination, and shows that resistance becomes central to the Islamists' postcolonial project of liberation. In their anti-imperialist politics, they reverse the terms, making their culture distinctive and superior to the West. While these Islamists see it as their duty to "wake up" those Muslims not positioned as they are, Tamimi argues that this attitude would (ironically) be misplaced in a western setting. The author and readers stand outside of postcolonial exigencies, in the very midst of the imperial core, and each location lays claim to equal but separate realities. The fragments of colonial empire have, as it were, relocated into the western imperial center. They are in need of a new jurisprudence if they are to maintain the essentials of Islam no matter how much these may be redefined in the process of translation. This new jurisprudence cannot be sited within the boundaries of a binary framework, located either in the world of the subordinated or in the world of the hegemonic. Its complexity/fluidity exceeds the binary structure of representation.

If the praxis and politics of life in Britain is one central theme of the excerpt from Tamimi's address, then the role of law is another. The explicit reference to a normative anchor in the form of a creative jurisprudence moors the ship at sea and constitutes its interpretive community (Muslims in the West). Through collective action of common believers as opposed to the ulama, the interpretive community becomes the locus of legal authority because it is called on to create this new jurisprudence. Tamimi takes his interpretion in a dramatic direction when he signals that a new system, based on new structures, is in formation or is about to come into being. The materials this takes from the older system assume a different value. The subordinate elements of the older structures can develop, and what was once incidental in the older system of meaning now takes on pre-eminence.

British scholars Steven Vertovec and Ceri Peach note that in "forging a new European Islam, young Muslim men and women are reclaiming the concept of ijtihad—'interpretation' or 'independent judgment' [in law] not as a special right of scholars but of all Muslims."[60] Ihsan Yilmaz also suggests that as a result of the Islamic metropole's nonrecognition of diasporic conditions, diasporic Muslim scholars have been producing new (neo-) ijtihads.[61] Textual analysis of the Qur'an and the Sunnah (traditions of the Prophet), debates about women's positions in Islam, and speculative reasoning about the roles of Muslim men and women in western societies are evident in the plethora of Muslim lay organizations materializing in Britain, especially among the urban youth. This kind of engagement can be seen as well in the emergence of Muslim women's groups in Britain. An example is the Muslim Women's Helpline, a counseling service established in 1989 that provides advice and counseling to Muslim women in Britain facing problems of sexual abuse, domestic violence, depression, and abandonment by their husbands. Other women's groups include Al-Nisa Association chapters in London and Northern Ireland, and an association launched in 2008 by the British prime minister's office, the National Muslim Women's Advisory Group, established, according to its Web site, in order to empower Muslim women and increase their civic participation in a manner that combats violent extremism.[62]

Practical concerns of daily life in Britain have subjected certain concepts and practices to a fundamental reframing, one that facilitates the emergence of a new identity that would seek to incorporate the marginal as a basis for empowerment. For decades groups such as the U.K. Islamic Mission, established as an offshoot of the Islamicized political party in Pakistan, *Jama'at Islami*, have organized networks and study circles in Britain. The Islamic Foundation (Leicester, United Kingdom) publishes materials written by British Muslims among others to discuss ways in which Muslim doctrinal views and an Islamic idiom may be accommodated in secularized local and global settings, and has initiated an outreach project to identify and address the specific needs of new British converts to Islam. Many other organizations and publications have been established in the last decade that try to speak to conventional western concerns within an Islamic idiom, including several Muslim charities (e.g., Islamic Relief International), and nonprofit research and advocacy groups such as the Islamic Human Rights Commission.

In articulating the need to take into account the specific realities of Muslims in Britain, Tamimi suggests that by being attentive to the diversity of the historical and local contexts of Muslims' lives around the world we may avoid reductionist tendencies that deploy orientalist depictions of a monolithic Islam. His considerations lead to a perspective that carves out a space for the "normalization" of discourse (i.e., for presenting norms), normalizing Muslim presence in the West within an Islamic discursive logic.[63] He remains doubly conscious of the politicization of difference (margins) in both normative terrains, and seeks both explanations for and solutions to marginalization and emerging problems on the basis of a rereading of sacred sources. To do this, the diasporic subject needs to be knowledgeable in the language and epistemic maneuvers of the dominant culture in two domains—Britain and the Islamic world—which in its everyday practice marks him or her as culturally marginal. The diasporic subject plays a very complex cultural strategy that positions him or her as a split subject.

In an interview published in the *Washington Report on Middle East Affairs* in December 1998, Tamimi claims that "Islam includes *faraghat*, that is, space. It allows for areas in which we as human beings act in accordance with respective needs and exigencies of time and place. Due to this provision for space, there is flexibility in which Muslims can devise suitable solutions for emerging problems."[64] In other words, religion is not a fixed set of beliefs and institutions that is determinative of social relations but is instead a resource from which individuals may draw symbols, practices, and discourses in order to respond to, reaffirm, and contest dominant social relationships. This way of thinking about religion places emphasis on the *agency* of individuals.[65] Similarly, in the 1995 address before the Muslim students of the United Kingdom and Northern Ireland from which this excerpt is taken, Tamimi argues that the problems between the West and the Islamic world—and he mentions specifically the Arab-Israeli conflict—are the product of geopolitical design and a set of social relationships contingent upon power relations and historical change in the region. Religion is not the basic ingredient of the dispute. Rather, it is the continued political and economic domination of the region, and religion is provisional to the pursuit of political/economic ends. Thus, Muslims in a different socioeconomic setting can use a religious jurisprudence that is tailored to their specific locality and represents a pluralization of Islamic idioms drawn from the contexts and the societies in which Muslims live.

A Mirror Image

If we return again to the excerpt, we see that in its final sentence, Tamimi metaphorically equates jurisprudence with a mirror that "reflects the conditions to realize the greatest good and impede corruption." As a mirror, this jurisprudence operates in a way that distances the subject from the object. Since a mirror reflects, it also creates visual space and distance because of the refraction of light and presents the image of an object rather than the actual object itself. In a metaphoric sense, jurisprudence is said to perform the function of "othering." It separates and creates the illusion of doubleness. This leaves the impression that there is an otherness to jurisprudence that is subject to supplementation.

What are the two dimensions that reflect one another in the mirror? Two dimensions permanently mirror one another, and presumably innovations in one dimension would alter the image reflected in the other. Jurisprudence is itself the mirror, the conductor of the images. Does it stay constant while the conditions that encompass it change? The metaphor strategically evokes a very often cited verse from the Qur'an (3:110) that enjoins Muslims to do that which is good and forbids all that is evil. The verse says, "You are the best of peoples, evolved for mankind, enjoining what is right and forbidding what is wrong, and believing in Allah." This injunction is used often to invoke consensus—the Muslim community will not agree on an error, or so the saying of the Prophet Mohammed goes, and jurisprudence is developed (historically, through consensus) specifically to implement shari'a, the divine law that offers moral regulation, to "enjoin what is right and forbid what is wrong." If jurisprudence is a "good" mirror in this sense, it will perform a community coalescing or consensus-forming function by drawing the interpretive community together to summon (or "invent") the mirror, so that the conditions to realize the greatest good and impede corruption become intelligible. The interpretive community is thus constituted: Muslims residing in the West must be conscious of, and attentive to, a mirror that reflects their own circumstances and particular needs and interests. The interpretive community has to read what is legible on its reflective surface.

But if the question we are interested in is, does jurisprudence-as-mirror remain constant as the encompassing conditions change?, then it is not the verisimilitude of the reflection in that mirror that concerns us. Rather, to understand the reflective properties of jurisprudence, I am turning my attention to the mirror itself and to its component elements. As Jacques Derrida would have it, the mirror itself is not a simple medium offering a "univocal signification" but an instrument of formation and permutation that "gives itself out" as something designed to be broken en route to the true source "to which it lures you."[66] The reflection in the mirror is a representation of a representation ad infinitum, which keeps the difference infinitely open. Thus the mirror, with its distortions and distorting properties, takes the place of reality, but it is no facsimile of the world that "comprehends the mirror which captures it and vice versa."[67] It is more accurately understood as a transformative medium to be passed through.

For the moment our attention is not fixed on the mirror's reflective surface. Instead, for the purpose of understanding how the interpretive community constitutes, one needs to consider the *tain*, the silver backing or tinfoil on the reverse side of the mirror. The tain is dull and lusterless, but without it, reflection and speculative activity would be impossible. As Rodolphe Gasche writes, "On this lining of the outside surface of reflection, one can read the 'system' of the infrastructures that commands the mirror's play and determines the angles of reflection."[68] This component of the mirror consists of materials, either selected by or thrust upon the interpretive community, from the numerous localities that compose the diaspora and from the dialogue of struggle and appropriation, of refusal and recognition, with and against Britain as much as Islam. The tain is synthesized—reframed, put together in a new way—from the endowments of each cultural (including legal) infrastructure, and the constitutive properties of articulation with these infrastructures determine the arcs of the mirror's limited play (i.e., the angles of reflection). This synthesizing process raises the question, what historical possibilities arise as a result of engagement and contention?

For Tamimi, those historical possibilities arise from what he calls the "most vital interests" of Muslims in Britain. According to Tamimi, they are as follows:

1. The general welfare of Muslims who *choose* to live in the West. These Muslims still face a number of challenges related to permanent residence in western societies. Solutions are impossible without interaction with or participation in public decision making.
2. The translation of Islam into a western idiom to make Islam comprehensible to western ways of thinking.
3. The continued involvement of Muslims in the nationalist affairs of their home countries, and their collective engagement in bringing pressure to bear on policy makers in the western governments able to affect circumstances in their home countries.[69]

While these are the priorities that Tamimi identifies, the challenges that remain include the intensified suspicion under which Muslims are universally regarded as the primary enemy of the West, the ignorance of westerners about Islam, and racial discrimination within western societies. These particulars of British life and the "politics of recognition" through which Muslims seek official endowments can be read on the reverse side of the mirror that is the metaphor for jurisprudence.

Conclusion

How relevant are these juridical discussions for today's Muslims in Britain? In this chapter, my goal has been to lay the groundwork for examining the frame of reference developed by those Muslims who wish to be regulated, at least to some extent, by Islamic law principles in whatever form they may take in the diaspora. These abstractions *do* matter because they set limits on conceptions of what is possible (and impossible), which themselves have been delimited in response to particular historical challenges and doctrinal developments. Legal conventions, including such topics as family law, dietary restrictions, and finance, engender critical discussions of conceptual inheritances and legacies. From one perspective, they provide a crucial point of entry to a discussion of the normative basis for social practices, particularly when addressing some vexing social problems. For many, these practices provide the resources to help normalize Muslim living in Britain not in relation to the dominant institutions of law and society but in an internally differentiated Islamic idiom. The boundaries of the "abode of Islam" are continuously contested and repositioned within a framework for which Islamic legal conventions remain a salient category. Even as a supplement, a new Islamic diasporic jurisprudence has been foregrounded by historical juridical debates about Muslim minority life. Yet at the same time, proponents of this kind of jurisprudence believe that Islam can make contributions other than the polarized positions that come from an idealizing tradition.

Often, when western scholars theorize about global Islam, they stress the Muslim subject's allegedly singular attachment to the Muslim ummah (community) as bounded, fixed, and stable. In this way, they overlook the multiple and shifting identities within communities identified as diasporic and the polyvalent organization of social relations in which both state and communal institutions play significant roles in the trajectories, moral or legal, that consciousness will take. Contemporary discourse in a consciously Islamic idiom reveals that there is just as much divergence over the very notion of global community as there is over what properly defines the abode of Islam. The features of community are contested, debated, challenged, and appropriated by various members and groups, as alternative definitions of justice and Muslim subjectivities materialize to "realize the greatest good and impede corruption." What we can see in the enunciation of a new jurisprudence in the diaspora is an attempt to maintain the resilience of Islamic values. The intersection of local practices, conditioned by Anglo-American conventions, and translocal knowledge generates a shift in the way people make sense of the world and adjust to their realities. I have indicated that there are struggles to generate an "ex-centric" structure of knowledge, one that is not entirely based on Anglo-American common law nor on Islamic law but is motivated by a wholly different and rival vision as Muslim subjects connect themselves to a diverse range of public spheres. These efforts say something about sets of social relationships contingent on historical processes and about the image that the interpretive community has of itself and its place in the world.

Jurisprudence brings to the fore a particular understanding of the self as legal subject, and elements constitutive of the community are discursively produced through law and through the experience of transmigration and translation. As we can see, texts (of a jurisprudential nature) circulate and are appropriated far from their origins of existence, that is, without the benefit of being surrounded by the social spaces which produced them or in relation to which they constructed themselves. To appreciate the call for a new Islamic jurisprudence governing Muslim life in the diaspora, it is necessary to consider how the texts appropriated in the opportunity spaces of Britain correspond to the lived experiences of individuals and groups. What Dipesh Chakrabarty calls "the art of conversing across differences" becomes all the more important to preventing insuperable barriers to comprehension.[70] Here I have suggested how to consider the dialogic process of appropriating certain discourses and significant moments in the construction of normative claims through law.

I began by asking whether diasporas offer women possibilities for reworking gender relations. I hope that I have begun to lay the foundations for a feminist analysis of a gendered vision of diaspora at least in an indirect manner. By questioning the binary view that depicts diasporas as subordinate and weak reflections of the Old World, the process of dislodging the authoritative element in the hierarchical relations between migrant communities and their places of origin has begun. Many of the issues that concern contemporary Muslim feminism are adumbrated in the weakening of the gendered construct of the diaspora. A commitment to the dismantling of patriarchal hierarchy and structures of control and exclusion associated with traditional systems of meaning can also challenge hegemonic understandings of cultural forms. The development of a Muslim subjectivity must be understood in relation to the wider social, political, and economic developments in Britain. While a diasporic jurisprudence may create an opening for a feminist reuse of legal concepts, to date the absence of women's input is conspicuous. The challenge will be to incorporate voices of women and minority positions in contested sites of local communal power in a way that contributes to the unique formation of a British Muslim diaspora. It is to this theme that I return in chapter 4, when I focus on the current struggle to overcome law's inadequacies.

3

The Qur'an and American Politics

The Cultural Logic of Symbols and Public Service

Midterm elections to U.S. Congress in 2006 marked a significant moment in American history. As a result of the elections, Congress became more religiously diverse. Keith Ellison, a Democrat from Minnesota, was elected to the House of Representatives and became identified in the press as the "first Muslim" ever elected to Congress (two Buddhists were elected as well). To a degree, this trend reflects the growing religious diversity of the general population in the United States, which is at an all-time high as a result of the 1965 liberalization of immigration rules. While religious outsiders are hardly new in Americans' historical experience, the range of faith communities in the United States is now greater than ever before. Is there public acceptance of these broad changes in the religious landscape?

This chapter examines the controversy that surrounded the election of the Keith Ellison to U.S. Congress, and specifically, his decision to use a Qur'an at his swearing-in ceremony. The focus is on oath-taking as a variant of the confessional speech act and how it is linked to our sense of self, to the truth *of* the self, and to the speech act's outward performance of commitment to the political community. I argue that Ellison's swearing of the oath—"to support and defend the U.S. Constitution against all enemies, foreign and domestic, and bear true faith and allegiance to the same . . . without any mental reservations or purpose of evasion"[1]—reveals a particular ideology at work in narrating the

FIGURE 3.1. Minnesota Democratic congressional candidate Keith Ellison poses prior to an interview with Minneapolis radio station, September 18, 2006. The first Muslim elected to Congress returned to his home state on December 24, 2006, and told fellow Muslims to observe their faith and work for justice. He spoke at a convention of the Muslim American Society and the Islamic Circle of North America, attended by about 3,000 people, the *Detroit Free Press* reported. (AP photo/Jim Mone; 060918035571.)

American nation. The oath extracts an allegiance to a "jealous" document, the Constitution, which demands exclusive loyalty to the rule of law above any particularistic loyalties to tribe, deity, or community. Yet a sacred text is ubiquitous in at least part of the ceremonial oath of office for any newly elected public servant, supplying an implicit yet undeniable assurance that the individual "bears true faith." This is a cultural logic that illustrates the contradictions and fissures within secularism and demonstrates that the sovereign authority of the secular state does not rest easily on the rule of law. Rather, the underlying volatility of the oath lies in the possibility that an individual who swears it bears false witness, is capable of treason, or is constituted in a way that makes him incapable of sharing the community's values, beliefs, or standards. All of this comes to bear on Ellison's public performance of a time-honored ceremony. I suggest that if we pay attention to the ways that outward appearance is understood to correspond with a particular inner mindset of values and intentions, we can better understand Ellison's struggle to prove himself a virtuous citizen.

FIGURE 3.2. House Speaker Nancy Pelosi of California, left, administers the House oath to Representative Keith Ellison, D-Minn., during a re-enactment swearing-in ceremony on Capitol Hill, Washington, D.C., January 4, 2007. Ellison's wife, Kim, holds Thomas Jefferson's Qur'an, which was provided by the Library of Congress. (AP photo/Lawrence Jackson; 070104018679.)

Sacred Text

"No 'American' Holy Book." So reads the title of the lead editorial in the *Chicago Tribune* of December 11, 2006.[2] The editorial, like so much of the media talk around the election of Keith Ellison to Congress, focused on the congressman's decision to take the oath of office for his elective position with his hand on the Qur'an instead of the Bible. Ellison sparked controversy when he announced his decision to substitute the Qur'an for the more commonly used Bible in a ceremony that really amounts to a photo opportunity. Whereas the official oath of office is taken by House members en masse on the floor of the chamber, without any books in hand, many representatives choose to have an additional swearing-in ceremony with the Speaker of the House, during which family members and cameras are usually present, and scriptural props (e.g., Bible, Torah, Book of Mormon) are often used.[3] The extra "photo-op" reenactment has become a tradition

FIGURE 3.3. Representative Keith Ellison, D-Minn., the first Muslim elected to Congress, places his hand on the Qur'an once owned by Thomas Jefferson as his wife, Kim Ellison, holds the two-volume book during his swearing in ceremony, January 4, 2007, at the U.S. Capitol in Washington, D.C. (AP photo/Haraz N. Ghanbari; 070104017895.)

since no cameras are permitted on the House chamber floor during the official swearing-in ceremony.

Ellison's decision was to use not just *any* Qur'an but a very rare Qur'an, one once owned by Thomas Jefferson. This particular selection of the Jeffersonian Qur'an was the product of the month-long debate that ensued when Ellison announced his decision to use a Qur'an for the re-enactment in late November 2006. It was contingent upon the specific discourse invoked by Ellison's critics, arguing that the use of the Qur'an in this context represented nothing less than the undermining of American civilization.[4] Conservative columnist and radio talk-show host Dennis Prager asserted that insofar as the oath of office is concerned, America is interested only in one book, the Bible. Further, Prager declared, "if you are incapable to taking an oath on that Book, don't serve Congress."[5] Similarly, in a letter addressed to his constituents, fellow congressman Virgil Goode (R-Va.) warned that unless immigration rules were tightened many more Muslims would follow Ellison's lead and run for elective office, then demanding the use of the Qur'an in swearing-in ceremonies.[6] Representative Goode proclaimed this anti-immigration jeremiad despite the fact that Ellison himself is not an immigrant and can trace his ancestors to 18th-century Louisiana.[7] In the face of pressures to apologize, Representative Goode stood by his statements in the letter, which had been widely circulated in the press and in cyberspace. In February 2007, during congressional debates on a nonbinding resolution criticizing President Bush's decision to send more than 21,000 more U.S. troops to Iraq (the "troop surge"), Representative Goode drew further attention to himself by commenting that "Islamic jihadists want U.S. currency to say 'In Muhammad We Trust,' with an Islamic flag flying over the White House and U.S. Capitol."[8]

Representative Goode's comments, both in his letter and in congressional debates, raise two salient points. First, he shows a strong tendency to conflate Islam and foreignness and to view Islam as a creed largely associated with an immigrant population, a tendency that has become de facto practice in public discourse. Even though Representative Ellison is not an immigrant but an African American (the first ever elected to Congress from Minnesota), Goode's rhetoric easily elides the boundaries between foreign and native precisely because Islam is "exotic," if not exogenous, to the American nation. In this way Goode's jeremiad—many other Others will follow Ellison across the border and run for elective office—reflects the spatial politics of power constructed around the figure of the Muslim as a foreign threat to domestic security. In Goode's terms, Ellison himself discursively becomes the embodiment of the disruptive foreigner in the domestic homeland and in the halls of power, even though he can demonstrate a long genealogy on American soil. He becomes estranged by his affiliation with Islam.

Other public officials have also used this polemic to frame the Islamic threat. For instance, Los Angeles police chief William Bratton suggested that African American inmates in U.S. prisons are prone to be the conduits of a radical form of Islam (referred to as "the Islam movement") that will spread among black communities and gang members who will then become "homegrown terrorists."[9] In the context of the anti-immigrant backlash and the "war" on terror, such images of brown and black collusion to dismantle and destroy the American nation testify to the technologies of power that could be exercised against the Other within the United States. Further, in Goode's view, that those "Islamic jihadists" outside the United States—in Iraq and elsewhere—might want to see an Islamic flag over the White House escalates the dangers represented by a limited number of lethal terrorist organizations "out there." Such organizations could, ideologically and materially, move stealthily into the homeland. Could a Muslim actually be president?

The management of risk and danger is always in process. In these two examples, links between criminal gang activity and terrorism on the one hand, and on the other, the category of race were forged and mobilized for different regulatory functions. Goode's rhetoric was to signify the notion of America as a territorially bound nation-state and is part of a broader discursive regime of an exceptionalist America. The rhetorical turn grabbed the opportunity to mobilize the already familiar representation of the "Islamic jihadist/terrorist," part of the dominant discourse since 9/11, to support an anti-immigrant project and to put in place more restrictive provisions governing immigration. For his part, Police Chief Bratton also made ready use of Islam as a rhetorical tool of argument. He revived older racial technologies to criminalize "the Islam movement" in a way that justifies the military training of metropolitan police officers. Both racial profiling and heightened prison security regimes became acceptable to many who before 9/11 would have objected.[10] Together, Goode and Bratton's remarks characterize Islam as a racialized danger. The process of othering in a variety of regulatory functions has produced a racialized Muslim identity, a racial formation that comes to fruition depending on forms of power and specificities of time and place. As shown later, this formation is one that recuperates older materials.

Briefly, the second point to which Goode's remarks draw our attention is the growing number and salience of faiths in America. This development extends beyond just the mere presence of multiple truth claims and religious styles of worship to questions about national identity. The idea that Islam is separate from the Judeo-Christian West is potent, although it is as illusory as it is influential. Yet as the following section shows, the construction of the American nation and its citizens' aspirations and obligations takes shape and reaches its limits discursively, in contextually specific ways.

The reaction to Ellison's choice on the part of conservatives spawned a counterreaction across a broad swath of liberal supporters. The image of multicultural America was used to counter the discursive construction of an exclusively Christian America that would see an oath on the Bible as a requisite for public service. A lively skirmish of the culture wars unfolded on the editorial pages of metropolitan newspapers, on radio airwaves, and in the blogosphere, where even liberal multiculturalists pledged their allegiance to the American nation.[11] Much of the newsworthiness of this debate can be attributed to the cultural dynamic it constructs between a culturally conservative Judeo-Christian nation and a secular humanist one. This dynamic reflects societal anxieties over the spatial politics and over the significant demographic changes alluded to earlier. In its coverage, we see the various media framing the swearing-in ceremony in divergent ways. The major metropolitan newspapers tended to frame this event as an occasion to celebrate American diversity and tolerance. They circulated the notion that the nation is constituted by the contributions of its various constituencies—the racialized and gendered subjects who see themselves as Americans ("Are we America or not?"). The majority of radio talk shows and many bloggers decried the lack of Americanness at the core of Ellison's choice. Some questioned Ellison's primary loyalty—was it primarily with an agenda of Islam or with his vision of the Constitution?[12]

Significantly, Ellison's speech act of swearing an oath—"to support and defend the U.S. Constitution against all enemies, foreign and domestic, and bear true faith and allegiance to the same . . . without any mental reservations or purpose of evasion"[13]—is a double declaration. In one respect, Ellison makes an outward statement, affirming his loyalty to the nation and promising to uphold the foundational document of that nation, the U.S. Constitution. He builds on distinctly national roots and sources to strongly affiliate with the nation-state, while at the same time maintaining his position outside it. And in another respect, the same speech act has an inner aspect, affirming individual values and intentions. In the former, Ellison's identity as a public servant is structural in nature, being dependent upon the roles assumed as an adult member of the community and as a person who has sworn to his duty as a defender of the rule of law. This structural identity, which is contingent upon institutional roles (member of Congress, lawmaker, attorney, citizen, voter, etc.), is markedly different from an *ascriptive* identity, which Representative Goode and the explicit culture call upon to define Ellison—or, for that matter, *any* Muslim—as categorically incapable of undertaking the role of public servant precisely because of the inner aspect of the speech act, the affirmation of values and intentions. This argument holds that Muslims, as believers in the Qur'an, cannot truthfully swear (whether on a Bible, a Qur'an, or any other totem) to defend the U.S. Constitution because Islam is opposed to republican ideals.[14] Being Muslim, it is argued, makes one automatically suspect because one can draw on religious authorities living in other, very different societies. This means that as Muslims, they categorically have an inherent capacity for disloyalty, marking them for exile from the political community.[15]

Notwithstanding, Ellison's double declaration of the outward and inner aspects of this oath defies his detractors' efforts to stigmatize. It is at one and the same time a declaration and a performative action.[16] The constative speech act simply corresponds to the world—it is a structural requirement of Ellison-as-elected-official to take the oath in the prescribed fashion. The performative function of the speech act of oath taking represents the positive affirmation of his intention to serve the public. The oath links the performativity of truth telling—of bearing one's soul to disclose one's true intentions—to the project of public service. In the performative aspect of Ellison's declaration of intent (to uphold the rule of law), we can grasp the continuing power of the sacred text as guarantor of sincerity. For even for those giving an affirmation of duty to speak the truth without the aid of a textual prop, the trace of religious authority is still present in the implication that falsehoods result in dire consequences—not just perjury but God's wrath.[17]

The political and legal controversy over the use of a book—*any* book— as a prop in swearing-in ceremonies brings us to the question of the relative position of iconic texts in the configuration of American heritage. The rivalry between religious and secular texts for symbolic supremacy traces the contours of a long-held tension about the role of religion in society and the government's relationship to the many religions embraced by its people.[18] Reflecting on the value we attach to the use of iconic texts to secure the verbal act of speaking the truth—illustrated here not just by Ellison's oath of office but also by reference to the use of the Qur'an in courtrooms—we may become aware of how close we still are to a political theology whose provenance dates to the religious oaths and confessional model of the 13th century. In the same way, we become aware of how closely linked our religious and secular symbols are. The confessional subject—in this case, the public servant or trial witness swearing an oath—is bound to self-examine and to affirm the results by testifying truthfully. In that process the state, via its legal apparatus, holds the power to legitimize the individual as a part of the broader community, a power that has its roots in religious authority. As Peter Brooks would have it, "what we are today—the entire conception of the self, its relation to interiority and to others—is largely tributary of the confessional requirement."[19]

Others have argued that the modern (popular) form of confession, the autobiography, owes something to the penitent practice of auricular confession. Even for those whose lives are relatively untouched by the Catholic Church or by religion of any kind, the confessional model of examining one's life (one's past, one's deepest thoughts and wishes) is now deeply implicated in our everyday morality. The confessional model appears in popular culture and official regulatory practices as a means to account for the individual self. Reflecting on Foucault's work, Brooks points out that the verbal act of confession takes place in relation to power, since one does not confess (or swear an oath) without the presence of the "agency that requires the confession, imposes it, weighs it, and intervenes to judge, punish, pardon, console, reconcile."[20] Thus the continuity between Christian methods of confession and modern technologies in governing crime (e.g., surveillance and interrogation) are consequential; the need to reveal transgressive thoughts and actions to an intermediary (priest) may have eventually lost its sacral dimension and spread to other relationships (e.g., psychiatrist or detective). Even so, the confession and the oath retain traces of their religious origin. Finally, were the spoken word considered to be sufficient to verify the truth, the presence of a scriptural text would not be necessary. In the case of oaths, the text becomes an icon of the remnants of religious authority, a supplement to the spoken word that shields the oath taker from the temptation to transgress the limits of community standards or common morality. The text becomes the supplement for the spoken word, which is underdetermined, and ensures the viability of law and maintains law's authority. Again, as shown in the previous chapter, this question of supplementarity introduces a potentially subversive element: Is the supplement adding on to or replacing the spoken word?

How can we better understand the slippage between the cultural urge toward confession and mistrust about the truth of this speech act? Taking a person at his word slips into "the truth of the Word" by virtue of the need to augment the spoken word with an oath sworn on a sacred text, which posits its own divine authority. In an increasingly secularized culture, the circumstances in which truth of the self is performed is still secured with reference to the Word (of God). Below I focus in more detail on Ellison's taking the oath of office, followed by a consideration of the use of the Qur'an for courtroom oaths, a subject of litigation recently in North Carolina. Both events yield cultural representations that are filled with ambiguities and normativity.

Swearing on Jefferson's Qur'an

The essential features of Ellison's Qur'an oath-taking controversy are as follows. In 2006 Democratic candidate Keith Ellison won election to the United States Congress, representing Minnesota's fifth congressional district (including the city of Minneapolis). The first African American elected to Congress from Minnesota, Ellison is also the first Muslim to hold an elected federal office, although many other Muslims have held municipal, county, and state-level offices. Ellison himself served two terms in the Minnesota House of Representatives. At the age of 19, Ellison converted from Catholicism to Sunni Islam while attending Wayne State University in Detroit, Michigan. During his election bid, it was reported in the press that while attending the University of Minnesota Law School, Ellison wrote articles in support of Louis Farrakhan, the leader of the Nation of Islam.[21] These articles caused a stir. In none of his electoral bids, neither in 2006 nor in previous elections, did Ellison make an issue of his Muslim American identity; he did not campaign as the "Muslim candidate." In his run for Congress, Ellison gained the endorsement of the publisher of American Jewish World, a Minneapolis–St. Paul newspaper, which helped to neutralize the effect of media coverage on the question of Ellison's previous support for Louis Farrakhan.

Two days after Ellison's election to Congress, the Council on American-Islamic Relations (CAIR), the largest Muslim advocacy organization in the United States, announced that Ellison would be a keynote speaker at their annual banquet in Virginia. However, on November 13, 2006, the Minneapolis Star Tribune published an article stating that Ellison would not be attending the CAIR banquet. The article quoted the congressman-elect as saying that the CAIR announcement that he would be a keynote speaker was the result of miscommunication. Instead of attending the banquet, Ellison sent a videotaped address.[22] Endorsements of Ellison from individuals working for CAIR had been a flashpoint in Ellison's election campaign, with critics asserting that CAIR is funded by Islamic extremists.

On November 14, 2006, in an interview on CNN *Headline News*, commentator Glenn Beck asked Ellison to prove that he is "not working with our enemies," adding, "and I know you're not. I'm not accusing you of being an enemy, but that's the way I feel, and I think a lot of Americans feel that way." Ellison replied that his constituents know that he has a deep love and affection for his country, and that he doesn't need to prove his patriotic stripes. Ellison also said that "Osama Bin Laden no more represents Islam than Timothy McVeigh represented Christianity."[23] Glenn Beck subsequently expressed remorse about the opening of his interview, saying that it was quite possibly the worst word choice of all time, attributing it to "my lack of intelligence."[24]

On November 18, 2006, Ellison addressed the Fourth Annual Body Meeting of the North American Imams Federation on the topic of imams (Muslim prayer leaders) and politics. It was upon their return from this annual meeting that six imams were ejected from a Phoenix-bound U.S. Airways plane, a controversy in which Ellison attempted to play a role in bringing together the concerned parties for dialogue.

On November 28, 2006, political commentator and talk show host Dennis Prager published an editorial on the conservative Web site townhall.com criticizing Ellison's announcement of his intent to use the Qur'an instead of the Bible at his photo-op reenactment of the swearing-in ceremony. Prager's critique drew responses from CAIR, the American Family Association (a conservative Christian organization), and, among others, the Anti-Defamation League (an advocacy group started by the B'nai Brith, dedicated to stopping the defamation of Jewish people).

In response to "scores and hundreds of emails" from constituents after Prager's editorial was published, Virgil Goode, a fifth-term congressman from Virginia, wrote a letter in which he said that, like Prager, he believed that Ellison's choice threatened "the values and beliefs traditional to the United States of America." In this letter, referring to himself in the third person, Goode also states that "if American citizens don't wake up and adopt the Virgil Goode position on immigration there will likely be many more Muslims elected to office and demanding the use of the Koran."[25]

On December 19, 2006, the text of Representative Goode's constituent letter was published on the c-ville.com Web site, a Charlottesville (N.C.) newsweekly. Subsequently the Web site smokinggun.com also posted the letter, and media attention continued to grow, with the story widely circulated by the Associated Press, Gannett, and others. Stories ran in major newspapers, such as the *Washington Post* and *New York Times*,[26] as well as smaller journals such as the *Roanoke Times* and *Richmond Times-Dispatch*. Advocacy organizations such as CAIR called for an apology, but Goode, through his staff, declined to apologize.

In December, Ellison's staff located a first edition Qur'an once owned by Thomas Jefferson. This edition, which was held in the Library of Congress, was an English translation by George Sale, published in London in 1734. Arrangements were made to use this edition for the reenactment. An Ellison staffer stated that the choice was significant because "it dates religious tolerance back to the time of our founding fathers."[27] In commenting on the Jeffersonian Qur'an, Ellison himself said that the Qur'an is "definitely an important historical document in our national history and demonstrates that Jefferson was a broad visionary thinker who not only possessed a Qur'an, but read it. . . . It would have been something that contributed to his own thinking." Ellison also said the fact that Jefferson owned a Qur'an demonstrated "that from the very beginning of our country, we had people who were visionary, who were religiously tolerant, who believed that knowledge and wisdom could be gleaned from any number of sources, including the Qur'an."[28]

After the swearing-in ceremony Ellison complained in interviews that he was tired of all the attention his choice of the Qur'an was getting and wanted to turn to the issues facing lawmakers. He struggled against being pigeonholed as the "Muslim representative." The overdetermination of his speech act had construed Ellison as the Muslim subject, and even his attempt to make his swearing-in ceremony into a multicultural space had essentially failed to resist the polemical logic of his critics who questioned the nature of his action. In effect, the spectacle around his oath had limited his ability to speak, to claim a position, and control the multiple meanings that were ascribed to his choice. To qualify for public service, Ellison had to mobilize a bit of Americana as a strategy to counter the discourse of American nationhood that had labeled Islam as the constitutive (and dangerous) "outside." The multiculturalism Ellison had attempted to perform had actually caused united, patriotic Americans to rise in opposition to his performance and in its turn, this reaction shaped Ellison's comeback to use not just any Qur'an, but Jefferson's. The materials available to Ellison to resist the nationalist discourse were already selected for him by the dominant narrative that posited a lack of Americanness at the core of Ellison's decision to use the Qur'an.

The choice of Jefferson's Qur'an begs the question, what was relevant to Jefferson about the Qur'an? This personal copy of the Qur'an was one of well over 6,000 books that formed the basis of what is now the Library of Congress. By 1814 when the British burned the U.S. Capitol and the Library of Congress, Jefferson had acquired a large personal collection of books. Congress purchased Jefferson's private library to replace the books lost in the fire. This acquisition included the two-volume Qur'an that was believed to have been purchased by Jefferson as part of his law collection. Jefferson also owned several books about the Ottomans and the "Barbary" pirates. Mark Dimunation, the Chief of the Rare Book and Special Collections at the Library of Congress, maintained that many of Jefferson's law books "refer to the Qur'an as an alternative view of certain legal structures."[29] In his own writing, Jefferson explored theories of religious toleration. For instance, in his auto-biography, Jefferson wrote about the struggle to enact the Bill for Establishing Religious Freedom in 1776, which prohibited religion as a disqualification from political office holding. He described the reach of the protections as "universal," to "comprehend, within the mantle of its protection, the Jew and the Gentile, the Christian and Mahometan, the Hindoo, and the infidel in every denomination."[30]

Yet Jefferson's orientation toward Islam was complicated. Like many of his generation, his use of Muslims and Islamic images demonstrated a well-established rhetorical tradition of his day. That is, he simply had to cite the similarities between his opponent's views and the purported beliefs of Islam as a way of discrediting arguments adverse to his own.[31] This style of argumentation was evident in the record of the constitutional conventions; the widespread use of "knowledge" of Islam, derived from observations of the despotic ways of the Ottoman Empire and other Muslim entities, supported political points in consequential debates. The construction of the American experiment in democracy created the necessary backdrop (Oriental despotism) to proclaim the new republic's superiority. In any event, it was Jefferson's rhetorical strategy of power to make references to Islam as a discursive act, to reinforce American superiority by delegitimizing Islam and confining Muslims in a liminal space. Behind this lurked a longstanding, ingrained attitude held by many in early America, based on Orientalist stereotypes about "Mahometans" and the "Saracens," especially images of the Muslim world as autocratic or opposed to liberty. Jefferson translated from French an essay that maintained that, historically, Islamic fanaticism had ruined flourishing civilizations in Egypt and Syria. According to historian Robert Allison, Jefferson was so impressed with a book written by a French philosopher about Islamic civilization, *The Ruins, or a Survey of the Revolutions of Empires*, which identified the despotism of the Ottoman caliphate as the cause of its decline, that when he was president he undertook a new translation into English, in 1802.[32]

How is it that North Americans before the 1800s came to know about Islam? Simply put, early Americans derived their impressions about Islam from widely circulated books, sermons, and narratives of North American and European captives in North Africa. Captivity narratives from as early as the 1670s portrayed Arab and Muslim captors as cruel infidels and helped frame a model of discourse that posited the superiority of Christianity over Islam. This discourse became a staple of religious polemics and established the global confrontation between Islam and Christianity for Anglo-Americans.[33] As Thomas Kidd puts it, "print allowed colonists to believe that they had legitimate and useful 'knowledge' of Islam, knowledge that appeared regularly in the print cultures of seventeenth- and eighteenth-century Anglo-America."[34] What many "knew" about Islam early in the 18th century came from religious debates and homilies that used Islam for religious purposes (e.g., Cotton Mather's "The Fierce Monsters of Africa" and "Mahometan Turks and Moors and Devils"). Later commentators often worked with this social imaginary to make use of Islamic categories in building political arguments. Kidd writes of this 18th-century practice that "associating an opponent with the imagined categories of Islam became a standard rhetorical move in religious, and later, political debate, as it empowered and legitimized the accuser as the defender of righteousness, obscuring moral ambiguities and masking strategies for religious or political hegemony."[35]

Iconic Texts

A nice illustration of this practice can be found in the ratification process in late 18th-century North Carolina. The very question of religious tests, which lies at the core of the imbroglio over Ellison's swearing-in ceremony, was central as well to opponents of the U.S. Constitution. William Lancaster, a delegate to the 1788 North Carolina Convention to ratify the U.S. Constitution, projected his gravest fears about the future of government: "But let us remember that we form a government for millions not yet in existence. I have not the art of divination. In the course of four or five hundred years, I do not know how it will work. This is most certain, that Papists may occupy that chair, and Mahometans may take it. I see nothing against it."[36] The chair to which this refers is nothing less than the presidency of the United States. Might a Catholic or a Muslim become president of the United States? In Lancaster's view, such a scenario would be certain if Article VI, Section 3 of the U.S. Constitution were approved. The second clause of this passage directs that "no religious test shall ever be required as a Qualification to any Office or Public Trust under the United States." In North Carolina, the state constitution of 1776 protected free white males who did not deny the "Truth of the Protestant Religion." The prohibition on religious tests contained in the draft Constitution presumably would open the door at the federal level to all non-Protestants and, according to Denise Spellberg, fueled a day-long debate in which "Mahometans" became central to the definition of American ideals of religious and political rights. Anti-Federalists opposed the ban on religious tests, seeing it as an incitement to "Mahometans" to become the enemy within, rather than merely the fearsome enemy abroad. They made ample reference to these fear appeals and the construction of the global confrontation between good and evil as a way of undermining the Federalists' arguments in favor of the prohibition. In their turn, without mentioning religion, the Federalists created a secular argument in favor of ratifying the Constitution, by defending the rights of all persons, even the unambiguously "bad"; anyone of any faith, *even a Muslim*, could become president. The prohibition of religious tests became the new foundation for American pluralism by creating political equality, not just for Protestants, but for all non-Protestants as well. By displacing religious tests as a guarantor of the public trust, the new republic bound the citizen (and elected official) in a common loyalty to the U.S. Constitution. This newfound loyalty was to be sealed by an invention, a civic oath. This simple move was of enormous symbolic and practical importance, decoupling the demands of religious discipleship from the obligations of democratic citizenship.

As a by-product of the contest among the framers of the Constitution, in the discursive space created at the historical moment of constitution-building, the standard 18th-century conception of "Mahometan" was invoked in domestic debates about religious identity and citizenship. The image that emerged from the North Carolina ratification debate was not simply the image of a faceless foreign threat but of individuated persons potentially possessing the rights of citizens. While in the discourse of the Anti-Federalists, all Mahometans, together with Papists were conflated as part of a monolithic threat to the new republic, the alternative discursive model offered by the Federalists was of Mahometans as individual believers with rights to be guaranteed under the new Constitution. In defense of a ban on religious tests, the Federalists developed, in theory, egalitarian ideals of Mahometan rights under the law. The transcripts of the debate show that the Federalists' arguments were just as inflected with prejudices against Mahometans as the opposition's arguments. Both sides cast Mahometans as inimical to emerging American ideals of political and religious freedom. Exactly how and why the Anti-Federalists and the Federalists invoked this image is interesting because it plays a significant role in forging American ideals in the founding period.[37] What is most significant is the impact this binary opposition between Islam and Protestant Christianity played in securing the ratification of the ban on religious tests, at least in the North Carolina debates over ratification.

The Federalists' position in favor of rights for Mahometans as non-Protestants was, however, purely strategic. No one believed that these rights would be claimed in practice. Neither the Anti-Federalists nor the Federalists could imagine a population of free American Muslims, but the Federalists alone argued that such a population would never reside in the United States.[38] The assertion of egalitarian political and religious status for Mahometans in the United States was only an invention, an outer frontier of what might be possible. The specter of the Mahometan was plainly a verbal fiction created to justify the ban on religious tests. Like Jefferson's argument in favor of religious toleration, Federalists argued in favor of a plural notion of democracy, defending the right of even a Mahometan to be citizen of the new republic. For opponents of the Constitution, the compelling totems developed for theological debates tracing back to the late 17th century and populating the sermons of Cotton Mather and other New England preachers (Muhammad as a false prophet, the autocratic and licentious Mahometan, the Muslim slave trader) served in these new debates about how to govern. The South Carolina and Virginia constitutional debates also attested to the power of Orientalist images about Mahometans, Islam, and the Ottoman Empire as a resource for politicians who harbored fundamental differences over church/state relations. For all their disagreements, these adversaries in the political arena could agree on one thing: Islam fostered religious and political repression. Who might exercise power in the nascent American republic? The peculiar thought that a Muslim would hold political power in the United States was almost too much to bear for many a delegate to the constitutional conventions.[39]

For their part, the Federalists thought the prospect exceptional—an exercise in defining the outer limits of theories of toleration—but mapped as pure fantasy. Their opponents, on the other hand, thought the danger was real. The three Anti-Federalists who invoked images of Islam when debating the proposed constitutional ban on religious tests at the North Carolina constitutional convention were all preachers—William Lancaster and Henry Abbott were Baptists, and David Caldwell, a Presbyterian. Among the Federalists, the two who spoke on this issue in 1788 were both Anglicans by faith and lawyers by profession. In his writings and speeches, James Iredell, the staunchest defender of the rights of Mahometans, relied on Blackstone as much as the Bible to fashion a sense of the law as almost a "science" and a "means to control politics" as well.[40] Two years later, Iredell was appointed to the U.S. Supreme Court.

The prospect that a Mahometan might be elected to office came up in speeches at the convention a half-dozen times, including references to the possibility that one might be president if there were a ban on religious tests. The first mention that a Mahometan might hold elective office was made by the Baptist minister Henry Abbott, who cautioned that *anyone* could become an elected representative if the religious test were absent: "pagans, Deists, and Mahometans might obtain office" if no religious test were required.[41] But there's some indication that Abbott believed his reference was so outlandish as to be comical. He continued in his oration to banter about oaths sworn not upon the Bible, but in the name of the supreme power of "Jupiter, Juno, Minerva, Proserpine, or Pluto."[42] The mere recitation of these ancient gods of Greece was meant to convey the absurdity contained in the very thought that anyone but a Protestant would represent the public. Abbot's reference to Mahometans and its echoes throughout the day raised the (by then, standard) visage of a foreign threat to the nascent American republic. It also forged the implausible new domestic conceptual category as yet unknown to the American public—the category of the feared believer of Islam as an American, even as a potential public servant. Known, inherited fears about Islamic political power were extended to statewide debates about ratification of the nation's constitution. In North Carolina and elsewhere, the ratification debates mobilized older materials to fashion a new category of inclusion in the new republic, moving a threatening population from the periphery to the center of political debate.[43]

The point here is that the fractious debates over adoption of the religious test in the U.S. Constitution contained the binary distinction between "us" and "them" that was inherited from centuries of global confrontation between Islam and Christianity. The Federalists did not win the day in 1788—North Carolina deferred ratification until after a second convention in 1789—but ultimately, the Constitution was adopted with the ban on religious tests intact. While Federalists used the abstraction to make a point about toleration but ultimately dismissed the conceptual category of Muslim-as-public-servant, their opponents considered what it would mean if the foreign threat were to be incarnated as "American" under the mantle of electoral politics. The nodal point for these discussions was the speech act of swearing an oath of office: Were officials to be taken at their word, without the aid of scriptural texts? Or was it necessary to invoke religious authority to supplement the political? Was it possible that non-Protestants, including believers of Islam, could fit with 18th-century notions about how to govern?

Another sociolegal field to consider is the courtroom. Oaths taken by witnesses and jurors in courtroom trials have long used scriptural props to compel the truth telling of the oath taker. As it happens, a controversy brewed in North Carolina in the early years of the 21st century, nearly simultaneously with the congressional oath-taking debate, concerning the use of the Qur'an for courtroom oaths. It is to this controversy I turn next.

What Power Lies in an Oath?

In the criminal justice system, the idea of using a scripture to secure an act of giving a promise—to tell the truth, *so help me God*—has its roots in *judicium dei*, divine judgment. This doctrine looked to physical signs of divine intervention to prove the truth of testimony.[44] The oath, then, was designed to incite both comfort and fear: Comfort was supposed to be experienced in the knowledge that the speaker will be truthful because of the fear in the speaker's heart of God's punishment. One who did not fear God could not be trusted to speak the truth. Since historically the penalty associated with falsehood imposed by the state—incarceration and fines for perjury—was not presumed in and of itself sufficient to elicit the truth, the concept of God's punishment has been present to add gravity to courtroom proceedings.

The required courtroom oath has evolved. While at one time the witness or the juror needed to rest her hand on a Bible while swearing in, now most courtrooms accept an affirmation of truth, giving those not willing to use the Bible an alterna-tive means to offer a pledge of honesty sanctioned by law. The oath, then, has served as a vehicle to relay the truth, and while extracted from its religious meaning its traces remain purposeful in courtroom procedure.

In North Carolina, the provisions of the law that stipulate the form that court-room oaths will take were challenged by the ACLU of North Carolina in a case involving a Muslim litigant. In 2003, Syidah Mateen appeared in court in a domestic dispute, and requested, upon raising her hand to swear on the Bible, whether she could have a Qur'an instead. Having no Qur'an available, the judge said she could take an affirmation of truth with no scriptural prop, which she chose to do. Two years later, not realizing that the absence of Qur'ans in the courtroom might have been mandated by law, the same woman returned to the Guilford County, North Carolina, courthouse with several Qur'ans that were donated by a variety of Mus-lim organizations for the purpose of stocking the public courtrooms with the holy book. The judge who sets the policy for the nine Superior courts in Guilford County said, "An oath on the Qur'an is not a lawful oath under our law."[45]

A short time later Mateen returned to court before a different judge, before whom she requested, and was denied, the opportunity to take the oath on a Qur'an. In refusing Mateen the use of the Qur'an this time, the judge cited a 1777 North Carolina statute, which states: "Judges and other persons who may be empowered to administer oaths, shall . . . require the party to be sworn to lay his hand upon the Holy Scriptures, in token of his engagement to speak the truth and in further token that, if he should swerve from the truth, he may be justly deprived of all the bless-ings of that holy book and made liable to that vengeance which he has imprecated on his own head."[46] Having been denied the chance to use the Qur'an as "holy scriptures," Mateen and the ACLU of North Carolina took the matter to court. The lawsuit sought a declaratory judgment to have an answer to this question: Can the term *holy scriptures* be understood to mean not only the Christian Bible but also the Old Testament, the Qur'an, and the Bhagavad-Gita? The lawsuit was dismissed since Mateen was given the opportunity to testify under an affirmation of truth when she appeared in court. The mobilization of the concept of choice is crucial here—what is decisive before the court is that she *chose* to take the affirmation of truth option instead of the oath—in conceptualizing Mateen as a liberal subject who is "free" to participate in a democratic "rule of law" project. When the case was taken up on appeal, a three-judge panel unanimously reversed the lower court rul-ing to dismiss the motion for declaratory judgment. The appellate ruling also men-tioned that the appeals court had received "affidavits from eight Jewish members of ACLU-NC who were residents of Guilford County and eligible for jury duty, stating they would prefer to swear on the Hebrew Bible rather than the Christian Bible if selected as jurors or asked to testify in court."[47] While declining to comment on the merits of the case, the appeals court panel ruled that the ACLU and Mateen had a justiciable controversy.

The case then returned to lower court. In May 2007 the Wake County Superior Court judge Paul Ridgeway ruled in favor of allowing the Qur'an in the courtroom, upholding an 1856 North Carolina Supreme Court decision, *Shaw v. Moore*, establishing that oaths must be administered in a form or upon holy texts that a witness or juror holds "most sacred and obligatory upon their conscience." The opinion in this lower court ruling states that "the highest aim of every legal contest is the search for the truth," and that impediments to truth telling had to be absent from the justice system. Interestingly, the court did not rule the state law unconstitutional or that the term *holy scriptures* stood for anything more than the Christian Bible. Instead, the court held that all persons share the absolute right to worship freely, and that this right is guaranteed by the state's constitution.[48]

The language of the North Carolina statute in question reads:

> Whereas, lawful oaths for discovery of truth and establishing right are
> necessary and highly conducive to the important end of good
> government; and being most solemn appeals to Almighty God, as the
> omniscient witness of truth and the just and omnipotent avenger of
> falsehood, and whereas, lawful affirmation for the discovery of truth and
> establishing right are necessary and highly conducive to the important
> end of good government, therefore, such oaths and affirmations ought to
> be taken and administered with the utmost solemnity. (N.C. Gen. Stat.
> Sec 11-1)

The 2007 ruling in Mateen's case upholds 18th-century reasoning and discursive connections between theistic power to compel the speaker to reveal her inner state and secular authority. Also, the ruling holds that in addition to what state law already allows (laying a hand over the Bible, saying "so help me God" without the use of a religious book, or affirming to tell the truth), the law must also allow any form or holy text deemed "sacred and obligatory" by a witness or juror before the court. Rather than seeing this as additive to other components of justice, opponents of this decision argued that sanctioning the Qur'an was a diminution of rights. For instance, Mat Staver, founder and chair of the Liberty Counsel, a Christian non-profit litigation and policy organization, believes that acceptance of other text options is a "secularization" of a religious oath, a sign of the creeping secularization of the judicial system. Taking the Christian Bible away from the process, he says, "changes the founding fathers' notion of accountability to God based on the Ten Commandments. . . . Our courts have weakened and watered down the religious history and the significance of oath-taking."[49] In Staver's eyes, the multiculturalist model of adding on religious texts detracts from the meaning and purpose of the

oath and violates the rights of Christians to live in accord with the political theology of the founding period. The vocabulary of attenuation is powerful in this
expression, constructing a nation discursively as drawing on something normative
that is other than its original promise, articulated by the generation that framed the
American Constitution. Other Christian advocates objecting to the court's ruling
called it a "war on Christianity," a battle in a larger war being waged in the courtroom and, as well, in the schools, the media, and the shopping malls.[50]

Similarly, Bill O'Reilly, commentator of the highly rated program on Fox
Channel *The O'Reilly Factor* and of his syndicated radio show, *The Radio Factor*,
argued that historically courtroom witnesses would swear on the Bible because it
was a symbol "you didn't mess with." When people do not swear on the Bible, they
"perjure themselves all day, every day." Secular progressives, according to O'Reilly,
"knock out any spirituality" when they expand the options beyond the mandated
religious oath in courtroom testimony. He averred: "But, look, the point of the matter is that it was there for about one hundred and—almost 200 years—where you
would go into court, and you would swear on the Bible to tell the truth, the whole
truth, and nothing but the truth. And the Bible was considered a symbol that you
didn't screw with, that you didn't mess with." In this and other oratory O'Reilly's
normative aim is most likely about the identification of secularists as the villains of
this piece, destroying what he imagines as a Golden Past, when people told the
truth. However, the key role players in his scenario include not just secularists but
also Muslims and immigrants as dangers to the victims and the virtuous.[51] He has
constructed a conceptual category of *anyone* of a different orientation who fails to
recognize the pre-eminence of the Bible as being a potential perjurer.

Conclusion

The election of a Muslim congressman for the first time in American history perhaps unexpectedly engendered not more ease with the growing diversity in America
as much as *unease* with the notion of the American nation "under siege" in the
world at large. Various laws passed in the aftermath of 9/11—the U.S.A. Patriot Act
among others seeking to increase security through more invasive intelligence gathering and stricter regulation of immigration—and narratives circulated by the
mainstream media, politicians and countless others further helped to elaborate reasons for fear and needs for a "culture of control,"[52] including which "enemies" must
be confronted by the government to protect citizens.[53] It is in this context that Representative Keith Ellison's swearing-in ceremony has been characterized as non-
American in essence and, more ominously, as a signifier of the risk all around us.
Race and religion intertwine tightly so that in the new millennium, systems intended

to manage the danger represented by Islam borrow from an older tradition of innovations of governance. This tradition, which runs from Jefferson's generation, also emerged in response to fear—a fear of power that corrupts, a fear of the Orientalist Other—and was highly influential in the constitutional debates. These uses of fear appeals may be separated by several generations but they share common traits.

Perhaps nothing describes the rising hysteria over Muslims as elected officials better than the conundrum raised in the aftermath of the 2008 election of Barack Obama as president of the United States.[54] Would he use his full name at the inauguration, when he had avoided mention of his middle name during the campaign? Putting aside the opprobrium that swirled around his Muslim ancestry—with his father from Kenya, not to mention the years of his youth spent in Indonesia, could he be loyal to the American nation? Once elected, it remained significant for some of his detractors that the president-elect's middle name is Hussein. Battling fears even more deeply rooted than the racial barrier he had to overcome in order to be the first black man elected president, Obama has a middle name that has proven to be worrisome. Might a Muslim be president? Members of the president-elect's transition team assured the press that Obama would take the oath of office on the Bible at the inauguration—after all, hadn't he done so in his public reenactment of the oath when elected to the Senate? Nevertheless, concerns circulated in the blogosphere and editorial pages of newspapers whether the oath would be taken on the Qur'an.[55]

In the semiotic communication of American pluralism, in which Islamic presence is a potent signifier, the Qur'an is highly productive. The Qur'an is one of the oldest rivals to the Bible as a text positing authoritative truth claims—Cotton Mather claimed upon reading an English translation that if only the Muslims would comprehend it as he had, they would see it pointed to Christ as the true messiah. In short, the Qur'an provokes a crisis of representation. Making the case for the simultaneous truth of world religions—that each has a legitimate claim to the truth—has rarely been popular with the American public; more often, it has been overshadowed by religious exclusivists such as Mather, who see only one mode of religious thought (their own) as true and all others false. I have shown above how claims to seek the truth are grounded in cultural specificity. The judge in the North Carolina case about the Qur'an in the courtroom proclaimed that "the highest aim of every legal contest is the search for the truth."[56] The Bible has long been privileged as the religious collateral necessary to secure the truth in the interest of justice, relaying a culturally embedded notion of justice.

In choosing the Jeffersonian Qur'an for Ellison's swearing in ceremony, his staff was faced with very limited options when it came time to demonstrate the congressman's loyalty to the nation. The discourse of American nationalism, including the nativist anti-immigrant backlash in some media commentators' and politicians' remarks, made it difficult for Ellison, or for that matter any Muslim subject, to "choose" what the signifiers adorning his private ceremony meant. The multiple meanings the Qur'an might have held in that setting were hijacked by the discourse about national belonging and by the wide range of mechanisms of power. Not only the institutions of the state but also a broader array of actors constitute a kind of rationality that acts upon and structures the dimensions of possible action. To counter the anti-immigrant tenor of his critics, Ellison's staff selected a Qur'an that was located in the seat of American power. But that Qur'an is imbued with Orientalist meaning and belonged to an American leader who, while arguing in the abstract for expanded rights and toleration, was not above using the rhetorical categories of his day, of Ottoman despotism and Barbary piracy. Ellison's speech act of swearing an oath of office for becoming a public servant was heavily marked by the governmentality that conditioned it. Throughout the media spectacle pundits, journalists, and politicians felt it necessary to warn of the fragility of an American way of life in the face of the terrorist threat. How did Ellison develop in that crucial moment as a specifically Muslim subject, as opposed to being primarily an African American, or Minnesotan? His strategic use of this Qur'an linked him, narrated him, into the American nation, and at the same time, asserted a differently racialized and religious origin in relation to the liberal nation-state. Together with Mateen's courtroom oath case, Ellison's speech act illustrates a lexical strategy to normalize Muslim cultural citizenship in a dialogic process, constructing the normative claim to be Muslim *and* American through law.

4

Britain's Fear of Shari'acracy

In the previous chapter, I discussed how in order to be normatively Muslim *and* American under the rule of law, a U.S. congressman discursively raised claims against the tide of cultural racism and the looming specter of an ill-defined Islamic radical. I showed how the nation's self-conception in the United States is imbued with the operating assumption of Muslim disloyalty, of a racialized fear of the outsider and of the new global threat to an American way of life. This fear is colorfully illustrated in a letter from another member of Congress who, in decrying Representative Keith Ellison's lack of Americanness, hoped to deliver a damning judgment against contemporary immigration to a nation of immigrants.

In this chapter, I turn my attention to a related process in Britain, in which the racialized Muslim subject is compelled to reproduce the dominant modes of thinking about civic virtue. In Britain, the public character of religion and arguments in favor of pluralizing the linkage between state and religion have emerged as part of the more general discourse about multiculturalism to become what one scholar calls a "moderate rather than absolute secularism."[1] For many, this trend is misguided as it tends toward a (deeper) state endorsement of religion. But for others, it almost seems to be the only way to address the discrepancy between the already existing institutional role of religious conscience in state affairs (e.g., the 26 bishops who sit in the House of Lords, not to mention the privileged position of the Church of England) and the failure of the public order to recognize religious minorities as political actors. As Tariq Modood has argued, if we can see that the public sphere is not morally neutral, we can begin to understand the phenomenon of Muslim groups seeking greater visibility and inclusion, engaging in the political process, and "not simply asking to be left alone or to be civilly tolerated."[2]

In February 2008, the archbishop of Canterbury and head of the worldwide Anglican Communion, Dr. Rowan Williams, gave a lecture at the Royal Courts of Justice. The lecture ruffled many British feathers.[3] In it, Williams suggested that British Muslims be allowed to live freely under shari'a law so long as the application of shari'a did not deny to anyone the rights guaranteed under state law. Williams's lecture signaled that there is something more than just the official British legal system alone. Williams argued that persons be given the option to choose the jurisdiction under which they will resolve particular matters under family law, financial arrangements, and conflict resolution. This speech not only highlighted the significance of legal pluralism—which the archbishop called "interactive pluralism"; it also raised the question of what it means to be a Muslim by conviction and free choice. In a subsequent radio interview, Williams observed that such accommodation was "unavoidable," given the demography of Britain, and in July of the same year, the High Chief Justice Lord Phillips publicly seconded what the archbishop had said. Thus, the highest authorities in law and religion in Britain equally acknowledged the multiple legal ordering of society and the presence of a religious system that does not depend upon official recognition for legitimacy.

This chapter focuses on the "shari'a debate" in Britain, normative ordering with respect to the public role of religion, and cognizance of the operation of shari'a councils in Britain, some of which are now on a par with other religious arbitration tribunals such as the Jewish Beth Din courts. I look at questions of agency and representation at a significant site, where the diaspora intersects with the national spaces it continually negotiates. Controversies over the place of alternative dispute resolution mechanisms, such as shari'a councils operating within the presumed uniformity of British law, call attention to the contrasting normative discourses long in gestation. From one direction, these discourses are infused with popular perceptions of an ominous rise in Islamic religiosity, and from another, they are instilled with a renewed relationship among faith, community, and moral obligation.

Shari'a or Not? Britain's Dilemma

In September 2008, far from the hue and cry brought on by the archbishop's lecture in the Royal Courts of Justice, the British government quietly announced that it had allowed the decisions of a network of shari'a councils in Britain to be legally enforced through county courts or High Court. Until that time, shari'a councils had operated on an unofficial basis (i.e., without judicial enforcement) and depended on voluntary compliance of Muslim disputants. The policy change was in effect for a year after September 2007 and involved the government classification of existing shari'a councils in London, Birmingham, Bradford, and Manchester (with two more planned for Edinburgh and Glasgow) as tribunals with legally binding authority, provided the disputing parties consent to the religious jurisdiction. The government found authority to classify these tribunals in a provision of the Arbitration Act 1996. Powers are limited to civil matters, primarily in family and financial disputes, and the network of councils is managed by Sheikh Faisal Aqtab Siddiqi of the Muslim Arbitration Tribunal.[4] The Labour government was roundly criticized by its opponents in Parliament for quietly sanctioning shari'a councils. Many politicians raised the alarm that the government's decision would entail the introduction of a parallel legal system. Conservative member of parliament (MP) and shadow home secretary Dominic Grieve felt that enforcement of shari'a council decisions was unlawful and said that "British law is absolute and must remain so."[5]

Yet the covetous defense of state law's uniformity found in the hostile reaction to the news bears little resemblance to the diversity experienced on the ground. Public dismay notwithstanding, religious tribunals have long operated in British society. Islamic shari'a councils have provided an unofficial alternative to the government's courts and have constituted a communal form of governance over the past thirty years. The rulings of Jewish Beth Din courts in dispute arbitration, marriage, and divorce have been routinely recognized within the British legal system for more than 100 years (being authorized under a precursor to the current arbitration law), and the majority of their arbitration awards that are contested have been enforced by civil courts, although they can be overruled. Orthodox Jewish couples can obtain a "get" or Jewish divorce through the Beth Din system but must also get a civil divorce in order to change their legal status. The same holds true for Muslims; a Muslim couple typically marries twice—once in a registered ceremony and once in a religious ceremony—and if the marriage dissolves, they must also get a civil divorce since a religious divorce certificate alone does not change one's marital status. In Britain, these religious courts cannot force anyone to come to them instead of using the government's courts in civil matters; in other words, disputants must agree to have their civil disputes adjudicated in these tribunals, and the settlements do not need to incorporate British law. However, British officials assert that if a specific settlement contravenes the broader objectives of legislative policy (e.g., fairness), the courts will not uphold the decision. So in theory, if the arbitrated settlement of a contract dispute were patently unfair, the civil courts would overturn it. Or, if a Muslim woman received a diminished share of property in an inheritance or divorce case, the civil courts might intervene. To have these shari'a decisions enforced, the British justice ministry maintains that the parties need to draft a consent order embodying the terms of the settlement and submit it to a court for approval.[6]

In arguing for a more inclusive understanding of religious practice in state law, the archbishop of Canterbury drew upon a large body of research that had analyzed the extent to which British legal system could already accommodate religious and cultural pluralism. Many scholars have contributed valuable insights into the plural legal framework in Britain. Notably, Werner Menski outlines for us the rise of "culture-specific hybrid legal tropes" that challenge our theoretical understanding of legal pluralism,[7] such as *angrezi shari'a* (English shari'a), a contested practice of Muslim personal law in the shadow of British law, which arose from the translocal migration chains from South Asia.[8] When Muslims encountered local obstacles to the continuation of their religious practices, they found ways to adapt Muslim law to the constraints of British legal imperatives. There is considerable evidence that Muslims living in Britain have been able to adapt shari'a to the British environment by taking cognizance of multiple levels of law. Muslims follow certain rules and have modified lifestyles in accordance with state requirements, in particular in the field of family law. For example, when refused exemptions from British public health and animal safety regulations, Muslim meat processors and consumers encountered an obstacle in their observance of halal dietary laws in Britain. The response in the 1980s was to obtain fatwas from jurisconsultants ruling that the method of slaughtering common in Europe would be acceptable for Muslims.[9] Therefore, rules of slaughtering without prestunning the animals were deemed not to be imperative. Subsequently, the British government granted the necessary exemptions, placing Islamic practices on a par legally with Jewish methods for producing kosher meat. Licensing of Muslim halal butchers is now common, but the main point is the consequence of the contact between British and Muslim laws. These are part and parcel of a wider adjustment process and create new spaces for a synthesis of obligation.[10]

Angrezi shari'a is one of the several ways in which Muslims in Britain have demonstrated social creative possibilities for subject formation. Menski posits that to understand the character of Islamic legal activity, it is useful to see it as part of a complex autonomous sociolegal field rather than as the polar opposite of state law. In other words, he draws our attention to the negative implications of familiar accounts, which describe Islamic personal law as "customary law" or unofficial law in Britain. Menski also warns us not to understand personal law as a discrete field, distinct from (and inferior to) official law; the very act of creating the oppositional framework of official/unofficial strongly encourages thinking about law that is organized methodologically around binary categories. Discursively, one can construct a narrative scaffold through which one can talk about law in a manner that implicitly privileges the first side of each oppositional pair used to describe law: official/unofficial, good/bad, universal/particular, impartial/partial, and so on. Inherently unstable, these categories invite conflict and partisan feelings, and underpin a Eurocentric defense of the status quo, insisting that personal law remain at the level of custom and not enter into the formal arena. Instead of wrongly privileging state law, Menski suggests, it would be more useful to consider how different understandings of law and legal postulates interact in a field which may be *dominated* by the laws of the government but which is, nevertheless, composed of multiple legal and normative orderings. It is important to note that, when the state recognizes the legitimacy, either in whole or in part, of the authority of one of the multiplicity of rule-based orders in society (e.g., canon law, ethnic minority law, professional guilds), then rules whose provenance lies elsewhere (i.e., outside the state's law-making apparatus) become a part of the system of adjudication and enforcement.

In this manner, we can see the recent shari'a debate as an example of the state being under pressure to amend "official" law by adding rules and concepts that had been clamoring "for transition from the 'unofficial' to the 'official' part of the whole structure of law."[11] This ad-hoc approach is too narrow and epiphenomenal to provide any stability to legal development or to bring legal scholarship in line with current realities. The "safety valve" approach taken by the British government (and other governments) of acceding to pluralizing demands whenever the pressure gets too great, offering forced and partial cognizance of existing pluralities, is not one that holds much promise for building into the legal system the plural structures needed to reconcile amalgams of the local and the global. The next chapter expands on this point in the American context, looking at how common law techniques of making exceptions to universal rules, applying seemingly neutral postulates of equity, appear to permit accommodation of certain legal claims in marriage and divorce. Yet the American approach may not be any more satisfactory than the British in meeting the challenges inherent in pluralism.

Among Britain's Muslims, there are sharply contrasting views about the advisability of incorporating shari'a councils into the wider legal system. A survey published in February 2006 stated that nearly 40 percent of Muslims in Britain aged 16 to 24 favor the introduction of shari'a in predominantly Muslim areas in Britain (compared to only 17% of those aged 55 and older).[12] This information is not particularly helpful since what is understood as shari'a could be anything from simply trying to live in accord with the prescribed practices (e.g., prayer, charity, fasting during Ramadan) to allegiance to an elaborate corpus of exegesis and jurisprudence from classically trained religious leaders. However, the information provided by the survey does beg the question about Muslim religious practices and loyalty to the state. The Muslim Council of Britain, one of the largest umbrella organizations, has opposed the idea of a dual legal system and many Muslim activists and scholars similarly fear "ghettoization." Yet others have argued that British law privileges Christian practices of marriage and other forms of family law; moreover, given the experience of British colonialism, in which a system of "personal laws" prevailed, individuals ought to have the option of being governed by concurrent systems of law. What is commonly understood by this reference to personal laws are the specific provisions of shari'a that prescribe sets of relations between men and women, as in marital law, where the husband must protect his wife, and the wife, in turn, owes him obedience. These provisions give rise to many other questions—whether the husband's permission is required before the woman can work outside the home; who controls the wife's earnings; how should the administration of different types of property be handled; who holds authority over the children; how should inheritance rights be controlled; and a host of questions over the dissolution of marriages, such as child custody, division of property, and so on. How will women fare once official recognition is granted to designated Muslim arbitration tribunals? Will these tribunals be active enforcers of patriarchal norms?

For many critics of the move toward accommodation, a series of dangers is associated with an "imposed Islamism," which would subordinate women and violate the human rights of any who contest the authority of conservative clerics. Apart from the adverse reaction of non-Muslim British commentators, fears of legal and cultural separatism of Muslims in Britain—of the "campaign for legal dualism"—have engendered internal Muslim resistance to the formalization of shari'a councils.[13] For instance, the advocacy group British Muslims for Secular Democracy, founded in 2006, is critical of the suggestion that shari'a be enforced in Britain since a move in this direction would be detrimental to Muslims and to society as a whole. The organization points out that a single set of Islamic laws could not be applied to British Muslims, who are diverse and hold divergent views about religious practice and cultural customs based on where they are from (geographical origins) and where they are (evolving a European identity). Parallel justice systems would in effect be a denial of inclusion and basic rights.[14]

In the following section, I outline the productive power of the main rationality underpinning the shari'a debate—the need to "rescue from culture" those most vulnerable to the practices of conservative structures of Islam. Before discussing the shari'a debate in more detail, I address the common fear of a spreading fundamentalism and the contingent normative ordering of citizen participation; second, I review the historical development of community organizations; and finally, I examine in detail the agentive voices of women as primary users of shari'a council services.

Defining Shari'acracy

The term *shari'acracy* was first coined by Ali Mazrui to describe the late 20th-century introduction of shari'a into the penal codes of 12 northern states of Nigeria.[15] Mazrui critiqued the turn toward adding the harsh criminal punishments associated with shari'a—stoning and amputation—and the removal of safeguards protecting human rights as a reaction against globalization, westernization, and cultural insecurity. Shari'a activists in Nigeria justify the return to their own separate laws by invoking the model of multiculturalism even in the face of mounting antagonism between Muslims and members of other religions who feel they have been excluded from the political process. These activists state that the stability of Nigeria depends on cognizance of cultural diversity and that implementation of shari'a will root out unwanted secular ideas of law, which were forced on Africans by colonial powers.[16] Several Nigerian opponents of the shari'a adoption—politicians, constitutional scholars, and others—have stated that if northern states want to enforce religious laws, then they cannot remain a part of the federal configuration of the secular republic. Mazrui disagrees, arguing that Britain, the former colonial power, "virtually invented asymmetry as a constitutional order"—Scotland has its own law and its own currency, Northern Ireland has its own separate regional assembly, and yet England has no regional representative body apart from the national parliament. Since the crown of the empire does not try to have symmetrical constitutional arrangements with its constituent parts yet has achieved national integration, then why cannot Nigerian federalism accommodate a similar lack of constitutional symmetry and allow for the existence of dissimilar normative orders in its various states? The decision to "go Islamic" need not be incompatible with Nigerian national integration.[17]

Since the invention of the term *shari'acracy*, others have developed it into a paradigm to refer more generally to the postcolonial rise of shari'a advocacy, combined with localized instances of shari'a implementation in former colonies of the British Empire, where governance according to the norms of shari'a is now advocated as the logical outcome of British intervention. Many accounts have portrayed the decisive trend toward restoration of Islam's authority as a project to retrieve an "authentic" heritage from the ill effects of western materialism and modernity. It is still contested in methodological debates whether one can or should posit shari'acracy as a category that extends universally, across differences of nation, region, religion, history, and so forth. Is shari'acracy specific to Nigeria or a project that can be transplanted? Put simply, the basic elements of this model of government boil down to (1) the authority of sacred law (and those who command the interpretive process) and (2) the premise that in Islam religion and politics are not separate. Accordingly, in nation-states that profess to embody an Islamic system of governance—for instance, Iran or Saudi Arabia—or in the context of a purportedly "secular" or "multi-religious" polity in which a Muslim minority is given a certain degree of autonomy—for instance, Kenya or Nigeria—religious jurists hold a unique ability to pronounce opinions on political questions with impunity. Religious leaders and jurists draw their influence from their knowledge of the textual sources of shari'a (the Qur'an, stories of the Prophet Muhammad's life, and the exegesis of Muslim legal scholars). By pronouncing the will of God through their fatwas, these authorities can give believers permission to disregard man-made laws that are at variance with Islam. Moreover, many treatises on Islamic political theory share one common feature—namely, that questions of governance and public interest must be understood in light of revelation.

Britain itself is immersed in a national conversation about the public character of religion. What is the relevance, if any, of the concept of shari'acracy in this conversation? The aims of Islamic revivalism and of aligning the public welfare with the will of God are moves that are significantly foregrounded in British political history. If we look back to Britain as an empire, we can see that the evolution of the public sphere in postcolonial countries such as Nigeria and, especially, India (as well as other Commonwealth locations from which Muslims have migrated to Britain) has been decisively shaped by the experience of British colonialism and the nationalist response to it. Instead of dealing directly with colonized subjects, the British state chose to rule through representational modes of governance, identifying elite representatives of discrete communities to represent the interests of their communities to the imperial state. This insured the elites—the interlocutors between community and imperial power—would have a stake in the colonial system of governance that granted them legitimacy and vested them with their own separate sphere of influence. Thus, public rituals celebrated diversity in British India, and identification with local community became the vehicle for identification with a larger entity. Furthermore, the imperial state set up a legal system that allowed the two major religious communities, Hindu and Muslim, to be governed by their separate personal laws dealing with family relations, family property, and religious practices. The imperial state then required the codification of these laws, and the British colonial administration enforced criminal law, laws of contract and of evidence, and anything else pertaining to "the public." Invariably, the imperial state was to leave the private sphere for the native elites to oversee. After the uprising known as the Indian Mutiny of 1857, the Queen's Proclamation of 1859 promised noninterference in religious matters as part of the project to reinstate imperial power. British policy was to shift from the Anglicizing aim of creating a class of westernized Indians to the courting of the more orthodox or traditional Indian groups. The result was accession to the autonomy of certain communities having their separate legal codes. For example, in the town of Deoband, north of Delhi, the establishment of *madrassahs* (schools, particularly of Quranic instruction) was an important means of Islamic reaffirmation under colonial rule, after the British dethronement of the last Muslim sovereign in Delhi in 1857. The boundary around the private sphere was sharply defined, and the activities inside the boundary were not to be interfered with either by colonial administrators or by the postcolonial Indian state.[18]

This historical digression is meant to show that the particular manner in which the British government and its Muslim constituents currently interact contains traces of its colonial legacy. It gestures toward a set of historically contingent cultural strategies that are connected with colonialism and its forms of knowledge. I am decidedly *not* making the argument that these are fixed communities that have been transplanted through chain migration, but simply that the reassertion of shari'a norms within Britain has been contingent on a particular set of historical relations. Colonial history illustrates a number of themes that are relevant to the current debates in Britain, including the precedence of representational forms of governance, demoralization of communal institutions and the capacity for state law to protect powerless minorities, contextualization of Muslim engagement in the national political process, and how to move forward. In this historical moment, the contemporary project of securitizing British state and society, with its marking of Muslim citizens as uniquely and exceptionally susceptible to an "anti-West" terrorist ideology, has created a particular crucible in which British Muslims encounter severe limits to their freedom. Invigorated laws on surveillance and investigation and extraordinary penalties for aiding terrorism have combined with the postcolonial legacy to prefigure certain individuals and groups as being outside the political community.

By the same token, much media focus is being directed on the "jihadi" salafist element, or, in other words, the disaffected youth living in inner-city Muslim communities within Britain who believe both government and community leaders are ineffectual. The young generation sees the same tendency to be controlled by "fake elites" that are propped up by artificial interests, just as Muslims in colonial societies were manipulated in the past. In their alienation, exclusion, and disempowerment, Muslim youth are now faced with momentous questions about economic marginalization and identity politics. Structurally, a multiculturalist framework that is truly inclusive is deemed to be lacking. Moreover, "young people have the ability to download problematic *fatwas* from websites," and unexpectedly the meaning of the word *shari'acracy* takes on an alarming affect.[19] The pejorative nickname *Londonistan* and blacklists of extremist bookshops reflect fears that British sovereignty and the "British way of life" are being undermined by transnational influences.

In the contemporary political climate, certain narratives intone the clash of values and seek either to expel or civilize the dangerous threat represented by Muslim groups and people. Images of shari'a militancy and assertions of the higher authority of God's law are countered by declarations of the superiority of the rule of law. The impression that Britain has a "Muslim problem" came to a head in 2006 after a series of interventions from Tony Blair's Labour government. Jack Straw's comments about women in full-face veils, followed by the abrupt end to government partnership with the Muslim Council of Britain in order to, in the government's words, "rebalance" its relations with community groups more willing to demonstrate their commitments to "antiextremism," indicated strategic shifts taking place in government policies vis-à-vis Muslim constituencies. The aim of these shifts has been to incorporate and legitimize religious diversity in the public sphere and to forge the logic of an operational framework that rewards loyalty to the state and civic engagement modeled on a "civic religion." According to Jonathan Birt, official discourse with respect to community leaders has framed Muslim community leaders in terms of a contrast between the "good" imam (prayer leader) and the "bad" imam, the former challenging the extremism of the latter. The bad imam, he writes, works outside the "opportunity spaces" provided for civic engagement and "may either be obscurantist and isolationist, or rejectionist, anti-West and possibly a supporter of violence and terrorism."[20] In contrast, the good imam is one who will work from an "Anglican template" to form Muslim religious leadership that will converge around values of interfaith tolerance, neighborly love, and active involvement in volunteer work. The formation of such a leadership will yield a brokerage of imams who are willing interlocutors between the government and community in the counteroffensive against extremism. This process of differentiation between "good" and "bad" has proceeded in the Brown government's continuation of the policy of rebalancing its relationship with Muslims in Britain. It relies on the promotion of self-regulation and has established several working groups to design means of engaging youth and women, facilitating community capacity building, and professional in-service training of imams to hone their managerial and pastoral skills under the rubric of "tackling extremism together."[21]

We see this when, after the terrorist attacks on American and British civilians in 2001 and 2005, British officials began to make use of the local imam to tighten security measures. For instance, there is the recent use of a therapeutic model to "cure" extremist Muslims in the prison system. In accordance with this model, inmates are being "deprogrammed" of their political beliefs in the same manner that members of cults are deprogrammed. In 2007, the ministry of justice established a special Extremism Unit to implement the deprogramming, employing roughly 150 imams to challenge inmates' beliefs on the basis of their own religious knowledge. Eleven percent of prisoners in Britain are Muslim, which is more than three times their proportion in the general population. Among these Muslim inmates, 90 are serving time for terrorist offenses, and as David Rose noted in an article in the *Daily Mail* on October 18, 2008, the justice ministry fears that if left untreated, their jihadist interpretation of Islam will spread in prisons. An unnamed source tells Rose that "the great fear is that kids from places such as Southall in West London, who feel pretty alienated anyway, could be vulnerable to recruitment. We don't have evidence this is happening—but we don't have evidence that it's not. We need to be aware of the possibility and act on it." Unable to prove the negative (no evidence that recruitment is *not* happening), the unit deploys imams into the prisons with a preemptive approach. One prison service official is quoted as saying, "We're looking to them to shoot down the religious justification for violence." At the same time, prison officials expect that imams "have to become a valve for the venting of prisoners' anger" over British policy in Afghanistan and Iraq, without lending support to what the authorities view as extremist tendencies.[22]

This service is at the focal point of the government's efforts to stem extremism. The classification of shari'a councils as arbitration tribunals with binding authority under British law may also prove to be a linchpin in the project of "fighting extremism together" as an extension of the neoliberal management of the Muslim population. In effect, the government privatized the resolution of conflict by shifting authority to family law courts and by differentiating between a few officially sanctioned practitioners who dispense Islamic justice and those placed outside the range of legitimacy. This turn toward authorizing selected shari'a councils institutionalizes more rigorously the historical colonial relationship that subordinates personal laws to the British government. For instance, the government delimits the scope of jurisdiction (e.g., no criminal law) and appoints the administrative staff, and the civil courts hold the power of judicial enforcement with the ultimate authority to overturn settlements. To appreciate the implications of these provisions, one needs to look at the historical development of shari'a councils in Britain as well as at the agency of women who bring the majority of claims to these tribunals. In the next two sections I outline the history and discuss the gendered discourse in conflict resolution.

History of Shari'a Councils

The widespread creation of mosques and other Muslim community organizations beginning in the 1960s and 1970s reflected what Philip Lewis has called a shift "within the migrants' self-perception from being sojourners to settlers."[23] Mosque formation has been closely aligned with the social, cultural, religious, and political cleavages of the local community each serves, generally reflecting salient ethnic, village kinship, and sectarian divisions. After World War II, Muslim migration was spurred by labor shortages in Britain especially in the steel and textile industries, and workers came mainly from the Mirpur district of Azad Kashmir or from the northwest frontier region of Pakistan or from the Syllhet region of Bangladesh (East Pakistan). Migrant workers also came from India (mainly from three large districts in Gujarat), and from East Africa (these migrants having their roots in Pakistan or Gujarat). In the 1970s, substantial numbers of workers came from Turkey and the Middle East and North African countries. Muslims from Yemen, though small in number, have had a very long history in Britain. Like others from Gujarat, Sind, Assam, and Bengal, Yemenis were recruited by the East India Company as sailors, and a handful settled in port towns in Britain as far back as the 18th and 19th centuries, establishing *zawiyahs* (places of prayer and congregation generally associated with Sufi Islam). More recently, Somali, Iranian, Arab, and Bosnian communities have been established in many cities in Britain. The 2001 national census shows that the largest group of Muslims in Britain originates from Pakistan, followed by Bangladesh, India, Cyprus, Malaysia, Turkey, the Arab countries, and parts of Africa.[24]

Until the 1960s, most Pakistani immigrants to Britain saw themselves as temporary workers who would return to their country of origin. But with changes in British immigration laws—the Commonwealth Immigrants Act 1962 closed opportunities to move freely between countries of the Commonwealth—transnational movement came to an end. Families had to choose whether to be together in Britain or to be divided for lengthy intervals between Britain and Pakistan. Between 1961 and 1966, the Pakistani community alone grew by more than 400 percent; between 1973 and 1981, an additional 82,000 Pakistanis came as settlers, almost all of them as dependents of men already in Britain.[25]

The decade of the 1960s marked a transition from sojourner to settler, and a wide range of institutions reflected the change. Migrants of Islamic faith became more self-consciously Muslim than had previously been the case and more observant in practice. A desire to build a corporate identity "in a situation of material disadvantage in an alien culture" fueled mosque formation, as Muslims became preoccupied with creating "a space for Islam" in Britain, a place to preserve life style and transmit traditional values in an enclave protected from western materialism and permissiveness. Mosques were "both a cause and consequence of increased self-definition" and, by the end of the 20th century, several hundred mosques and Islamic centers in Britain provided the "infrastructure for continuity and belonging."[26]

Similarly, Islamic shari'a councils have emerged under the auspices of these mosques to offer spiritual and religious guidance in close relationship with mosque leadership. Most shari'a councils are affiliated with a mosque and the imams of the related mosque often sits as a member of the council. Thus, often the history and development of mosques and shari'a councils are intertwined. Just as mosques across Britain grew from strong ethnic and regional affiliations—Punjabis, Gujaratis, Mirpuris, Pathans, Bangladeshis, Yemenis, Somalis, and so on—the emergence of shari'a councils in Britain can be understood in similar terms. Moreover, as many scholars have indicated, in the larger communities in Britain different Islamic schools of thought and politics prevail, most notably the Barelwi, Deobandi, Jama'at-i-Islami, Ahl-i-Hadith, Shi'a, Shi'a Ismaili (a minority view within Shi'ism), and Ahmadiyya. These schools offer variations in doctrinal teaching, which result in diverse interpretations of shari'a.[27] Many concerns of the community involve defining the Islamic way of doing things, and shari'a-related questions got referred to a jurisconsult (religious scholar) for a fatwa.

Just as significantly, the formation of British shari'a councils coincided with the development of local religious and cultural organizations under the rubric of multiculturalism. In the 1980s state-sponsored policies of multiculturalism encouraged what Steven Vertovec calls "ethnic governance," and while communities have autonomously created their own "idioms of mobilization" as well as their own strategies of engagement with the secular state, the impact of the availability of opportunity spaces on the formation of an Islamic normative discourse is conspicuous. Contributing to the religious identification and definition of Muslim subjectivity, exigencies such as cultural diversity, legal pluralism, and state responses to demands generated by newly settled diasporic communities have resulted in the emergence of a semiofficial community regulatory framework that can best be described as a highly differentiated sociolegal field. "The emergence, development and management of shari'a councils in the Muslim community has to be considered as part of the process of cultural and legal contestation and the 'hybridization of lived legal cultures'" in Britain.[28]

It is estimated that there are between sixty and seventy shari'a councils currently operating in Britain, a number that may increase, given the recently granted official status of some shari'a councils' rulings. An interesting feature of most shari'a councils in Britain is that, unlike mosques, they are not considered "voluntary bodies" and are not subject to public body regulation under British law. That is, they do not have to reveal details of their organizational structure or their financial status. Certainly, this is likely to change now that a few shari'a councils are formally recognized as tribunals, undoubtedly placing them under more uniform government scrutiny and regulation. In fact, in arguing in favor of official accommodation of certain aspects of shari'a, the archbishop of Canterbury maintained that in making shari'a councils a part of the public process, people will no longer be allowed to do what they like in private in ways that intensify oppression within a given community.[29] Not to be forgotten is this argument that official recognition will lead to greater levels of state regulation and, presumably, protection of disadvantaged individuals within the community. A second feature worth noting is that while mosques historically have been organized along ethnic and kinship allegiance to reflect the specific needs of different groups of Muslims in Britain, shari'a councils often aim to bridge interethnic differences, to cater to the needs of all Muslims regardless of ethnic, racial, or national background.[30]

Notwithstanding this effort, though, these councils are highly variegated in the degree they are tied to a parent mosque and in terms of the diversity of membership and clientele. Some councils are indirectly influenced by the deliberate recruitment of imams from Pakistan, done by mosques in order to sustain village-kinship networks and localized cultural practices. These councils rely heavily on Pakistan-based experiences in their deliberation even in spite of the objective to draw on a wide range of Islamic schools of thought. This results, as one scholar puts it, in reformulating "cultural practices of the specific Pakistani Muslim communities in Britain to fit with [the specific council's] framework of dispute resolution," and the resolution becomes an expression of a highly ethnicized idiom.[31] In this process, it is easy to see how globalization has contributed to legal pluralism in Britain, and that council development reflects Muslims' settlement patterns.

Sometimes British shari'a councils are not only, or even primarily, adversarial tribunals within Muslim diasporic communities of various national origins. Many have also functioned as liaisons to the local or national government in Britain, providing advisory opinions about legislative matters and problems arising in provision of public services. For instance, what is the Islamic position on genetically modified foods?[32] How can medical services best be provided in public hospitals and clinics in ways that do not cause offense? What does Islam say on the status of the human fetus? Or what is the Islamic perspective on banking and finance? Often the larger shari'a councils in metropolitan areas in particular find themselves representing the ethical and social values they believe are best embodied in Islam, in public debates over how best to govern British society. On the other hand, the workload of many shari'a councils consists primarily in addressing matters of internal concern to Muslim communities, such as securing Islamic divorces and determining questions of child custody and inheritance. In these cases, the councils serve as nodal points for the propagation of fatwas (alternatively, *fatawa*), or religious/legal opinions, in response to queries for guidance in daily life. The Islamic Sharia Council, an association of the Islamic Central Mosque at Regents Park, the U.K. Islamic Mission, the Muslim World League, the Jamia Mosque and Cultural Centre at Birmingham, the East London Mosque, the Dawatul Islam, and other organizations, reports that it has heard thousands of cases since inception in 1983, many of them involving marital disputes.[33]

Gendered Discourses and Disputing

The Islamic Sharia Council maintains that 95 percent of the queries it receives are about marital problems, and the majority of clients who use the council's services are women seeking an Islamic divorce. While it is often presumed that divorce is solely a man's prerogative under shari'a, an Islamic divorce can be acquired in a number of ways—*talaq* (the unilateral repudiation by the husband); *khul'* (alternative spelling, *khula*; the divorce initiated by the wife either with her husband's agreement, or on condition that she will forego her right to support); and *ubara'at* (divorce by mutual consent). There is flexibility within each of these three categories, and even when the husband's consent is not obtained, a Muslim woman can still seek the intervention of a religious scholar to determine whether an Islamic divorce is possible.[34] Thus women have become frequent users of these alternative dispute resolution bodies, demonstrating a particular kind of personal legal consciousness as they seek to obtain a Muslim divorce certificate. Some Muslim women in Britain actively pursue claims in shari'a councils, telling stories that challenge the circumstances of their lives. Yet ethnographic work reveals an uneasy tension between the women's expectations (an Islamic divorce) and the intentions of members of the council whose objective is to keep families together. As Sheikh Abdullah, a member of the Shariah Council of the United Kingdom (Tottenham, North London), is cited as saying: "As Muslims, we have a duty to live according to the Qur'an and Sunnah even though we may have chosen to live in non-Muslim countries. I think it is incumbent upon us to live up to this responsibility because of the effect of western influences upon our children and ourselves. It is easy to neglect our duties in this secular environment."[35]

    Thus in the diasporan frame, the use of these dispute resolution bodies has been transformed from an option into a moral obligation in the diaspora. Living in accordance with shari'a is spoken of as a *duty* for Muslims especially for those living in non-Muslim societies where it would be easy to fall into neglect. Hence councils are a focal point for the project of strengthening allegiance to a prescribed way of life and a sense of belonging to a wider Muslim ummah. Discursively the route leading to shari'a councils in Britain (many of which are affiliated with community mosques) has become inextricably tied into a sense of diasporic Islamic identity and has a decisive impact on the formation of a distinctly Muslim legal consciousness.

    Practically speaking, much of the work of shari'a councils has been narrated through the lives of British Muslim women. This may be so because women have fewer contexts in which they can narrate the difficulties they experience in marriage. Of course, that women are the primary users of shari'a dispute resolution services does not mean that most British Muslim women support official accommodation of some form of shari'a into the British legal system. Many Muslim women in Britain are critical of the recent turn by the British government. For instance, Samia Bano argues that people have many different reasons for subscribing to variable combinations of "secular and/or religious beliefs" when it comes to disputing and conceptions of justice, and a "fixed and homogeneous understanding of Muslim identity does not sufficiently engage with the complexity of Muslim identity" in British society nor with the "alternative narratives" within the community in question.[36] The differences that manifest and operate in people's agency vis-à-vis dispute resolution must be understood as multifaceted and sometimes contradictory. For some individuals, positivist law—or the law of the state in Britain—may not be up to the task of recognizing the legal pluralism inherent in a multicultural society or the contextual nature of justice; nor can it even be sufficient to preserve the liberal norm of equality before the law, particularly when it comes to Muslims. However, cognizance of the law's inadequacies does not necessarily mean that one supports the move toward official recognition of religious forms of communal dispute resolution in matters of family law. To understand Muslim subjectivity, there must be an interrogation of the complex engagement between shari'a and secular civil law and the ways in which Muslims engage with shari'a in Britain.

Why are women motivated to interact with shari'a councils? Some say the need to obtain a religious divorce certificate is vital to some Muslim women's religious identity. According to community norms, a Muslim woman cannot marry again under shari'a unless a divorce granted by the state is "Islamized." Also, the contractual sum of a *mahr* (dower) is stipulated in the Muslim marriage contract, and the husband must pay this to the wife in the case of divorce. A woman's claim to the mahr must be pursued through an Islamic divorce.[37] Another factor to consider is whether a woman is willing and able to live without community. Marriage is used to reinforce kinship networks, and unless a woman has economic means and more options to leave communities (e.g., housing), she may not be inclined to abandon community. As one observer puts it, for many Muslim women in Britain, the norms of the religious idiom include the notion that an Islamically sanctioned divorce is superior to civil divorce; she found in her fieldwork that "for these women, the importance that the *talaq* divorce assumed was a logical concomitant of the strength of their religious identity and practice."[38] Thus, some women act within the constraints of community, the home, and family to create ways to register complaint that stay embedded *within* the narratives and norms of an Islamic idiom.

Women's agency in seeking justice in the "privatized space" of the shari'a council is mediated through important family networks. Women experiencing difficulties in their marriages often look for guidance first from family members and friends, sometimes even consulting the local imam, before contacting a shari'a council. Reaching this stage is extraordinary, however, since there is considerable evidence that Muslim families are reluctant to seek intervention from nonrelatives. Admission of marital trouble would bring shame on the extended family honor (*izzat*).[39] Samia Bano found in the four shari'a councils she studied in Britain that women made initial contact with these alternative dispute resolution bodies through the intervention of relatives and/or an imam, a practice that might suggest that the decision had not been entirely autonomous. Another researcher found that women who called the Muslim Women's Helpline seeking intervention in domestic violence cases were also referred confidentially to the Muslim Law (Shari'a) Council at Ealing, London. Parenthetically, he reports that callers often said their husbands "would never agree" to mediation, and so indirectly, whether consciously or not, women may be choosing to initiate an Islamic divorce as a way of aligning themselves with the masculine authority of an imam and shari'a council to correct the power imbalance in their relationships.[40] Many women in Bano's study reported that they had little knowledge of the existence of shari'a councils prior to seeking an Islamic divorce, and it was often a family member who acted as the initial point of contact by providing an address or telephone number.[41]

As Susan Hirsch found in another context, marital breakdown is particularly problematic for communities since it is in the narrating of difficulties that a family's vulnerabilities are exposed. Maintenance of family honor and status in the community turns on whether the married couple can keep "dirty little secrets" rather than air their laundry in public. Furthermore, while the law configures gendered approaches to disputing—men and women have different access to the law's provisions— Hirsch points out that it is just as important to see that speakers in courts are influenced and constrained by perhaps more subtly embedded *cultural* conceptions about what men and women are allowed to say. In other words, with respect to marriage and divorce, the expectations and duties of men and women are different, and thus it is accepted that disputing parties will make only those claims that are specific to their gender roles. In fieldwork observation, Hirsch found that when a woman speaks in a manner thought inappropriate for her gender, she is silenced by the judge, or her complaints are ignored. Negotiations for a divorce, resting on claims of abandonment, bigamy, impotence, infertility, emotional abuse, domestic violence, forced marriage, and so on, are speech acts that draw on and produce gendered assertions about rights and responsibilities in marriage. By providing accounts of troubles in the "story world" of narrated conflict, disputants often engage in performative speech—accusing, blaming, persuading, justifying—to effect change in social relations through dispute resolution. Thus divorce proceedings can best be understood as a point of struggle vis-à-vis a discursive frame of reference that positions men and women differently. In these circumstances, speakers interact in ways that often reinforce but sometimes transform assumptions about gendered status.[42]

In the current social context in Britain, Bano shows through her interviews with Muslim women seeking an Islamic divorce certificate that many were initially unaware of their options under shari'a. She writes that "a number of women expressed surprise upon discovering that, under Islamic law, they had the right to instigate divorce proceedings against the wishes of their husbands." Many were informed by elder relatives about the steps they would have to take. Nevertheless, in their pursuit of a religious divorce decree, these women found themselves to be confronting the central tenet of the council members whose main focus on keeping family honor intact and rescuing the marriage worked against the female applicants' stated desires. The women's individual interests in ending their marriages were sidelined as they were coaxed into unofficial reconciliation and mediation with their spouses, facilitated by a religious scholar. The councils' intervention sought to reconcile the parties by establishing a dialogue between the female applicant and her husband, even when the women had already exhausted this option before contacting the shari'a councils. Typically, when a woman files an application to obtain a divorce, the council contacts the husband to see if reconciliation is possible and, if he consents, the services of a trained counselor are provided for the couple. The counselor frames the discussion of trouble from an Islamic perspective and reminds the disputants of their Islamic duties as husband and wife. The counselor's directive force comes from his framing of the reconciliation process as both a moral duty (preserving the sanctity of the Muslim family) and a religious obligation (a divorce cannot be pronounced without attempts at reconciliation). The deployment of an Islamic idiom here shapes the discussion in specific ways in an effort to rework social relations between the disputants. Typically, men assert their rights to their wives' labor—household duties—and sexual access, while wives complain of abuse, neglect, or a lack of financial maintenance. The application forms used to file for a khul' (female-initiated divorce) require the production of formal petitions and certificates of marriage, birth, and civil divorce used in the British administrative channels. Although the typical language used in these forms is the authoritative language of procedural and evidentiary rules (see figure 4.1), formal language is rarely applied in a mediation. Instead, discourse about conflict draws on cultural, rather than institutional, conventions. The mixture of discourses reflected in the application forms indicates legal pluralism.

Predictably, given that women have already tried other ways to resolve their problems before seeking the councils' assistance, divorce remains the most common outcome regardless of the shari'a councils' insistence upon reconciliation. In the process, the councils give an advantage to the husbands who sometimes use their positions to leverage favorable terms in exchange for the man's pronouncement of a talaq divorce. For instance, husbands have secured greater access to their children, even in cases in which there were protective injunctions issued by civil

The Islamic Shari'a Council

مجلس الشريعة الاسلامية

34 Francis Road Leyton London E10 6PW
Tel.0208 558 0581

CB_____   Date: _____

APPLICATION FORM TO FILE A DISSOLUTION/ KHULA/ DIVORCE
(Please read carefully and complete all sections of the form in capital letters, otherwise we shall return the form)

WIFES DETAILS	HUSBANDS DETAILS
1. Name _____	1. Name _____
2. Address _____	2. Address _____
_____ Post Code _____	_____ Post Code _____
Tel (Home) _____ Mob: _____	Tel (Home) _____ Mob _____
E-Mail _____	E- Mail _____
3. Date & Place of Birth _____	3. Date & Place of Birth _____
4. Nationality & Status : _____	4. Nationality & Status : _____

5. Date & Place of Nikah : _____

6. Date & Place of Civil Registration in UK: _____

7. Amount of Dower (Mahr) Agreed: _____

    a) How much has been paid: _____

    b) How much was deferred: _____

8. Have you received any Jewellery/ Land/ Money from your husband, please give details: _____

9. Main reason for asking Divorce: _____

10. Have you been married before?   Yes ☐   No ☐

    If **Yes**, please provide proof of your previous Divorce Certificate _____

11. Details of Children from *this* marriage:

Name	Age	Name	Age

12. Date since complete separation from husband: _____ Please read section D for information.

13. Have you applied for Civil Divorce? **Yes / No** If **yes**, date of decree absolute, if applicable: _____

    If **No**, please read section A and if applicable consult your solicitor: _____

14. Did your husband defend the divorce petition in court? **Yes / No** if No, Send copy of D10 form _____

DECLARATION
I have read Section A, B, C, D before submitting the form. I testify in the name of Allah (SWT) that the information which has been given is true.

Please see overleaf for instructions

SIGNED:	DATED:

FIGURE 4.1. Divorce (Khula) form provided by the Islamic Shari'a Council.
http://www.islamic-sharia.org/about-us/about-us-7.html (accessed June 2, 2007).

CHECK LIST

You must answer all the questions in the application form otherwise it may cause a delay in your case being processed.
To help us process this application quickly, we would like you to provide with as much information to support your Khula application **by way of evidence**.

Please enclose <u>COPY</u> of the following & post / submit it to:

The Islamic Sharia council
34 Francis Road, Leyton, London, E10 6PW   YES   NO

    1) Photo ID (your <u>passport or driving license</u>)   ☐   ☐

    2) Your Nikah Nama and Civil - Marriage Certificate,   ☐   ☐

    3) Your Decree Nisi or Decree Absolute (if applicable),   ☐   ☐

    4) Letters from solicitors or court (if applicable)   ☐   ☐

Please Do Not Send Originals

Please see section C for payment details:

Amount paid _____ cheque/ postal order / Credit, Debit Card*

Cheque number _____ Date of Cheque_____

*If paying by Card, please provide below contact details to enable the accounts dept to collect details:
Name of Card Holder_____ Contact Number_____ Convenient time_____

FIGURE 4.1. (*Continued*)

PLEASE RETAIN THIS SHEET FOR YOUR INFORMATION

A. Important information for British citizens regarding civil divorce:

1) You have to apply for civil divorce:

   i) If your marriage took place in any country abroad (like Pakistan, Bangladesh) in accordance to the law of that country. **It does not matter you have sponsored your spouse or not.** For details please see Foreign Marriage Act 1892.

   ii) If your marriage took place in the UK and registered in a civil registry.

2) Civil divorce is not required if your marriage took place in the UK but was never registered in a civil registry.

B. Islamic Sharia Council (ISC) procedure for KHULA / Marriage Dissolution (When Wife is the Petitioner)

1. All new and prospective applicants must attach the main reasons for seeking a Khula / Marriage Dissolution, on a separate sheet, with their application form.

2. Your application will be registered with the relevant details. It is imperative that you provide a contact address for the husband.

3. The Council will issue the first letter to the husband, informing him that his wife has approached the ISC for Khula / Marriage Dissolution. The applicant will receive a copy with a reference number for future correspondences. If the husband fails to reply within the allocated period, the ISC will issue a second letter which will be followed by a third letter if no reply was received within the allocated time. The allocated period for husbands residing in the UK is one month otherwise two months for those residing abroad.
 (If the wife has obtained the Civil Divorce, evidence has to be provided that the husband did not defend it. In this case, the issuance of one letter may be enough provided that the address is verified).

4. If the husband failed to respond to the third letter, the Council will request the applicant to verify the respondent's address. However, if the husband responded at any point, a joint meeting between both parties and the ISC representative is an integral part of the proceedings to carry out fair and just meditation. Failure to attend this meeting by the applicant may delay the case or result in its closure.

5. The above procedure is subject to the nature of the contact details of the husband.

6. Once the Council has received verification of the husband's address, it will issue an interview request letter to the wife and the husband (provided he is legally able to do so) to see one of the ISC representative in their area (if applicable). The representative will produce a report accordingly.

7. If the husband does not attend the interview in given time, the Council will issue a final notice and copy of 1st, 2nd, 3rd letters will be sent to him via recorded delivery.

FIGURE 4.1. (*Continued*)

8. A request is sent to the wife asking her confirmation to take the file to the next panel meeting, which is on last Wednesday of every month. However, before a case is presented to the panel meeting, all the above criteria must be met.

9. Once the case goes to the panel meeting, if any conditional decision of dissolution is made by the panel then divorce certificate is issued subject to compliance of these conditions. If the wife breaches any conditions which she agreed to, the council may revoke the divorce certificate.

*For Civil divorce, a solicitor must be consulted as this is an Islamic Divorce. The Shari'a Council does not deal with legal matters.

C. Payment Details

In order to register with Islamic Shari'a Council, please fill in the enclosed application form and return it to us with your payment.

The total fee for this service is £250 pounds <u>OR</u> you can pay in the following instalments.

a) **£150** pounds fee with your application form covering registration charges (**£75** for those on income support)

b) **£100** pounds final payment, before the issuance of divorce certificate (**£50** for those on income support)

Cheque and postal order to be made payable to The Islamic Shari'a Council

<u>Please note registration fees are not refundable.</u>

D. Definition of Separation

Separation is counted from the day when matrimonial relationships were halted completely i.e. No on and off contact took place.

<u>Instructions for communication with ISC</u>

1) General enquiries: Please quote reference number when calling
2) For Change of Address: Written information is required
3) Case closure / pause and reopen: Written Notice should be submitted

FIGURE 4.1. (*Continued*)

courts to prohibit access. In many ways Bano observed that the women were encouraged to conform to cultural norms and acceptable patterns of behavior if they were to be issued a divorce certificate.[43]

The interview data reveal that some women were uncomfortable in the reconciliation sessions because they felt the religious scholars regarded them as unwilling participants. For these women, the unease related to the lack of validation; many reported being encouraged to accept their husbands' limitations because Muslim women are supposed to be more open to compromise. And as Bano puts it, "the language of reconciliation embodies dynamics of power that place emphasis upon the woman's divinely ordained obligations to stabilize marriage and family relations, and in this way the assumption remains that the women will seek reconciliation."[44] In some cases women reported they were ignored or silenced when narrating their troubles, contesting and challenging the religious ideals of family and female submission to male authority. For instance, one interview excerpt reads, "It was weird but it felt as though I was the one being told off and when I tried to put across what I thought was wrong . . . it's as though he [the imam] didn't want to hear it."[45] And in another instance, "I told him [the imam] that I left him because he was violent but he started saying things like, 'Oh, how violent was that? Because in Islam a man is allowed to beat his wife'! I mean, I was so shocked. He said it depends on whether he really hurt me! I was really shocked because I thought he was there to understand but he was trying to make me admit that somehow I had done wrong."[46] Here women's voices are positioned precariously. Patriarchy is performed through the imam's words and, in the latter case, the husband's physical abuse and the women's words are muted. In each account, the speaker produces framing devices and offers her perspective at the time. These words tell stories that confirm women's oppression, but in part they also indicate the transformative impact of the experience. Outside the councils, these women communicate shock over the indignities they suffered, indicating disjunctures to be dealt with as Muslim women challenge conventions in pursuit of greater autonomy within an Islamic context.

The most striking fact is that these women portrayed their participation in the shari'a council process of reconciliation and divorce as an element of belonging to the Muslim ummah. Bano reports that, overall, the women's impressions of their experiences ranged from ambivalence to outright resistance about a process they saw as instilled with male dominance and conservative interpretations of doctrines regarding the position of women in Islam (as daughters, wives, and mothers). Outside the councils, women complain about the treatment they experienced. Yet many indexed a preeminent place for these councils in imagining cultural continuity. Even though many had not expected that they would need to submit to reconciliation with recalcitrant husbands, and the process often took six months or more, women by and large were not refused what they were after—an Islamic divorce certificate. Most cases resulted in dissolution of the marriage, and participants engage in the process in divergent ways. Some of the women whom Bano interviewed said they were able to challenge certain practices (e.g., forced marriage) as "un-Islamic" and antithetical to the values of their faith. Regarding the question whether the shari'a councils should be recognized as a part of the larger British legal system, one of Bano's informants said: "To be Muslim is to be part of the Muslim ummah. If they [shari'a councils] are recognized, I think that's great, an important development for all Muslims."[47] And another offered this opinion: "If it's about community control, I think they [shari'a councils] should be honest about that but I don't know if it is. I mean women want the Islamic divorce and I guess they are providing a service. It's just the way some of them do it that's the problem."[48]

If we pay attention to these narratives of cultural survival, we can see that even when women are unable to fully control the discourses used in the shari'a council to frame their discussions of marital trouble, they still find the councils to be useful. This forum is a site of contestation over the meaning of Islam and women's rights within it. The legitimacy of this legal process is rooted in the individual's belief in and acceptance of the normative ordering it represents, even when that individual is distrustful of its implementation (e.g., "It's just the way some of them do it that's the problem"). We can also find that these women understand the councils to be an important resource for the diasporic community to provide continuity and connection with the larger global community of Muslims, the ummah. This space is constituted as an alternative to the dominant sociolegal framework, a move that might be understood as a culturalist expression of a sense of superiority vis-à-vis the surrounding secular society. As Abdullahi An-Na'im has suggested, it is when communities perceive themselves to be under siege that they are most likely "to turn inward and reinforce the very practices that those on the outside are seeking to change."[49] Many researchers have demonstrated the growing politicization of a Muslim identity in Europe with the concomitant strengthening of affinity for connection to the Muslim ummah. The concept of a united global community of Muslims has been discussed as a contributing factor in the subject formation of a diasporic Muslim identity regardless of ethnic origins. The position that some Muslim women take, albeit in tepid tones, of valorizing shari'a councils as vehicles for social cohesion becomes comprehensible in this light, particularly in this historical moment when so many western democracies have made it an imperative to rescue Muslim women from their patriarchal communities.

Bano's data analysis indicates little about the socioeconomic status of the women she interviewed. The shari'a councils that were the sites for her study described themselves as community organizations providing a service "with minimal charge and no financial gain."[50] The presumption is that these councils would offer affordable access to a form of justice for economically disadvantaged women and couples who could neither afford nor choose to seek out the costly legal and therapeutic services provided by (possibly non-Muslim) professionals in the larger society. An important consideration is whether the women who seek an Islamic divorce have economic means, since presumably poverty would limit their options at least as much as religious beliefs or community strictures do. The relationship among class background, cultural values, and educational attainment is crucial. Other large-scale surveys have indicated that Muslims in Britain are among the most disadvantaged on most measures of socioeconomic status, particularly for Pakistanis and Bangladeshis.[51] I would argue against treating gender as a unitary explanatory model standing apart from other sociological variables, just as I would argue against treating religion as the only practice that subordinates and constricts opportunity. A complex assessment of all the circumstances and structural processes affecting women's lives, including not only family and community but also the state apparatus and economic opportunities, can yield a full picture of the forces that produce a Muslim woman's subjectivity.

Conclusion

The move toward neoliberalization, as illustrated by the removal of the resolution of family disputes from public courts in the presence of particular cultures (e.g., Muslim or Jewish) is an explicit gesture toward cognizance of the multiple normative ordering in society. Yet in formalizing shari'a councils has the British government privileged one form of Islamic practice and doctrine while marginalizing alternative narratives? Through this action the government has authorized certain discursive subjects by granting them institutional standing. Forms that diverge are devalued in comparison. The official act authorizes some discursive practices and not others, implicitly marginalizing those using unauthorized forms of dispute resolution and often inculcating in them feelings of outsiderhood.

Scholarship about other societies claims that, for many reasons connected to their subordinate status, women generally are not inclined to address their problems through Islamic institutions.[52] And yet, while it is true that most Muslim women do *not* make use of Britain's many shari'a councils, they are still overwhelmingly the primary users of these alternative dispute resolution bodies. These courts have come to serve as an increasingly important resource for women in troubled domestic situations who live in complicated networks of extended family and community. Analogous to the situation observed by Susan Hirsch in kadhi courts in Kenya, the situation observed in Britain indicates that the position of these courts in Britain facilitates women's agency in making claims yet also causes their success to be problematic. Individual women who win claims may experience changes in their personal situations, which alleviate their oppression by specific men. But the women's use of the courts represents an ambiguous form of resistance to male domination.[53] The complexity of the legal field in which these courts operate, especially in light of the neoliberal trend to "privatize" the resolution of culture-specific family relations, calls into question any clear application of the concept of resistance. I would argue that it warrants further attention to see whether the agency and representation of Muslim women changes, while the shari'a councils administered as officially recognized tribunals gain legal force.

Discourses of disputing can retain their gendered quality, particularly in view of a hierarchical ordering or rights and obligations and depending on who has direct access to the discursive power to invoke the organizing principle of hierarchy. This chapter is an attempt to illuminate how normative ordering is associated with civic virtue, and how gendered positions are constructed through the available discourses of family conflict. Personified by two figures—the virtuous citizen and the gendered Muslim subject—these notions are both reinforced and contested in an Islamic idiom. They offer sites for investigating the connections between political conflict and personal status.

The focus of the next chapter shifts back to the United States to describe the standing of Islamic legal principles in American case law. In the context of anti-Muslim discrimination, alternative dispute resolution, family law, and contract law, I call attention to the points where religious and secular laws intersect.

5

Si(gh)ting Muslim Women
on the U.S. Legal Landscape

Posted on a U.S. State Department Internet Web site are statistics and
testimonials about Muslim life in the United States. Quoted on the Web
site, a California-based Muslim engineer avers, "American values are, by
and large, very consistent with Islamic values, with a focus on family,
faith, hard work, and an obligation to better self and society."[1] The "faces
of Islam" section, a photo gallery meant to illustrate the "extraordinary
range and richness of the way American Muslims live," features several
photographs of Muslim girls and women purchasing vegetables at a
farmers' market or competing in a high school relay race, in which all
females are clad in the modest attire of the hijab. If one were to limit
investigation of Muslim life in the United States to this official version,
one would come away with the impression that the history and social
practice of Muslims in general and U.S. Muslims in particular confine
women to wearing this concealing clothing. To be authentically Muslim,
it would seem, requires that women conform to a stereotypical and
narrow notion of Muslim existence, reducing the scope of that
"extraordinary range and richness" of Muslim life to specific perceptions
of what constitutes Islam.

The Web site was conceived of by an advertising executive, Charlotte
Beers, who, as undersecretary of state for public diplomacy, produced
media products that would sell the United States as a hospitable place
for Muslims to live after the terrorist attacks of 9/11. As part of a major
media campaign, four videos were made about American Muslims. The
videos were shown in the United States and abroad, in Muslim countries

such as Indonesia. The main point of the videos (known as the "apple pie" series) was to underscore that the United States is a misunderstood place and that Islam is universally tolerated in the U.S. Portraits of Muslim women are, again, confined to images of women with their heads covered with an Islamic head scarf.[2] Such images beg the question, how do official versions of Muslim life in the United States affect the prospects of Muslim American women? While the hijab is a volatile emblem— viewed as a symbol of male oppression of women or as a symbol of religious and cultural outsiderhood—it remains an important indicator of Muslim presence in the United States. It demonstrates how gendered the purported clash of civilizations is. In the othering and homogenising discourse of Orientalism,[3] the hijab has been construed as a symbol of enforced silence and submission, imposed by a patriarchal faith, which may signify a radical brand of Islam and anti-American terrorism. In this chapter, I look at how far the U.S. justice system has gone to protect Muslim women's rights, and whether that has been productive of a particular kind of knowledge about Muslim women.

How is a society that is based on the principles of tolerance and egalitarianism supposed to accommodate the demands of an increasingly heterogeneous public? In the United States, this question lies at the heart of cultural and legal pluralism and the multicultural accommodation of newcomers. There has been a growing trend towards the acceptance of myriad cultural practices and identities as legitimate forms of self-expression. But, at some critical points of intersection between "mainstream" society and its component parts, important trade-offs ensue. For instance, while tolerance of, and respect for, difference are valued concepts, so is the equality of women. When the precepts of a so-called foreign belief system offend the equal rights of women, which is to hold sway? According to contemporary American legal standards, the civil rights of women by and large trump the civil liberties of religious or cultural minorities whose inherited traditions, perhaps incidentally, result in sexist or discriminatory treatment. Often in the U.S. case law women's rights to equal treatment and job security have prevailed over the asserted right of a community to religious liberty. For instance, in one case, when submitted to a limited frisk search by a female correctional officer, a male Muslim prison inmate objected on religious grounds to being touched by a female other than his wife or mother. When taken to the courts, this religious belief was judged not to be protected by the First Amendment because of the state's overriding interest in providing equal career opportunities to women as correctional officers.[4]

Tensions between Islamic practices and women's rights continue to be engaged, argued about, harmonized, negotiated, and renegotiated in varying ways. The prevalent ingredients of this dialogue, unfortunately, are views that tend to be reductionist—ones that discredit Islam as a peculiarly sexist religion, or feminism as a hazardously ideological movement that pits women against men. At one end of the constructed continuum is a patriarchal culture, with specific gender-based presumptions contained in the law; and at the other, an equality gender structure that results in a court system that refuses to enforce the perceived gender bias of its contrast. As scholar Ann Elizabeth Mayer points out, "where Islam is concerned, the Western inclination to totalize a non-Western culture seems especially strong, although even a moment's reflection should prompt doubts" about whether all Muslims and the diverse variations in Islam can realistically be lumped together as a coherent and unified whole.[5] These inclinations to elide differences are not particularly helpful in working through the controversies that efface the complex nature of both Islamic and western societies.

The struggle over the so-called clash of civilizations purports that the values of secular society are at odds with Islamic beliefs, that Islam and democracy are incompatible, and that Islam is inherently inimical to human rights and the interests of women in particular. Muslims in the United States are confronted with the dominant paradigm, which maintains that Muslim family law—including the personal status of women—is constitutive, universally, of *the* Muslim way of life. The social environment in which Muslims, and others, live in the United States is built around such presumptions about Islam and is additionally based on particular precepts about church-state relations, identity politics, and civil rights that have played momentous roles in U.S. legal history. The separation of religion and state has been preserved by policies that, while seeking broader inclusion of religious and ethnic minorities in the public square, have the effect of discouraging specific faith-based practices, which are seen as a threat to the civic self-definition of the United States. In this milieu, Muslim women have found themselves subject to the normalizing pressures of prevailing official standards that demand greater conformity to a secular vision of America, one that discourages outward, public displays of religiosity and faith.

These contests are nowhere more apparent than in American courts of law. As Muslims become more confident and assertive of their rights as members of a religious minority in American society, a struggle to balance the sometimes clashing requirements of religious law and secular law ensues. Besides inevitable conflicts that arise between Muslims and non-Muslims—such as between a Muslim inmate and prison officials as in the case cited above, or in an instance of employment discrimination—American courts of law are also more frequently confronted with demands to resolve disputes *among* Muslims, often on issues of Islamic family law. Some Muslims are pressing American courts to apply Islamic legal rules in instances of family law, making the resolution of disputes arising from the realities of Muslim life in the United States an important although complex part of the American legal terrain. In this chapter I first look at the problem of anti-Muslim discrimination as it affects Muslim women in the United States, including accommodation of Muslim practices in the workplace, school dress codes, and matters of public security. Next, I consider instances of divorce and child custody, in which stipulations of Islamic law pertaining to marriage and divorce, child custody and inheritance, are evaluated in U.S. courts. In the United States, courts commonly refer matters to religious tribunals for alternative dispute resolution—Christian, Mennonite, Jewish, and Muslim.[6] It has been common for courts to enforce decisions made by Jewish courts known as bet dins, and as I will show, courts have upheld Islamic principles in matters of divorce and child custody. In 2003, a Texas state appellate court referred a matter of divorce to a tribunal called the Texas Islamic Court.[7]

With respect to the experiences of Muslim women in American courts, this encounter has been highly productive. In their work on gender, power, and identity among evangelical Christian and Muslim women in the United States, sociologists John Bartkowski and Jen'nan Ghazal Read point out that religion has provided unique cultural repertoires, which enable women to affirm their religious values while refashioning their convictions to fit their post-traditional lifestyles.[8] In the same vein, the law—whether sacred or secular—also contributes in important ways to the repertoire women use in the process of negotiating their place in American society, staying current and engaged with broader social trends (such as prevailing gender norms) while simultaneously tailoring their own religious identity.

Protection from Anti-Muslim Discrimination

The problem of anti-Muslim discrimination, complicated as it is by the historical relationship between Muslim societies and the West, has become especially pronounced in the United States since the terrorist attacks of September 11, 2001. The FBI has reported an increase of more than 1,600 percent in harassment and anti-Muslim hate crimes between 2000 and 2001.[9] Some local law enforcement agencies also reported significant increases in violent crime against Muslims and Muslim or Arab-owned property during the same period. Many of these cases involve women, most commonly related to the wearing of a head covering. In monitoring workplace discrimination, the Equal Employment Opportunity Commission (the EEOC), the federal agency responsible for monitoring and enforcement of several federal civil rights laws, has documented that since 9/11 it has received many hundreds of complaints annually from individuals who allege backlash discrimination because they are—or are perceived to be—Muslim, Arab, Middle Eastern, South Asian, or Sikh.[10]

In apparent retaliation for the 9/11 attacks, extralegal forms of backlash violence have targeted persons who appear to be Middle Eastern or Muslim. Homes, businesses, and places of worship have been firebombed or vandalized. Individuals have been attacked with guns, knives, fists, incendiary devices, and words. Women wearing the hijab have been spat upon, shoved, and beaten. Children in schools have been harassed by their teachers, classmates, and parents of other children. The EEOC has created a separate category just to handle the sudden increase in the volume of 9/11–related complaints. In this context, Muslims in the United States are increasingly concerned about their continued ability to freely practice their faith in the face of what many are calling "Islamophobia," a widespread fear or apprehension of all things Islamic.

Americans seem to find it difficult to talk about Islam without discussing gender relations, and the practice of veiling or wearing the hijab. Wearing Islamically prescribed clothing is considered an important marker, not only of gender but of social regulations when women choose or are expected to wear it. There are divergent views among Muslims about whether Islam requires women to cover, and these views are especially pronounced in a religiously pluralistic and publicly secularized society such as the United States. Most Muslims, however, are tolerant of different perspectives. Many Muslim women in the United States who *do* wear concealing clothing feel that their sisters who do *not* cover their heads still are considered to be "good" Muslims.[11]

For many American Muslim women, the hijab is not about coercion but about making choices, about "choosing" an identity and expressing a religiosity through their mode of dress. Some women say that by veiling they are making a statement against imperialism, which sees Muslim piety as a sign of terrorism, and against conservative Islam, which seeks to impose a traditionalist understanding of Islam that oppresses women. Some view the hijab as projecting images of purity of women and view it as a means of controlling female sexuality. Many young Muslim women wear the hijab as a means of expressing identity and spirituality, as well as modesty. Some Muslim women have expected that wearing the hijab would end the objectification of their bodies but have found, paradoxically, that as covered women, they became even more frequent "objects" of the western gaze. For American Muslims in general, wearing the hijab is seen as the political reappropriation of Islamic religiosity and way of life, wresting it from the control of traditionalist Islam and placing its meanings within the control of the Muslim women who wear it. For most non-Muslim Americans, no other symbol reconstructs Islam as "other" quite so directly as the hijab. Women in hijab are targets of discrimination in the United States, ranging from hate crimes and violence to discrimination in employment and education, as illustrated in the following cases.

On September 30, 2002, the EEOC sued Alamo Rent-a-Car Company because a customer service representative in its Phoenix office, Ms. Bilan Nur, was denied permission to cover her head with a scarf during the Muslim holy month of Ramadan. Alamo had granted Ms. Nur permission to cover during Ramadan in

1999 and 2000, but in December 2001—just three months after the terrorist attacks, the rental company refused to allow her to observe her religious beliefs. Alamo subsequently disciplined, suspended, and fired Ms. Nur for failure to remove her scarf. Several cases like Ms. Nur's have been brought to the courts to adjudicate claims of anti-Muslim discrimination in the context of the workplace and beyond. Women and girls who wear the hijab or the more concealing niqab for religious reasons have long been the subject of discrimination lawsuits.[12]

A highly publicized post-9/11 bench trial in Florida, *Sultaana Lakiana Myke Freeman v. State of Florida*, involved a Muslim woman who wished to have her driver's license issued either without her photo on it or with a photo of her wearing dress that covered her entire body except for her eyes. The state of Florida had issued Ms. Freeman a license with a photo of her fully covered, but 10 months later, some three months after September 11, 2001, the Florida Department of Motor Vehicles sent Ms. Freeman a letter stating that her existing license was suspended, and she was to present herself for a photograph without her niqab. Citing security concerns after 9/11, the state of Florida insisted that the woman's driver's license was her primary form of identification, and that law enforcement personnel ought to be able to determine the woman's identity efficiently with the aid of her license. A license photo of a motorist fully covered would not be very helpful in this endeavor, the state argued. The judge in this case agreed with the state, writing in her ruling that while Freeman "most likely poses no threat to national security, there likely are people who would be willing to use a ruling permitting the wearing of fullface cloaks in driver's license photos by pretending to ascribe to religious beliefs in order to carry out activities that would threaten lives."[13]

The upshot of the court's ruling is that a Muslim woman who was not suspected of any crime was associated with the threat of terrorism merely on the basis of her appearance. While *she* is not a terrorist, the court said, others who intend to plot terrorist attacks may take advantage of the liberties protected by the Constitution to allow women to dress like this woman in order to disguise their identities. When taken up on appeal, the Florida appellate court affirmed the trial court judge's ruling, stating that while "we recognize the tension created as a result of choosing between following the dictates of one's religion and the mandates of secular law . . . as long as the laws are neutral and generally applicable to the citizenry, they must be obeyed."[14] In both the bench trial and the appeal, the record notes the fact that both sides in the case presented expert witnesses on Islamic law. For the state, the expert witness averred that exceptions to the practice of hijab are made because of necessity. The expert stated that even in Saudi Arabia women are required to have full-face photos on their passports and for exam taking. Since the primary purpose of the hijab is to avoid sexual enticement, and since the state had made efforts to accommodate by having a female photographer and no males present when the photo was taken, the necessity of providing security warranted an exception to the Islamic practice. Another expert witness testified on Ms. Freeman's behalf, stating that Muslim women must cover themselves. The witness referred to numerous passages in the Qur'an and the Sunnah to support his position. In his opinion, no exceptions would be permissible. The trial court judge, Circuit Court Judge Janet Thorpe, asserted that she would not choose between contending interpretations of shari'a provisions and agreed with state officials that letting people show only their eyes would compromise efforts to stop terrorists.

The ACLU has taken up the cause of fighting against anti-Muslim "backlash" discrimination since the attacks of September 11, 2001. The civil liberties organization defends persons charged with crimes related to espionage and terrorism under the U.S. Patriot Act and other federal intelligence-gathering laws; it has also defended Muslim women who have been discriminated against. In June 2004, the Nebraska chapter of the ACLU filed a civil rights lawsuit against the city of Omaha on behalf of Mrs. Lubna Hussein, a Muslim woman who was told that she would have to take her head scarf and cloak off if she wanted to accompany her children at the municipal swimming pool. Pool employees told Mrs. Hussein that she could not be in the pool area with her "street clothes" on, even though she was not planning on swimming. The city's policies required persons around the pool to be in swimsuits. Hussein saw that others were permitted in the pool area wearing clothing other than swimsuits and explained, to no avail, that she merely wanted to watch her young daughters while they swam. The ACLU filed a claim of civil rights violations on the basis of race, national origin, gender, and religion. In February 2005, the city of Omaha and the Nebraska ACLU announced a settlement, according to which the dress code at the public pool was amended to allow a variance to accommodate religious and/or medical needs.

Post-9/11 Security

Samar Kaukab, a 23-year-old U.S. citizen of Pakistani origin born and raised in the United States, was detained at O'Hare Airport on November 7, 2001, while passing through airport security, and ultimately "strip-searched." In accordance with her religious beliefs, which require modesty in public appearance, Kaukab covers her hair and neck with a scarf at all times in public. At the time of the incident, Kaukab resided in Columbus, Ohio, and worked for the national service program Volunteers in Service to America (VISTA). After attending a VISTA conference in Chicago in November 2001, she went to O'Hare to fly home to Columbus. She was wearing trousers, a long sweater, and ankle-length boots as well as her hijab and carried some hand luggage. While she was waiting in the security line with a group of other

VISTA conference participants, she noticed that occasionally someone would set off the metal detector. When this happened, the security staff did a quick, relatively nonintrusive additional search with a hand-held metal detector, and then the person was allowed to go on his or her way. Kaukab saw a woman wearing a scarf on her head, and some people with baseball caps, walking through the checkpoint without being stopped or asked to remove their head gear. According to Kaukab, none of these people appeared to be of South Asian or Pakistani descent, or wore clothing that would identify them as Muslim. Kaukab walked through the metal detector without setting it off. When she went to retrieve her bags, security staff surrounded Kaukab as if to prevent her from leaving the checkpoint and at the direction of Mr. Vargas, the National Guardsman who ordered the search, searched her multiple times with a hand-held metal detector. A female member of the security staff passed the wand of the detector over Kaukab's head and upper body, down her legs and her crotch, and stuck the detector into Kaukab's boots (while she was wearing them). She then conducted a pat-down of Kaukab, pulled the hooks and straps of Kaukab's bra, and asked Kaukab to lift her sweater. She then ran the detector over the portion of Kaukab's body that had been covered by her sweater. Despite numerous and extensive passes over Kaukab's head and body, the detector produced no audible signal. During this time, Vargas glared at Kaukab as the security staff carried out his orders to search her. With a crowd beginning to gather, Kaukab felt embarrassed and humiliated.

After the female security staff completed the pat-down search, the three staff members, after conferring with Vargas, ordered Kaukab to remove her head scarf. Kaukab explained she could not remove her hijab in public for religious reasons. The staff insisted, and Kaukab stated that she would remove her headscarf in a private room or behind a screen and only in front of a woman. Her request was not honored. Feeling violated and upset by the demands to remove her hijab, Kaukab repeatedly stated that she would not remove her hijab for religious reasons in public or in front of a man. After a lengthy discussion among the staff and Vargas, a male security guard ordered Kaukab to follow him to a room where he insisted that he search Kaukab while his female colleagues stood outside to guard the door. Kaukab, feeling harassed and frightened, repeated her objections. Finally, the security staff agreed that Kaukab could go into the room with the two female security guards.

One guard then conducted what Kaukab calls a "demeaning and overly intrusive" search of Kaukab's head. When told to remove her hijab, Kaukab complied. Then the security guard ran her fingers through Kaukab's hair and touched and rubbed Kaukab's scalp and neck. Despite Kaukab's compliance with the order to remove her hijab, the security guard proceeded to perform a complete body search, including removing Kaukab's sweater and placing her hand inside of Kaukab's bra, as well as unbuttoning and unzipping her trousers to place her hands inside her trousers and checking her crotch. During the entire search, the other female security guard watched. Finally dressed again, she was allowed to leave to catch her flight. During this stop and search, Vargas and the security personnel found no weapons or contraband.

In her claim, Kaukab alleged that the defendants violated her First Amendment rights to practice her religion, her Fourth Amendment right to be free from unreasonable searches, and her Fourteenth Amendment right to equal protection under the laws. She also claimed that the defendants deprived her of the full enjoyment of the terms and conditions of her passenger contract with United Airlines on the discriminatory grounds of race, ancestry, color, and/or ethnicity. Finally, she complained that the defendants falsely imprisoned her and committed battery against her. The lawsuit, filed on behalf of Kaukab by the ACLU of Illinois, sought a federal injunction to require airport guards to be trained not to base searches solely on religion or ethnicity, plus unspecified financial damages. Her case was settled out of court for an undisclosed amount. The case illustrates the point that the right of a person to be free from being profiled for purposes of search and seizure based on one's apparent Muslim religion or Arab or South Asian ethnicity has been compromised by national security and shows that it is difficult to strike a balance between legitimate security concerns and personal freedoms.

Discrimination and Accommodation in the Workplace

Maysa Mounla-Sakkal was delighted when, after earning a medical degree and working nine years as a researcher and nurse in her husband's medical practice in Aleppo, Syria, she was accepted as a first-year resident at Case Western Reserve University Hospital's Pediatric Residency Training Program in Cleveland, Ohio. As she went through her monthly rotations at Case Western Reserve, physicians on the teaching staff at the pediatric department completed evaluations of her performance. At the end of her first year, Dr. Mounla-Sakkal's residency was not renewed, and she brought a lawsuit against the pediatric department alleging religious and national origin discrimination, harassment, and retaliation. Her suit was dismissed before trial because of a lack of direct evidence, although her deposition shows that before she was even hired, the teaching staff had made comments about her Arab origin and wanted to know her position with respect to the Arab-Israeli conflict. A female physician on the teaching staff told Mounla-Sakkal that if she wanted to continue to second-year residency, she would have to take off her headscarf and not pray in public, adding that "babies are afraid" of the hijab. The attending physician allegedly discussed the resident's heritage with others on the staff, claiming that Muslims ride camels and are backward thinking, that Muslim women walk behind their husbands, and that Islam is inferior to Christianity. Although the incidents that Mounla-Sakkal could point to were inappropriate, the court considered them neither frequent nor harsh enough over the course of a year to constitute harassment.[15]

The intersection of personal and professional lives is never more complicated than in the realm of religion. While the free exercise of religion is enshrined in the U.S. Constitution, the very expression of religious belief in daily life evokes consternation when it overlaps with work responsibilities. When an employee displays a scriptural passage in a work space, or reads the Qur'an at lunch break, or starts a conversation about religion with coworkers, red flags are raised in a way that rarely happens when an employee talks about the home town professional baseball team. Religion is a sensitive area of life that makes many people uncomfortable, and the issue of religion in the workplace is not an easy one to handle. The regulation of religion in the workplace often leads to litigation. On the one hand, an employee who is censored in her religious expression at work may bring a lawsuit against her employer for infringement of her First Amendment rights or for discrimination on the basis of religion. On the other hand, an employer who liberally allows religious expression may face a religious harassment lawsuit from employees who are made uncomfortable by its implications. What is more, if the employer is part of the public sector, then an opening is created for a lawsuit based on the establishment clause of the First Amendment, which prohibits the "endorsement" of religion by the state.

In the face of such difficulties, what is an employer to do? Recent developments in civil rights legislation may provide some guidance for determining how to deal with religious expression in the workplace. In 1997, the Clinton Administration released guidelines on religious exercise and expression in the federal workplace.[16] The standard articulated in the guidelines presents a high threshold: Restrictions on religious expression are allowed only in cases where an employee's interest in the expression is *outweighed* by the government's interest in efficient provision of public services. In addition, if a government employer allows nonreligious speech that has a negative effect on productivity or efficiency in the workplace, then it must also allow similar religious speech, even if it reduces workplace efficiency. To put it another way, if public employees linger at the water cooler to discuss professional sports and their supervisor does nothing to put an end to it, employees with a religious message must also be permitted the same liberty as long as it does not slow down their productivity any more than the discussion of baseball did. The 1997 guidelines point out that several forms of expression generally do not amount to harassment of other employees who may not want to hear or see such expressions. For instance, keeping a Qur'an at one's desk to read during breaks, or discussing religious views with coworkers in the cafeteria or the hallway, or wearing religious jewelry, does not in most circumstances amount to harassment of other employees. According to these guidelines, to qualify as religious harassment the speech must reach the level of religious *intimidation,* ridicule, or insult.

How does one know the difference between protected expression and harassment? Employees in both the public and the private sector have petitioned the courts to receive guidance about what constitutes religious harassment in the workplace. In *Venters v. City of Delphi,*[17] a federal appellate court reasoned that religious harassment is analogous to sexual harassment for the purposes of determining legal liability. In other words, previous court decisions that have delineated what constitutes *sexual* harassment in the workplace can be helpful in determining what kinds of behaviors constitute *religious* harassment as well. Thus employees' claims of both the "quid pro quo" and "hostile work environment" variety of harassment have been accepted in the courts for evaluation. Quid pro quo religious harassment may take the form of a supervisor requiring an employee to engage in an unwelcome religious activity in order to keep a job or a job benefit. For instance, a supervisor who requires attendance at prayer meetings as a condition of employment can be said to be harassing his or her employees.

In comparison, a "hostile work environment" claim of religious harassment can occur when an individual employee makes disparaging remarks about another employee's religious beliefs, or places literature that insults that employee's religious beliefs in the employee's mailbox, or threatens an employee with physical harm. In such cases, the work environment is poisoned by the hostility of a coworker or supervisor. However, because the perception of what constitutes a "hostile" work environment is subjective—every individual has different levels of tolerance for unwanted pressures—the courts require that the complainants show that not only they find the harassment severe but that a "reasonable person" in their shoes would have found the work environment hostile (an objective criterion). Moreover, the courts have held that the *occasional* utterance of distasteful comments or hateful epithets that an employee may find offensive is not enough to create a hostile work environment. The *totality* of circumstances has to include evidence of severe and pervasive conduct, which means that the sheer number of overtly hostile comments or behavior has to be frequent enough to allow a jury to believe that the harassment interfered with the employee's work performance or created an intimidating working environment.

Various examples of charges of discrimination in the workplace that could not be successfully prosecuted can be cited, including the case of Dr. Mounla-Sakkal with which this section began. Another case is that of *Sheveka Gibson v. The Finish Line, Inc., of Delaware.*[18] A Muslim woman sued her former employer alleging claims of a hostile work environment and wrongful discharge (i.e., that she was improperly fired) because of her religion. Ms. Gibson worked as a cashier for The Finish Line, a sporting goods store in Kentucky. In March 2000, she began to talk about the possibility of her religious conversion from the Baptist church to Islam. She informed a coworker that she had learned more about the Nation of Islam, was attending services at a mosque on a regular basis, and was closer to deciding that she wanted to be a Muslim. The assistant manager of the store was within earshot of this conversation and out of Gibson's presence discussed with the manager what she had overheard. The assistant manager, who was white, said that she perceived the Nation of Islam to be a racist organization, "worse than the Ku Klux Klan," and that she did not feel comfortable continuing to work with Gibson. Gibson pressed charges, but the federal court held that Gibson had failed to show that the conduct of the assistant manager of the store in which she worked had created a hostile work environment. The court held that the assistant manager's single comment, made to employees other than Gibson and not in Gibson's presence, was not objectively hostile. Neither the frequency nor severity of the discriminatory conduct met the definition of a hostile work environment.

Yet another unsuccessful case is that of Firoozeh Butler, a practicing Muslim of Iranian descent, who had worked in various capacities for a software company since 1993. During the first few years of her employment, she consistently received favorable performance evaluations. However, after she complained to the Human Resources department in 2000 and 2001 regarding derogatory remarks made by coworkers about her ethnicity and religion, management "engaged in a calculated and deliberate effort to malign [her] job performance, to target her for termination, and to ostracize her from her fellow employees." She was demoted from her senior software engineer position to software engineer II in June 2001, and no adequate reasons for the job demotion were given. Butler also alleged that her supervisor threatened to terminate her health benefits, suggested that she resign, contacted her physician without authorization, and placed a bogus verbal warning in her personnel file while she was on short-term disability leave for a stress-related condition. Fellow employees, she says, "ridiculed her religious beliefs and national origin by inquiring whether she was to blame for terrorist activity and by referring to her as a 'camel jockey.'" In 1997 her supervisor commented to Butler that Iranians are crazy and put dirty laundry on their head. The supervisor's manager is also alleged to have made remarks that "Middle Eastern people smell and . . . [are] crazy." In 2000 another supervisor told her that cultural differences between them made communication impossible, and that "American people do not forget that Iranians take hostages." Finally, Butler was offended when, in October 2001, her supervisor posted a photograph in the workplace of Taliban leader Mullah Muhammad Omar with a caption using the word *jihad*. Butler sued, claiming a hostile work environment and discrimination according to national origin, race, and religion under

Title VII of the Civil Rights Act of 1964, as well as intentional infliction of emotional distress. The case was tried in 2003, and the jury returned a verdict in favor of the employer. Upon appeal, the appellate court held that the work incidents did not occur with sufficient frequency to constitute a pervasive or continuing violation. In other words, because the offenses were spread out over five years they were not evidence of an "organized scheme' against her.[19]

While most employers maintain and regularly train employees on their anti-discrimination and antiharassment policies, employers' enforcement efforts have not traditionally focused on prevention of discrimination on the basis of national origin or religion. Although the cases cited here were not successfully prosecuted, it may be that awareness of the potential for discrimination or harassment on the basis of national origin or religion is growing, particularly as employers see that such actions may well result in the same sorts of penalties as discrimination on the basis of race, gender, and disability.

School Dress Codes

If dress is an issue involving considerable controversy in the workplace, it is also very important in the context of American public schools, where religious symbols are banned because schools are considered secular institutions for the public education of its future citizens. From this perspective, the absolute prohibition of religiously inspired attire such as the hijab strengthens the boundaries of the secularized public sphere against any religious interference and upholds the separation of church and state. A number of cases that have reached the courts involve school girls wearing Islamic dress. Nashala Hearn, a sixth-grade student at Ben Franklin Science Academy in Muskogee, Oklahoma, for example, was suspended twice from school for wearing the hijab in violation of the school's dress code, which bans bandannas, hats, and other head coverings. Nashala said, "I didn't know it was going to be a problem because on Aug. 18, 2003, my first day of school last year, I explained to my homeroom teacher that I am Muslim and I wear a hijab and that I also pray between 1 and 1:30. She said that was fine and that she had a room for me to pray in. From that day forward, I received compliments from other kids as well as school officials." All that changed, however, when another teacher approached her in the cafeteria and said her hijab looked like a bandanna or a handkerchief, both head coverings being banned under the school system's dress code. She was suspended from school until the U.S. Justice Department interceded and had her reinstated in March 2004. Her parents filed suit against the Muskogee School District, and the Justice Department filed a motion in federal court in support of Hearn's position. According to the government's attorney, "No student should be forced to choose between following her faith and enjoying the benefits of a public education." The government alleged that the school district violated the equal protection clause of the 14th Amendment, which bars states from applying dress codes in a discriminatory manner. A settlement was reached whereby the school district agreed to change its dress code to accommodate attire worn for religious reasons. Testifying before senators in a U.S. Senate Judiciary subcommittee hearing in June 2004, Nashala said that her insistence on wearing the hijab set off "a battle between being obedient to God by wearing my hijab to be modest in Islam versus school dress code policy."[20]

Other cases involve the apparel of teachers, and it is worth considering a number of these in some detail. In 1984, Dolores Reardon, a Muslim who believes that Muslim women are required by their faith to wear a concealing headscarf and long, loose dress in public, was fired from her job as a substitute teacher in Philadelphia's public schools pursuant to Pennsylvania's "religious garb" statute.[21] The statute prohibits teachers and other Pennsylvania public school employees from wearing religious dress, marks, emblems, or insignia while performing their duties in public schools. The statute was enacted in 1895 on the heels of a very unpopular Pennsylvania Supreme Court ruling that allowed Catholic nuns teaching in public schools to wear traditional religious habits in the schools as long as they were not conveying religious instruction during school hours. Any public school principal who fails to suspend or fire an offending teacher is subject to a criminal penalty. Ms. Reardon had been working in the Philadelphia school district for twelve years when she decided in 1982 that her religious beliefs required her to adopt the hijab. She continued teaching after 1982 wearing the hijab and received no complaints from either the community or the school administration for about two years. At the end of 1984, Reardon was told that she could not teach while wearing the hijab by three different school principals on three separate occasions. She was not allowed to teach as a substitute while wearing the hijab, and she was sent home on all three occasions because she arrived at the schools so dressed.

In November 1984, Reardon filed a Title VII complaint with the EEOC against the school district of Philadelphia, claiming discrimination on the basis of religion. The EEOC investigated the complaint and, finding it to be valid, attempted reconciliation meetings with the school board. Reardon was reinstated as a school teacher in November 1985 and was allowed to teach full time as a substitute in the Philadelphia school district while wearing the hijab. However, she was not awarded back pay, and the school board refused to concede that the religious garb statute was applied in a discriminatory fashion. As a result, the U.S. Justice Department sued the Philadelphia school board alleging that the school district discriminated against individuals who wear certain attire as an aspect of their religious observance by failing to accommodate their religious beliefs.[22]

Ms. Reardon's complaint of religious discrimination in the workplace raised the following question for the first time: Does the Pennsylvania religious garb statute violate the prohibition on workplace discrimination on the basis of religion contained in Title VII of the 1964 Civil Rights Act? Additionally, her case raised a constitutional question: Would compliance with Title VII mean that the school district would be violating the establishment clause of the First Amendment to the U.S. Constitution, by conveying the impression that the public school "endorsed" Ms. Reardon's beliefs? One might add to this a third question: Does the "religious garb" statute position the school board and the commonwealth of Pennsylvania as openly hostile to religion (in violation of the establishment clause) because it singles out and punishes only employees using symbolic speech with religious content, while permitting its employees to wear "garb," including jewelry containing secular messages or no messages at all?[23] Initially, Reardon's case was successful. The district court held that Title VII prohibited the enforcement of the religious garb statute, and Reardon received back pay for the length of time she was denied employment as a substitute teacher. The court called the school board's application of the religious garb statute to Reardon selective and disparate treatment, because several other individuals in the school system wore religious symbols or garb without complaint or incident, and there was no evidence that any student perceived such garb as an endorsement of a particular religion. The school board was enjoined from continuing the enforcement of the religious garb statute.

However, on appeal, the Third Circuit Court of Appeals overturned the lower court ruling in favor of Reardon. The appellate court accepted the school board's argument that the accommodation of Reardon's religious practices would constitute an undue hardship for the school district in two ways: First, it would put individual school principals in the position of violating a valid state law, thereby exposing administrators to the risk of criminal prosecution, and to the loss of their jobs, pursuant to the "religious garb" statute; and second, it would require Pennsylvania to sacrifice a compelling state interest in preserving the secular character of its school system. The mere prospect of criminal prosecution, no matter how remote, when combined with the establishment-clause interest in maintaining a separation between church and state, was sufficiently strong to persuade the court to reverse the ruling of the lower court. The appellate court decision held that the 1964 Civil Rights Act does not prevent the school board in Philadelphia from denying Reardon the opportunity to teach while wearing the hijab. In fact, the ruling implies, but never explicitly holds, that Title VII's requirement of accommodation of religious practices in the workplace might place the public official at risk of violating the establishment clause of the First Amendment by creating the impression of the official endorsement of religion.

Islamic Law in American Courts

The foregoing sections have examined litigation involving Muslim plaintiffs versus non-Muslim (often public) defendants, in circumstances of anti-Muslim discrimination. The purpose of this analysis has been to see how far court officials will go to protect Muslims' civil rights under American law. Next, I turn my attention to legal disputes between Muslim litigants to examine the courts' recognition of Islamic law or shari'a provisions in the American context. While the details of the law are too extensive to be fully treated here, it should be noted that the process of fiqh, or application of the law, is a primary activity among observant American Muslims trying to understand what regulations genuinely apply to persons living in non-Muslim majority countries. With no Islamic school of law predominant in the United States, and with traditional notions of family relations often at odds with prevailing American ideologies and public policy, Muslim leaders are spending considerable time and attention in helping their constituencies understand what is right, appropriate, legal, or not legal in the American context. The implementation of Islamic law in daily life actually becomes more important for some in a non-Muslim environment, where it is thought to be too easy to slip into so-called secular ways without the behavioral constraints imposed by a Muslim-majority society. Many periodicals and Internet Web sites are devoted to the exploration of shari'a and the Qur'anic injunctions that would apply to everyday life. Essays, commentaries, and fatwas provide guidance about several topics ranging from dating and married life to divorce, child custody, the prescriptions of the hijab, prayer, hygiene practices, inheritance, economic rights, female genital cutting, and sexuality.[24]

What follows are some court cases that illustrate the relationship between state (secular) law and shari'a in the United States. Most involve state rather than federal courts since matters of marriage, divorce, and child custody fall within the jurisdiction of the states. In general, when judges are asked to enforce the provisions of a ruling obtained from a court located in a foreign country, they follow the international rule of comity, giving full force and effect to rulings obtained in accord with the procedures of the official courts in the particular country, provided that they do not fly in the face of public policy in the United States. In this manner, courts affect a kind of legal pluralism by incorporating the rulings of foreign jurisdictions. The rule of comity thus serves as a source of hybridity in American law.

Marriage and Divorce

While some Muslims in the United States ignore Islamic law altogether and choose instead to rely exclusively on secular American law, many selectively combine key provisions of Islamic law with American conventions on marriage. In these cases, in addition to obtaining an official marriage license, the couple has the marriage religiously sanctioned in accordance with Islamic law, which treats marriage as a matter of contract. Traditional legal rules—such as those allowing Muslim men to marry up to four wives at one time—are rarely observed because they are considered anachronistic. In the view of the vast majority of Muslims, such rules are inherently biased against women and fail to embody the ideals in Islam that portray marital relations as mutually supportive.

On the other hand, rules about the payment of the mahr (dower), are often observed in American Muslim marriages, if only symbolically; that is, before getting married, the couple negotiates an Islamic marriage contract in which it is stipulated that the groom will pay to the bride an immediate mahr—an honorific sum of money, jewels, gold, or other goods—when the marriage takes place and will also commit to pay a "deferred" mahr—another specific sum of money—in the event that the marriage ends in divorce. The couple may customize their marriage contract by adding stipulations that generally guarantee the rights of women vis-à-vis their husbands. For instance, women frequently stipulate that they keep their finances separate from their spouses' and control their own investments. Women can reserve the right to work outside the home without getting their husbands' permission, as well as the right to use contraception, or even that they will not cook or clean the house.

Azizah al-Hibri argues that women need to protect themselves by drafting carefully constructed marriage contracts.[25] She argues that women's Islamic rights are unrecognized and therefore underused; the right to insert conditions into marriage contracts, to modify conventional marital relations in a manner that enhances women's freedom, is chief among these.[26] Should an American court, in the name of multiculturalism, substitute the mahr provision for the usual provisions of alimony and child support, or for the equitable division of community property called for in state law? If a married couple has signed an Islamic marriage contract—either as U.S. residents or in another country before migrating to the United States—should the provisions of that contract supersede existing state laws governing the dissolution of the marriage? To appreciate the potential economic and social inequalities that could occur in such cases, we need to keep in mind the purpose for which the mahr is practiced.

Historically, the ostensible purpose of the mahr provision has been to protect the wife in the event that the husband suddenly decides to divorce her. In its origins, mahr was meant to compensate for the fact that women are vulnerable in marriage to the man's privilege to execute a unilateral talaq-style divorce. Women have virtually no recourse against this method of repudiation. Thus, the mahr provision serves as a guarantee of maintenance, particularly important for women who have not earned salaries during their marriages. Even though U.S. courts seldom recognize the talaq divorce as valid, given that its omission of notifying the wife violates American standards of due process, the use of the mahr provision is increasingly popular in the United States. Asifa Quraishi suggests that the record of Muslim marriage litigation in the United States shows evidence that Muslims generally do continue to include the mahr provision in their contemporary marriage contracts, making the question of whether mahrs are valid under civil law a relevant one. It is important to keep in mind that a mahr does not serve the same purpose as a prenuptial agreement under American law. In contrast to mahr provisions, which are created in order to protect women from the harsh effects of unilateral divorce under Islamic law, the prenuptial agreement is used to draw an enclosure around the assets of an individual in order to protect him or her from the potentially acquisitive grasp of the partner. While the mahr is gender specific, providing maintenance for the wife, the prenuptial agreement is gender neutral and can be used by either spouse to protect his or her property. In many cases that have appeared before the courts, the decisions have been made by treating the mahr provision as if it were a prenuptial agreement. Ultimately, however, in determining the relationship between U.S. law and shari'a in cases on the dissolution of marriage, the issue of whether the mahr provision should be honored turns on the question of whether the woman would be economically worse off with mahr than under state laws governing the dissolution of marriages.

The following are brief synopses of a number of cases of Muslim divorces that illustrate the types of problems, as well as solutions, that have arisen in this area. It is important to keep in mind that both sets of American civil law that have a bearing on Islamic marriage contracts—marriage and divorce laws and contract law—fall under state jurisdictions in the United States. Consequently, because of the independence of states, the decisions in the cases are a mixed variety of rulings that are supportive of Islamic legal claims in some states and prohibitive in others. The landscape that emerges, therefore, is neither consistent nor predictable. In the case of *Odatalla v. Odatalla*, the couple had been married in an Islamic ceremony conducted by an imam.[27] The terms of the mahr had been agreed by both parties before the marriage. The husband was to pay the wife one gold coin during the marriage ceremony and a deferred mahr of $10,000 in the event of a divorce. Several years later, the wife filed for divorce and sought enforcement of the mahr provision in a New Jersey court. The husband objected, arguing that enforcement of the mahr would violate the establishment clause of the First Amendment by putting public officials in the position of implementing what was essentially a religious agreement.

The trial court rejected the husband's argument, and held that the enforcement of the mahr provision would neither excessively entangle the court in questions of religious doctrine nor infringe the "free exercise" rights of the husband (both infringements of First Amendment guarantees). While included as part of a religious ceremony, the mahr provision of the contract had a secular purpose, the court reasoned, because it was intended to address the financial support of the wife after the marriage ended. The award of the mahr to the wife was thus within the judicial authority of the court; the court also determined that the mahr provision complied with New Jersey standards for contract law and thus was enforceable.

In New York, the state Supreme Court accepted the concept of the mahr provision in the case of *Habibi-Fahnrich v. Fahnrich*,[28] ruling that *in general* it is enforceable in a state court of law. Nevertheless, the court held that the specific mahr provision contested in this case was not legally valid, because the terms of the payments were simply too vague to be upheld in accordance with the law. The immediate mahr was a ring and the deferred mahr was to be half of the husband's possessions. However, since no specific means were presented in the contract to determine which assets, calculated at what time during the marriage, the court found the terms to be too indefinite.

In *Re. Marriage of Shaban*, the couple divorcing had been married in Egypt in the early 1970s.[29] Their marriage contract provided for an immediate mahr of 25 piasters (about one American dollar). The mahr to be paid in the event of a divorce was equal to about $30. At the time of the marriage, neither spouse anticipated that the couple would emigrate to California. Once there, the husband became a successful physician, and the couple subsequently divorced. Had the court found that the deferred mahr was a valid agreement, the wife would have received only $30 instead of half of the $3 million estate she shared with her husband. In this ruling, the court refused to substitute the mahr for the equitable division of community property under California divorce law.

In many instances, the courts have referred marital disputes to religious tribunals. This occurs when both parties consent to religious adjudication, and the rulings of these tribunals are taken by government courts as advisory, along the lines of "special masters" of the court. Typically, judges enforce the rulings of religious tribunals in cases in which the outcome would not contravene the justice principles of civil law. An example of this is seen in *Jabri v. Quaddura*, in which the deferred mahr for the wife provided her half of the value of a particular house and $40,000 in the case of divorce.[30] Also stipulated in the marriage contract was the provision that any dispute arising under it would be referred to the Texas Islamic Court. When the couple divorced, all parties to the proceedings (including the husband's brother, who was part owner of the house, and the wife's parents) submitted to binding arbitration before the Texas Islamic Court. When arbitration proceedings broke down, the wife petitioned the state court to compel arbitration. When the wife lost at the trial court level—the court held the provision for religious adjudication contained in the marital contract was not covered by the Texas Arbitration Act—she and her parents appealed. On appeal, the Texas judiciary ruled that the agreement to arbitrate in the Texas Islamic Court was enforceable under state law.

However, the courts have recognized the mahr as superseding the provisions of state law in a number of cases. In *Chaudry v. Chaudry*, a New Jersey court held that the mahr superseded any alimony or division of the property of the husband, a millionaire physician.[31] The court based its decision on the fact that the husband had gone back to Pakistan and obtained an Islamic divorce. In accordance with the international rule of comity, decisions rendered procedurally in foreign courts will be upheld in American courts unless they fly in the face of U.S. public policy. Consequently, the court viewed the mahr agreement as a waiver of the Muslim wife's right to equitable distribution of the couple's jointly-owned property under state law in the American legal system.

Cultural Arguments

Western distortions and unfavorable portrayals of Islam and Muslims have been replete in popular culture and official circles in the United States for generations, manifesting in contextually and historically specific ways. The less than hospitable reception of Islamic symbols and the mixed record of accepting Islamic legal norms in the courtrooms and law offices of the United States are yet other examples of such an Orientalist stance. As more Muslim Americans grapple with the role that religion plays in shaping their lives, American courts will increasingly be faced with instances of people negotiating between Islamic and civil sources of law. A desire by the courts to give Islamic law due respect forces them to decide what constitutes the appropriate interpretation of Islamic law to fit the particular circumstances before them. What is important about the cases discussed in this chapter is the body of knowledge being produced about Muslim women. Certain stereotypes about Muslim life, embodied in the symbol of the hijab, denote Islam as a backward religion that is the cause of the problems that Muslim women face—submission, ghettoization, patriarchy, and so forth. This view of Muslim women as subjected to the practice of hijab tends to deflect responsibility away from mainstream society for incorrect assumptions about Islam that result in prejudice and institutional barriers against Muslims in the United States. Muslim women, according to this logic, are kept out of the American mainstream not because of discrimination against them as Muslims, but because Islam is oppressive of women, keeping them shrouded in religiously mandated clothing. Simplistic generalizations that are both inaccurate and reductionist are made about Muslim women. These generalizations legitimize exclusions and devalue the position of Muslim women as inferior against the standards of western feminism.

Cases of divorce, discrimination in the workplace and schools, hate crimes, and racial or ethnic profiling in the aftermath of 9/11 are all instances that display tensions between individual freedom and the authority of the state. The law is central in determining the relationship between the individual's right to religious liberty and the state's power to protect and promote such general interests as national security and gender equality. In some instances, the state occasionally protects a woman's right to wear a particular mode of dress for religious reasons despite resistance on the part of an employer or a school that seeks to promote other objectives. In other cases, the state jeopardizes a woman's right to self-expression by singling her out for extraordinary scrutiny and by making religious freedom secondary to competing interests. The practice of hijab is not the only issue that places women in the crucible of American domestic law—some American courts apply Islamic rules of marriage and divorce. Issues such as domestic violence, child custody, inheritance, and female genital cutting raise further questions about women's rights under Islamic law. Do these offer potential sites for a collision between religious law and public policy? Does this offer an opening for an Islamic feminist jurisprudence to emerge? Can the interpretation of legal codes in the diaspora offer women possibilities for actively reworking gender relations within their own communities? Or will the articulation of Islamic law continue to carry its historically entrenched masculinist properties in our contemporary times?

These questions raise a set of issues that have been marked as specific practices of belonging to the group or community, in this instance the feminist interpretive community. Islamic feminism has emerged as a discursive field predominantly in western societies among feminist thinkers who claim the authority to read the Quran and Islamic traditions from a feminist (and for some, a womanist[32]) perspective. Central to this feminism is the point that the Qur'an was revealed to a male authority. The question is whether the Qur'an endorses male authority exclusively, determining that rule by father and husband is divinely ordained. Asma Barlas, a political scientist, defines Islamic feminism as a kind of Qur'anic hermeneutics that allows Muslims to argue against patriarchy from within an Islamic frame of reference. She urges Muslims to recuperate the Qur'an from its patriarchal modes of reasoning and authority to reframe it as a text of gender equality and social justice and a mandate for the practice of rights.[33] Many others have similarly argued for the project of rereading the Quran and Islamic traditions and shari'a from a woman-centered point of view. This proposition challenges the authority of traditional interpretive communities, and writers such as Asma Barlas and Amina Wadud are claiming for themselves the authority to produce religious knowledge and argue for gender equality by reinterpreting foundational Qur'anic principles.[34] Riffat Hassan, religious studies professor, has called the Qur'an the "Magna Carta" of human rights.[35]

Some feminist scholars have mapped how a masculinist bias became institutional during the first centuries of Islamic history and actively seek the reform of Islamic law as a means of ending gender discrimination. They use the concept of ijtihad (personal interpretation) to bring to the table new, feminist interpretations of standard legal principles. Others argue that Islam is patriarchal and misogynist because of its social, economic, and cultural underpinnings. This factor, the argument continues, is one among several that determine the subordination of Muslim women. For these women, Islamic materials mandate a hierarchical order and sexual inequality, and thus engagement in an interpretive project focused on the Quran and shari'a is pointless.

Cultural testimony has been provided in courts of law in cases that raise claims of cultural bias. An interesting example of expert testimony offered by an advocate of Islamic feminism appears to have played a pivotal role in one such case from 2004. In this case, which involving claims of disc.·imination violative of Title VII, Dr. Riffat Hassan testified as an expert witness on behalf of a Muslim woman, Dr. Zakiyyah Muhammad. Dr. Muhammad was fired from her position as principal of an Islamic school in Orange County, California. She successfully sued the Islamic Society of Orange County for unlawful race- and gender-based discrimination, retaliation, fraud, and intentional infliction of emotional distress, receiving a jury award of punitive damages on most of her claims. The defendants appealed the jury verdict because of the use of expert testimony about cultural bias, which, they argued, was more prejudicial than probative. The appeals court found that the expert testimony was neither unfairly prejudicial nor insufficient evidence to uphold the judgment against the defendants because it was directly related to Dr. Muhammad's effort to show that her termination was the result of gender stereotyping.

The disputed testimony provided by Hassan was given in the following context. Dr. Muhammad, an African American Muslim woman with advanced degrees in Education from Columbia University, had been principal of the Orange Crescent School in Garden Grove, California, for approximately five years and had a considerable record of achievement. The school was operated by the Islamic Society of Orange County. The court record notes that when Muhammad was hired, the school board's decision to hire her was not unanimous. Those expressing reservations thought that as an African American, she would have trouble running the school. Most if not all of the teachers and students were not African American. In 2003, in a contentious election for school board president, the female president was "asked to step aside" to allow one of the defendants named in the lawsuit, Dr. Mirza, a male psychiatrist from Pakistan, to run unopposed. Upon his election to the top position in the school board, friction began at Orange Crescent School between Dr. Muhammad, as principal, and Dr. Mirza, as school board president.

The evidence at trial indicated that Mirza tried hard to remove Muhammad from her position.

In the court trial, Riffat Hassan qualified as an expert witness to testify on Muslim cultural beliefs and attitudes. Hassan testified that in South Asia and the rest of the Muslim world, there is a "very strong patriarchal bias" in the interpretation of the Qur'an, and "according to patriarchal assumptions it is regarded as self-evident that women are inferior to men and men are superior to women." In her own experience, she said, the "overwhelming majority of people are patriarchal in their thinking." Further, she offered, Muslim societies are very traditional and tend to divide public space, the purview of men, from private space, such as the domestic sphere, which belongs to women. The "Islamic order of things" is thrown into jeopardy when women occupy public roles. The view of gender equality in Islam, she testified, is influenced by a verse in the Qur'an, which appoints men to be the managers of women and affirms that men are "qawwamun" (guardians; see Q4:34) with regard to women. Other verses in the Qur'an that she mentioned indicate among other things that women are inferior to men in prayer because they are to abstain from praying during menstruation. These and other reasons are cited to deny gender equality is possible in Islam. Hassan went further to explain that in India and Pakistan, the Hindu caste system is powerful, and that darker-skinned persons are looked down upon. Thus when Muhammad was seen to challenge the authority of lighter-skinned males, she would be viewed as acting out of place.[36]

Much of what Hassan testified to was questioned on cross-examination. She admitted that such generalizations do not apply to all persons coming from South Asia, but that she believes that "most Pakistanis" believe that women are inferior to men. While the major world religions developed in patriarchal cultures, she testified, most adherents have risen above the patriarchalism through historical evolution and adaptation. However, "if you compare say Muslims in general with Christians in general and Jews in general, . . . Muslim communities in general are far more patriarchal today than the Jewish communities and the Christian communities are."[37] Furthermore, she testified to seeing many examples in the United States where Muslim men bond together and exhibit autocratic behavior toward women, in particular where there are also differences in ethnic origins. In sum, given what this testimony looks like on the record, it would seem that Muslim men from South Asia would be inherently incapable of dealing with an outspoken, well-educated woman in the workplace, particularly when that woman has dark skin color.

In the closing argument, the counsel for Dr. Muhammad asked the jury, "What's driving [the defendants]? What's driving them are these feelings of honor and loyalty. And this woman, how dare she ask for [a hearing] because women don't do this, they don't speak up, they don't criticize, they don't have rights, they are not allowed to go in front of the Majlis and they sure as heck don't deserve an apology for what I did to her.... Was this a big surprise that this woman was treated this way by the Muslim men? Was it a big surprise to you? Do you think we told you something you didn't already know?"[38] Together the expert testimony and the lawyer's queries in the closing argument posited a particular "knowledge" of Islam that would affirm what presumably jurors "already know"—namely, that women are oppressed and Islam is irremediably patriarchal. Muhammad's lawyer emphasized the generalizations introduced into evidence by the expert witness and invited jurors to give in to their prejudices. However, in reaching its decision, the appellate court held that the expert testimony was not prejudicial in part because of an action taken by the jury in deliberation. Before delivering its verdict, the jury sent a note to the court saying, "We the jury, feel it is important for all the parties involved in this litigation to know, and understand, that we do not consider Islam to be on trial.... Both sides in this matter have also evidenced a sincere commitment to faith and the education of children—both honorable and very American.... We have been empowered to deliver a verdict, but are powerless to deliver peace and understanding. You must seek that elsewhere."[39]

The jury here seems to be resisting the notion that cultural generalizations apply to individual defendants on trial and that broad indictments of whole cultures, and specifically Islam, as oppressive and patriarchal by definition are troubling. Faceless though the jury may be—and we do not know anything about this jury, in terms of gender, ethnicity/race, age, income, religion, education, media exposure—we do see that the jurors felt it necessary to put in writing that "Islam is not on trial" in this case. Implicitly perhaps this statement suggests that there is as a general perception that Islam *is* on trial in other venues, such as the media, or just simply that the jurors felt the cultural testimony was off base. The verdict went against the defendants, but the jurors were anxious to communicate that the reasons had little if anything to do with the "knowledge" of Islam and South Asian cultures produced in that courtroom. In any event, in their own words, what the jury had to offer was (only) a verdict, not peace and understanding. For that level of amity, the litigants would have to go somewhere other than a court of law.

Epilogue

The inspiration for the title of this book came from the classical Islamic dichotomous formulation of dar al-Islam (the abode of Islam) and dar al-harb (the abode of the unbeliever). The notion of the unfamiliar abode implicitly challenges the dichotomy embedded in the social imaginary by focusing on Muslim life and legality voluntarily outside the dar al-Islam. Historically, Islamic jurisprudence has recognized many situations in which Muslims live outside the main fold—in dar al-darura (abode of necessity), dar al-ahd (abode of treaty), and dar al-sulh (country of truce).[1]

Consequently, over the years jurists have developed mechanisms to facilitate compromise. This final chapter reflects on the diasporic brand of inventiveness and intellectual production that enjoys currency among contemporary Muslims in the West.

The facility for making meaning out of a fragmentary situation is driven by a contradictory tendency to derive norms from lived experience (pragmatism) on the one hand, and on the other, to index, at the same time, a comprehensive set of tenets and general principles that guide interpersonal relations and community (idealism). This mix of pragmatism and idealism has encouraged the application of human reason to the project of interpreting God's will. Thus, Muslims in the diaspora currently engage in differentiating between "the universal principles to which the Muslim consciousness must seek to be faithful" and those doctrines that developed at a given point in history and must be limited to their given context.[2] Many classically trained religious scholars accede that this process of transplantation/adaptation of Muslim living has continuously occurred throughout Islamic history, and in today's western countries, permanent settlement is permissible provided that "holy law" is still maintained and enforced. Even though they keep classical Islamic categories as the frame of reference, most of these scholars recognize that while many people may try to live in accordance with shari'a, they will always interpret the law in ways that are contextually specific.

Various Muslims in the West have fashioned methods to bring Islamic principles in line with the realities of their lived experiences. According to Ihsan Yilmaz, classical Islamic jurisprudence has offered space for eclecticism through the sophisticated device of *takhayyur* (the selective use of legal rules from a variety of juristic opinions) or *tarjih* (the process of evaluating hadiths and choosing the "preferred" one to apply to the problem at hand). In looking for the solution to a novel problem, the jurisconsult may choose to base a solution on a minority opinion within a historical *maddhab* (school of thought) or to pick and choose from across boundaries separating schools of thought. This approach represents the dissolution of maddhab boundaries and instigates within the context of legal pluralism the opportunity spaces for what Yilmaz has called the practice of neo-ijtihad.[3] These mechanisms might be indispensible for the realization of a diasporic legal consciousness in an Islamic idiom. Tariq Ramadan explicitly addresses the conditions for ijtihad, the independent reasoning of a jurist to infer the rules of shari'a in novel situations facing his community. The legal instrument of independent reasoning is the rational elaboration of laws by a qualified jurist; however, for historical reasons this instrument was sidelined in favor of *taqlid* (imitation of one's predecessors, or loosely understood as blind application of precedent). As a result, the impetus to formulate personal judgment on the basis of the direct study of the sources of law (Qur'an and the Sunnah) was lost. Ramadan argues that through its religious scholars, the contemporary Muslim ummah should be engaged in the project of independent reasoning. He calls for an ijtihad that uses the tools of electronic databases of important reference works. He also calls for computer-aided classifications and authentication of *ahadith* (sayings attributed to the Prophet Muhammad), which will "make the work of the mujtahid easier and more effective."[4] Through a renewal of ijtihad practice, Ramadan asserts that Muslims will be guided by the right mix of pragmatism and idealism, or the vicissitudes of their daily lives and the fundamentals of Islam.

One of the more striking aspects of the growing field of contemporary Islamic religious scholarship is the number of treatises debating the legitimacy of legal interpretation in the minority context. A few Muslim scholars question the wisdom of a *fiqh al-aqalliyat* (jurisprudence of minority), which consists of a series of legal opinions in step with the legal systems of western societies often made available to the public through Web sites. The cognizance of a minority perspective is applauded, yet scholars such as Tariq Ramadan and Mohammed Khalid Masud (former Academic Director of the Institute for the Study of Islam in the Modern World, in Leiden, the Netherlands) suggest that to think in terms of minority status elaborates a mode of thinking that places Muslims at the margins of political and social relations. Rather, there is no longer a place of origin from which Muslims in the West are distanced or exiled, and Muslims in western societies need to consider themselves fully enfranchised in their natural domain. Moreover, to expect that shari'a will resolve the contradictions created by the impact of modernity on Muslim life is impractical. Instead of relying on classical legal conventions, Masud suggests that jurists will have to "dig deep into social norms" to translate the principles of shari'a into a functional normative system of law. As a dynamic legal system, Islamic jurisprudence will have to continue to interact with changing societal norms.[5]

Numerous conceptions of living neither "in peace" under dar al-Islam, nor in the domain of dar al-harb ("the unbeliever," in the unsettled condition of war, which is the literal translation of *harb*) provide new spaces within which to nurture creative approaches to living in the present. To invoke a metaphor already used in this book, living in an untried diasporan context requires examination of the *tain* (reverse side) of the mirror, freighted with meanings about community, difference, and change. The purpose of this examination is to find cultural endowments that facilitate and define the arc of the mirror's reflective properties. No doubt, we can find in the mirror distortions of the Other, but we may also find images of reclamation and new possibilities. This possibility prefigures the normative basis for dialogue—the "interactive pluralism" recently indicated by the archbishop of Canterbury, which entails the acknowledgement that a conversation partner even exists with whom one is willing and able to interact.

The title claim, "the Unfamiliar Abode," which implies that the social imaginary of the West is unfamiliar, may be overstated and provisional. It is *not* meant to suggest that Muslim subjectivities are without any certain abode, or *right* of abode, in the United States or Britain. Neither is it meant to say that Islam constitutes a civilizational opponent vis-à-vis western societies. Nevertheless, the phrase *unfamiliar abode* offers a key insight into displacement and belonging as central features of contemporary Muslim life, law, and society. Muslim life, with its subjectivities within law and social structures, has its own (exceptional) specificities of time and place that make it quite different from other ethnic or religious minorities with transnational connectivities. The phrase inspires hope for the transformative possibilities contained in the diaspora but also draws our attention to the limits set by the legal strictures, discursive dynamics, and cultural understandings embedded within the diasporic framework.

As I mentioned in earlier chapters, I am interested in the kinds of subjectivities that emerge from the various assemblages (loosely strung abstractions about Islam, secularism, and neoliberalism) produced by the regimes of security common to the early 21st century. It is widely accepted that Islamic norms are important. And yet, the logic of the dominant secular form of governance in the United States and Britain struggles to define a public role for religious values. Muslims see these governments disingenuously empowering some expressions of religiosity over others. One fundamental premise of secularism is that the government should play the role of neutral arbiter, staying out of debates internal to religious communities about competing religious orthodoxies and conceptions of the good, and refraining from differentiating citizens' rights on the basis of religious identity. But the experiences of many Muslims reveal the contradictions and inconsistencies of this premise. "Being tough on Muslims," Sherene Razack writes, "is one significant way in which contemporary Western governments secure both their domestic base [through appeals to the conservative right affirming the idea of a monoculture] and their international stature (through appearing to be active participants in the 'war on terror')."[6] What this means for Muslims residing in the United States and Britain is that the burden of a policy of toughness abroad falls squarely on their liberties at home. Increased surveillance, diminished due process rights, and social stigmatization have made it clear that responses to Muslims have been organized around beliefs that they pose a credible threat to the modern nation.

The objectification of Muslims and Islam as dangerously Other in western democratic societies is neither new nor astonishing in the current political context. Scholars such as Edward Said documented that the ideological underpinnings of a global confrontation between the West and Islam have long been present in political, media, and theological discourses. The clash of civilizations thesis expressed in Samuel Huntington's work is merely the most recent popularization of the dichotomous variable of insider/outsider or Muslim/non-Muslim that has taken over a significant portion of political and academic analysis. The political and legal processes through which Muslims are depicted in American and British societies extend the fallacy further. The legitimate defense of national security in response to the threat of terrorism becomes inextricably bound to the indefensible inclination to stigmatize those who "do not share our values" or "hate us for our freedoms." Appeal to the clash of civilizations thesis justifies a form of politics that presents citizens of the Muslim faith with an impossible dilemma: Prove the negative ("I am not a terrorist") by demonstrating civic virtue ("join us in fighting extremism together"), or renounce your religion as premodern and antisecular.

Official efforts to overcome the deleterious effects of popular distrust of the Muslim Other and the stereotyping of the Muslim communities in the West have been in tension with official agendas to combat terrorism. This state of things has resulted in an uneven terrain, which Americans and Britons of the Muslim faith must navigate. For instance, in the United States one witnesses the appointment of an Islamic scholar-in-residence to the U.S. Department of Treasury, and efforts made by the Treasury to teach the principles of Islamic finance to U.S. banking regulatory agencies. But one can also witness the freezing of assets of American Muslim charities in the interest of security, notwithstanding admissions by the Treasury that most of the charities' funds went to worthy causes. A U.S. Supreme Court justice recently held that the practice of ethnic profiling of Arabs and Muslims not only makes sense but is very likely constitutionally valid.[7] In Britain, in the aftermath of a security crisis, the government can be seen engaging in dialogue with a narrow range of Muslim interlocutors, mainly spiritualists (Sufis), women's groups involved in gender equality campaigns, and "moderate" religious scholars and journalists. Yet this dialogue gives license to operationalize suspicions and stereotypes about the growing Islamic extremism in Britain's inner cities, in particular in the Midlands, and dilutes the administration of justice.

The years since terrorist attacks on American and British civilians have started in earnest have been a time of unprecedented intellectual and organizational growth among Muslims in Britain and the United States. In this study, I tried to convey the notion that the diasporic project of building capacities for defining the terms of discourse—developing an idiom that pivots on an Islamic frame of reference— aims to create the space that will allow contestation and maturation to happen. The prevailing popular discourse about a Muslim presence in the West is often based on oppositional frameworks portraying Muslims as fanatical/rational or integrated/ separated, which are at variance with the complexity of Muslim subjectivity. I contend that the dividing line is "wrong" both in the normative and in the factual sense: Normative because it leaves us with no meaningful strategies to consider when faced with the necessities and opportunities for dialogue; factual considering that such generalizations are all too often incorrect and thus are not a useful foundation for knowledge, opinion, or policy formation.

The emerging and multifaceted Muslim legal consciousness and diasporic subjectivity are interesting sites for the study of power relations because they represent some of the most apparent and blatant invocations of difference. All power relationships involve contests between the subordinate and the powerful. Yet here, the situations are unique in that they unfold in the midst of a growing securitization of the state's defensive apparatus—not only through the force of arms but also through the discursive constructions of rationales to support the use of force, such as interrogation, investigation, and diminution of civil rights. I suggest that as scholars, we should pay further attention to the polyvalent organization of social life in which official state institutions and community organizations play a significant role. Only through deeper analysis of pluralism can we comprehend the significance of the impact of translocal knowledge production and the important shifts in the ways people make sense of the world.

Notes

INTRODUCTION

1. I borrow this term from Arjun Appadurai, *Fear of Small Numbers: An Essay on the Geography of Anger* (Durham, N.C.: Duke University Press, 2006).

2. Invasions first of Afghanistan and then of Iraq were designed principally as "forensic" wars, to make certain discoveries about who exactly the enemy is: What is Al-Qaeda? Who is Osama Bin Laden? And who really are the Taliban devotees? These invasions were also "forensic" in the sense of discovering who were the supporters of the United States and Britain, forcing many fence sitters to declare their loyalties and even to join in the construction of the "coalition" forces in "Operation Iraqi Freedom" (ibid., 20).

3. See, for example, Nasar Meer and Tehseen Noorani, "A Sociological Comparison of Anti-Semitism and Anti-Muslim Sentiment in Britain," *Sociological Review* 56 (2008): 195–219; David Theo Goldberg, "Racial Europeanization," *Ethnic and Racial Studies* 29 (2006): 331–64; and William E. Connolly, *Pluralism* (Durham, N.C.: Duke University Press, 2005).

4. The term *normalize* came up in a personal interview with a British Muslim intellectual activist, Dr. Azzam al-Tamimi. This interview is discussed in chapter 2. In the United States, another term commonly used is to *indigenize* Islam.

5. For a discussion of the constitutive theory of law, see John Brigham, *The Constitution of Interests* (New York: NYU Press, 1996), and Michael McCann, *Rights at Work: Pay Equity and the Politics of Legal Mobilization* (Chicago: University of Chicago Press, 1994).

6. However, in "A Sociological Comparison," Meer and Noorani make a compelling case that Jews were similarly scapegoated by associating them with anarchist movements in Europe in the late 19th century.

7. Sherene H. Razack, *Casting Out: The Eviction of Muslims from Western Law and Politics* (Toronto: University of Toronto Press, 2008), 6.

8. For an illustration of this idiom, see Engin F. Isin and Myer Siemiatycki, "Making Space for Mosques: Struggles for Urban Citizenship in Diasporic Toronto," in *Race, Space, and the Law: Unmapping a White Settler Society*, ed. Sherene H. Razack (Toronto: Between the Lines, 2002). The authors cite a Canadian urban planner who notes approvingly how an architectural plan to redesign a building into a mosque will transform a "plain church" into a "different cultural idiom . . . completely crossing cultural lines from the historic, simple Protestant idiom to the exotic, romantic, eastern design" (206).

9. See Abdullahi Ahmed An-Na'im, *Islam and the Secular State: Negotiating the Future of Shari'a* (Cambridge, Mass.: Harvard University Press, 2008), 35–36.

10. Tariq Ramadan, *Western Muslims and the Future of Islam* (Oxford: Oxford University Press, 2004), 22.

11. Ibid., 33.

12. Ibid., 4.

13. Pnina Werbner, "Islamophobia: Incitement to Religious Hatred; Legitimizing a New Fear?" *Anthropology Today* 21 (2005): 6.

14. Meer and Noorani, "A Sociological Comparison," 198.

15. Isin and Siemiatycki, "Making Space," 207.

16. The phrase *the path that leads to the spring* refers to shari'a, the religious law of Islam. See Ramadan, *Western Muslims* and An-Na'im, *Islam and the Secular State*.

17. For an interesting overview of doctrinal foundations for affirming Muslim residence in non-Muslim contexts, see Ramadan, *Western Muslims*.

18. Ibid., 64.

19. Ibid., 63.

20. Razack, *Casting Out*, 10.

21. The two dates, of course, refer to terrorist attacks in United States and London, England. The coordinated series of bomb attacks on London's public transportation system during morning rush hour, which occurred on July 7, 2005, is referred to as "7/7," replicating the pattern established by the use of "9/11" to refer to the terrorist strikes of September 11, 2001, in the United States. Aside from the obvious lyricism, this framing of "9/11" and "7/7" does a lot of ideological work in constructing Americans and Britons as shared victims of religious violence.

22. Inderpal Grewal makes a similar point when she writes that "looking Middle Eastern" has become a neoracist idiom, a new racial formation that lumps together South Asians, Arabs, Iranians, and many others. Grewal also argues that this assemblage is not new but has colonial roots and is used to serve a new purpose (governmentality). See Inderpal Grewal, *Transnational America: Feminisms, Diaspora, Neoliberalisms* (Durham, N.C.: Duke University Press, 2005), especially 208–17.

23. By globalization, I refer to the current restructuring of the global economy, that is, to the political economy of the integration of nation-states into a global "free market"; the accelerating transnational flow of labor migration, infonilation and capital, and the central place of information technologies in facilitating this flow. These phenomena are characterized by the rapid growth of transactions and institutions outside the framework of

interstate relations, including but not limited to various transnational judicial forums, and the growth of such regional organizations as the European Union and the North America Free Trade Agreement (NAFTA). In this essay, *global* is not meant to mean *universal*; it is meant to convey a sense of not nation- or society-specific. There is much controversy over the meaning and implications of the term *globalization*. See Arjun Appadurai, "Disjuncture and Difference in the Global Cultural Economy," *Public Culture* 2 (1990): 1–24. Many observers have argued that the language of "globalization" disguises the continuity of colonial processes of modernization and uneven development. See, for instance, Susan S. Silbey's extended discussion of globalization, "Let Them Eat Cake: Globalization, Postmodern, Colonialism, and the Possibility of Justice," *Law and Society Review* 21 (1997): 207–36.

Others argue that globalization is an "ultraliberal ideology" that aims at limiting state sovereignty. Several book-length treatments of globalization have appeared of late. See, for instance, Akbar S. Ahmed and Hastings Donnan, eds., *Islam, Globalization and Postmodernity* (London: Routledge, 1994); Priyatosh Maitra, *The Globalization of Capitalism in Third World Countries* (Westport, Conn.: Praeger, 1996); Roger Burbach, Orlando Nunez, and Boris Kagarlitsky, *Globalization and Its Discontents: The Rise of Postmodern Socialisms* (London: Pluto Press, 1997); Saskia Sassen, *Globalization and Its Discontents: The New Mobility of Money and People* (New York: New Press, 1998); James H. Mittelman, *Whither Globalization? The Vortex of Knowledge and Ideology* (London: Routledge, 2004); Ankie M. M. Hoogvelt, *Globalization and the Postcolonial World: The New Political Economy of Development*, 2nd ed. (Baltimore, Md.: Johns Hopkins University Press, 2001); and A. S. Bhalla, ed., *Globalization, Growth and Marginalization* (New York: St. Martin's, 1998).

24. For a discussion of legal consciousness, see Laura Beth Nielsen, *License to Harass: Law, Hierarchy, and Offensive Public Speech* (Princeton, N.J.: Princeton University Press, 2004), and Sally Engle Merry, *Getting Justice and Getting Even: Legal Consciousness among Working-Class Americans* (Chicago: University of Chicago Press, 1990).

25. Patricia Ewick and Susan Silbey, *The Common Place of Law: Stories from Everyday Life* (Chicago: University of Chicago Press, 1998), 17.

26. For this characterization, see Proceedings of the 5th Annual Association of Muslim Social Scientists (U.K.) Conference, University of Westminster, London, February 2004, http://www.islamonline.net/english/Contemporary/2004/03/janfinal.pdf (accessed August 22, 2008).

27. For a discussion of discourses of rights as material resources, see Linda Fisher, "Guilt by Expressive Association: Political Profiling, Surveillance, and the Privacy of Groups," *Arizona Law Review* 46 (2004): 621–700, and Geoff Gilbert, "The Burgeoning Minority Rights Jurisprudence of the European Court on Human Rights," *Human Rights Quarterly* 24 (2002): 736–80.

28. See, for example, Hammed Shahidian, "Saving the Savior," *Sociological Inquiry* 69 (1999): 303–27.

29. Manazir Ahsan, former director of the Islamic Foundation in Leicester, U.K., refers to Muslims who have "embraced laws other than Islamic" (whether in Muslim countries or in the West) as casualties of extensive Westernization. See Manazir Ahsan, "The Muslim Family in Britain," in *God's Law versus State Law: The Construction of an Islamic Identity in Western Europe*, ed. Michael King (London: Grey Seal, 1995), 21–30.

30. Cited in *Fiqh Today: Muslims as Minorities* (proceedings booklet of the 5th Annual Association of Muslim Social Scientists [U.K.] Conference, University of Westminster, London, February 2004), http://www.islamonline.net/english/Contemporary/2004/03/janfinal.pdf (accessed August 22, 2008). Many other organizations promote fiqh as dynamic and inventive, a means to show how the laws of shari'a are to be applied in non-Muslim contexts (e.g., Fiqh Council of Europe, Fiqh Council of North America, the Muslim Council of Britain).

31. See J. M. Balkin, who generally argues that we are all "the bearers of this cultural information; indeed we are constituted by it. And its constitution of us is our constitution as historical beings. It is the source of our historical existence." J. M. Balkin, *Cultural Software: A Theory of Ideology* (New Haven: Yale University Press, 1998), ix. He further asserts that the differences in worldviews that people possess are the product of the evolution of cultural information.

32. See Ihsan Yilmaz, *Muslim Laws, Politics and Society in Modern Nation States: Dynamic Legal Pluralisms in England, Turkey and Pakistan* (Aldershot, U.K.: Ashgate Publishing, 2005); and Muhammad Khalid Masud, ed., *Travellers in Faith: Studies of the Tablighi Jama'at as a Transnational Islamic Movement for Faith Renewal* (Leiden: brill, 2000).

33. Muhammad Khalid Masud, Brinkley Messick, and David Powers, eds., *Islamic Legal Interpretation: Muftis and Their Fatwas* (Cambridge, Mass.: Harvard University Press, 1996).

34. Ibid., 4.

35. Notable works done on the interaction of Muslim law and customs with British law have been done by Prakash Shah, *Legal Pluralism in Conflict: Coping with Cultural Diversity in Law* (London: Glass House [Cavendish] Publishing, 2005); Prakash Shah, ed., *Law and Ethnic Plurality: Socio-Legal Perspectives* (Leiden: Martinus Nijhoff, 2007); Prakash Shah and Werner Menski, eds., *Migration, Diasporas, and Legal Systems in Europe* (New York: Routledge-Cavendish, 2006); and Yilmaz, *Muslim Laws*. In the United States, see Khaled Abou al-Fadl, *The Great Theft: Wresting Islam from the Extremists* (New York: HarperSanFrancisco, 2005), and Kathleen M. Moore, *Al-Mughtaribun: American Law and the Transformation of Muslim Life in the United States* (Albany, N.Y.: State University of New York Press, 1995).

36. Sally Engle Merry, "Law, Culture and Cultural Appropriation," *Yale Journal of Law and the Humanities* 10 (1998): 577.

37. Isin and Siemiatycki, *Making Space for Mosques*, 193.

38. Jane I. Smith, *Islam in America* (New York: Columbia University Press, 1999), xiii.

39. See Barry A. Kosmin, Egan Mayer, and Ariela Kaysar, American Religious Identification 2001 Study, "Statistical Abstract of the United States, 2004–2005," U.S. Department of Commerce, Bureau of the Census, http://www.census.gov/prod/2004pubs/04statab/pop.pdf (accessed June 30, 2008).

40. Tom Smith, "The Muslim Population of the United States: The Methodology of Estimates," *Public Opinion Quarterly* 66 (2002): 404–17.

41. For a discussion of the reasons for these discrepancies and the best available information for estimating the size of the American Muslim population, see Smith, "The Muslim Population of the United States."

42. Appadurai, *Fear of Small Numbers*, 42.

43. See King, ed., *God's Law*; Philip Lewis, *Islamic Britain: Religion, Politics and Identity among British Muslims* (London: I. B. Tauris, 1994); Jorgen S. Nielsen, *Muslims in Western Europe*, 2nd ed. (Edinburgh: Edinburgh University Press, 1995); Tariq Modood, *Multicultural Politics: Racism, Ethnicity, and Muslims in Britain* (Minneapolis: University of Minnesota Press, 2005); and Yilmaz, *Muslim Laws*.

44. See, for example, Steven Vertovec and Ceri Peach, eds., *Islam in Europe: The Politics of Religion and Community* (London: Macmillan, 1997); Philip Lewis, *Young, British and Muslim* (London: Continuum International, 2007).

45. Modood, *Multicultural Politics*, 20.

46. In "Racial Europeanization," Goldberg refers to this phenomenon as the "deafening silence" of Europe about its colonial legacy. Further, he points out that while the "relational frame" of race thinking in Europe largely has been binary (black/white) there has been, at least since the 15th century, a "third major artery," the trajectory of European Muslimania, positing the Muslim as a figure that is inherently dangerous and inferior.

47. See in particular Lewis, *Islamic Britain*, and Nielsen, *Muslims in Western Europe*, for details about the origins of the linguistically, culturally, and historically diverse Muslims in Britain. For the purposes of this study, it is significant to note that it has been difficult for Muslims to unite just the Deobandi and Barelwi traditions within the communities of South Asians, not to mention the numerous sectarian and linguistic differences with Muslims of other geographic origins (e.g., Turkish, Arab, Iranian, West African, Malaysian).

48. Meer and Noorani, "A Sociological Comparison," 202, and Lewis, *Islamic Britain*, 13–18.

49. Vertovec and Peach, *Islam in Europe*, 24.

50. Fred Halliday, *Arabs in Exile: Yemeni Migrants in Urban Britain* (London: I. B. Tauris, 1992).

51. Samia Bano, "In Pursuit of Religious and Legal Diversity: A Response to the Archbishop of Canterbury and the 'Shari'a Debate' in Britain," *Ecclesiastical Law Society* 10 (2008): 283–309.

52. *Nyazi v. Rymans, Ltd.*, Employment Appeal Tribunal (EAT/6/88), May 10, 1988 (Eng.). For discussion see Vertovec and Peach, *Islam in Europe*.

53. Modood, *Multicultural Politics*, 109.

54. *R (Shabina Begum) v. Headteacher and Governors of Denbigh High School*, [2004] EWHC 1389 (Admin), [2004] ELR 374; [2005] EWCA Civ 199, [2005] 1 WLR 3372; [2006] UKHL (Eng.) 15, [2007] 1 AC 100.

55. For an excellent analysis of similar instances of the neoliberal management of racialized minorities who are scripted to be premodern in Canada, see Razack, *Casting Out*.

56. Barbara Hewson, "Visible Justice," *New Law Journal*, 157 (2007): 717.

57. "Muslim Veil Allowed in Courts," *BBC News*, April 24, 2007, http://news.bbc.co.uk/2/hi/uk_news/england/staffordshire/6588157.stm (accessed November 26, 2008).

58. *Azmi v. Kirklees Metropolitan Borough Council*, Employment Appeal Tribunal [2007] ICR 1154, [2007] IRLR 484, [2007] ELR 339 (Eng.).

59. See Bano, "In Pursuit of Legal and Religious Diversity."

60. Razack, *Casting Out*, 18.

61. See Yvonne Yazbeck Haddad and Adair T. Lummis, *Islamic Values in the United States: A Comparative Study* (New York: Oxford University Press, 1987); Yvonne Yazbeck Haddad and Jane Idleman Smith, *Muslim Communities in North America* (Albany, N.Y.: State University of New York Press, 1994); Smith, *Islam in America*); Sulayman S. Nyang, *Islam in the United States of America* (Chicago: ABC International Group, 1999); and Philippa Strum and Danielle Tarantolo, eds., *Muslims in the United States* (Washington, D.C.: Woodrow Wilson International Center for Scholars, 2003).

62. Although ultimately Muslim suspects were not accused of these terrorist acts, initial media coverage of these events did assert or assume that the perpetrators were likely to be "Middle Eastern looking." The earlier bombing of the World Trade Center in New York (July 1993), for which a handful of Arab Muslim defendants were convicted, left an indelible imprint on the public mind and may have led people to assume all too quickly that those responsible for the 1995 bombing of the Murrah Federal Building would be Muslims. For an analysis of U.S. public opinion on Muslims and public safety in America, see Kathleen M. Moore and Stephen R. Pelletier, "Weaving New Fabric: The Challenge of Immigration for Muslim-Christian Relations," *Islam and Christian-Muslim Relations* 10 (1999): 177–96, and Kathleen M. Moore, "United We Stand: American Attitudes toward (Muslim) Immigration Post-9/11," *Muslim World* 92 (2002): 39–58.

63. See, for instance, Council on American-Islamic Relations, *A Rush to Judgment: A Special Report on Anti-Muslim Stereotyping, Harassment and Hate Crimes Following the Bombing of Oklahoma City's Murrah Federal Building* (Washington, D.C.: Council on American-Islamic Relations, April 19, 1995), and Council on American-Islamic Relations, *The Search for Convenient Scapegoats: The Crash of TWA Flight 800 in the Media* (Washington, D.C.: Council on American-Islamic Relations, 1996).

64. Kathleen M. Moore, "Anti-Muslim Discrimination and Violence," in *Social Issues in America: An Encyclopedia*, ed. James Ciment (New York: M. E. Sharpe, 2006), 142. For a discussion of Muslim-American civil rights history, see also Moore, *Al-Mughtaribun*.

65. Emphasis added. See Cindy Swirko, "Middle School Suspends Muslim Student," *Gainesville Sun*, October 1, 1998, A-8.

66. See the following for these rights claims: Kathleen M. Moore, *Al-Mughtaribun*; Kathleen M. Moore, "The Hijab and Religious Liberty: U.S. Anti-Discrimination Law and Muslim Women in the United States," in *Muslims on the Americanization Path?* ed. Yvonne Y. Haddad and John L. Esposito (New York: Oxford University Press, 1998), 129–58; Kathleen M. Moore, "Muslims in the United States: Pluralism under Exceptional Circumstances," *ANNALS of the American Academy of Political and Social Sciences* 612 (2007): 116–32; and Kathleen M. Moore, "Legal Pluralism in Britain: The Rights of Muslims after the Rushdie Affair," in *Europe's Other: European Union Law between Modernity and Postmodernity*, ed. Peter Fitzpatrick and James Henry Bergeron (London: Dartmouth/Ashgate, 1998).

67. For example, see Appadurai, "Disjuncture and Difference in the Global Cultural Economy," 1–24, and Paul Gilroy, *The Black Atlantic: Modernity and Double Consciousness* (Cambridge, Mass.: Harvard University Press, 1993).

68. Moore, "Muslims in the United States."

69. Connolly, *Pluralism*, 6.

CHAPTER 1

1. Arjun Appadurai, *Modernity at Large: Cultural Dimensions of Globalization* (Minneapolis: University of Minnesota Press, 1996); Brian Keith Axel, *The Nation's Tortured Body: Violence, Representation and the Formation of a Sikh "Diaspora"* (Durham, N.C.: Duke University Press, 2001); and Aihwa Ong, *The Buddha Is Hiding: Refugees, Citizenship, and the New America* (Berkeley: University of California Press, 2003).

2. See Thomas A. Tweed, *Our Lady of Exile: Diasporic Religion at a Cuban Catholic Shrine in Miami* (New York: Oxford University Press, 1997), and Garbi Schmidt, *Islam in Urban America: Sunni Muslims in Chicago* (Philadelphia: Temple University Press, 2004).

3. *Islamism* is a highly contentious term that has been used variously to refer to the belief that Islam is not only a religion but a political system, strongly suggesting that Muslims must return to their roots and unite politically; Salafi movements; Islamic revivalism led by such organizations as the Muslim Brotherhood; and the general malaise under which Islamists argue that they are losing their culture to western styles of clothing, music, values, lifestyles, language, and identity.

4. Anthropologist John Bowen asks a similar question about the French context. See *Why the French Don't Like Headscarves: Islam, the State and Public Space* (Princeton, N.J.: Princeton University Press, 2007).

5. See Nazli Kibria, "The 'New Islam' and Bangladeshi Youth in Britain and the US," *Ethnic and Racial Studies* 31 (2008): 243–66; Inderpal Grewal, *Transnational America: Feminisms, Diaspora, Neoliberalisms* (Durham, N.C.: Duke University Press, 2005); and Lori Peek, "Becoming Muslim: The Development of a Religious Identity," *Sociology of Religion* 66 (2005): 215–42.

6. Connolly, *Pluralism*, 41.

7. Peter Berger, *Facing Up to Modernity: Excursions in Society, Politics, and Religion* (New York: Basic Books, 1977).

8. Peter L. Berger and Thomas Luckmann, *The Social Construction of Reality: A Treatise on the Sociology of Knowledge* (New York: Doubleday Anchor Books, 1966).

9. Ibid.

10. Roger Waldinger and David Fitzgerald, "Transnationalism in Question," *American Journal of Sociology* 109 (2004): 1179.

11. Stuart Hall, ed., *Modernity: An Introduction to Modern Societies* (Cambridge, Mass.: Blackwell, 1996).

12. Cited in Jon Butler, "Theory and God in Gotham," *History and Theory* 45 (2006): 54.

13. Other former government officials have expressed their belief in the importance of religious perspectives in solving domestic problems and international conflicts. See Madeleine Albright with Bill Woodward, *The Mighty and the Almighty: Reflections on America, God and Global Affairs* (New York: HarperCollins, 2006), and Jimmy Carter, *Our Endangered Values: America's Moral Crisis* (New York: Simon and Schuster, 2005).

14. James Madison, "Federalist Paper No. 10," in *The Federalist Papers*, ed. Isaac Kramnick (London: Penguin, 1987 [1787]), 124.

15. Cited in Wade Clark Roof, "Pluralism as a Culture: Religion and Civility in Southern California," *Annals of the American Academy of Political and Social Sciences* 612 (2007): 87.

16. See Louise Cainkar, "The Impact of the September 11th Attacks and Their Aftermath on Arab and Muslim Communities in the United States," *Global Security and Cooperation Quarterly* 13 (2004): 1–21, http://www.ssrc.org/programs/gsc/publications/quarterly13/cainkar.pdf (accessed September 21, 2006), and Erik C. Nisbet and James Shanahan, *MSRG Special Report: Restrictions on Civil Liberties, Views of Islam, and Muslim Americans* (Ithaca, N.Y.: Cornell University, Media and Society Research Group, 2004), http://www.comm.cornell.edu/msrg/report1a.pdf (accessed March 12, 2006).

17. For a discussion of the role played by Arab American and Muslim political action groups in the 2000 general elections in the United States and of the political adjustment of Muslim Americans to the political realities of the election process, see Yvonne Yazbeck Haddad, "Muslims in U.S. Politics: Recognized and Integrated, or Seduced and Abandoned?" *SAIS Review* 21 (2001): 91–102, and Mohamed Nimer, "American Muslim Organizations: Before and After 9/11," in *Muslims in the United States: Identity, Influence, Innovation*, ed. Philippa Strum (Washington, D.C.: Woodrow Wilson Center, 2006), 5–18.

18. Former *New York Times* reporter Chris Hedges calls the investigations into possible ties to terrorism of Islamic organizations in Virginia "part of a ruthless campaign to strip Americans of fundamental rights because of their religious beliefs," or part of an effort to disenfranchise Muslim Americans. See Chris Hedges, "Democrats Won, but Arabs in America Still Suffer from Bush's War on Terror," *AlterNet*, December 6, 2006, http://www.alternet.org/rights/45100/ (accessed December 6, 2006).

19. Two of the Pew Forum's projects, the Pew Research Center for the People and the Press and the Pew Forum on Religion and Public Life, conducted an extensive nationwide survey of Muslim Americans and released a report entitled "Muslim Americans: Middle Class and Mostly Mainstream" (Pew Research Center, May 22, 2007), http://pewresearch.org/assets/pdf/muslim-americans.pdf (accessed June 10, 2007).

20. See http://www.columbia.edu/cu/ssw/news/aug06/kaushal911.html (accessed December 6, 2006).

21. Bill Maurer, *Pious Property: Islamic Mortgages in the United States* (New York: Russell Sage Foundation, 2006), 6.

22. Ibid., 5.

23. Ibid., 34.

24. Ibid., 12.

25. See http://www.universityislamicfinancial.com/file/Fatwa/SHAPE%20Profit%20Sharing%20Fatwa.pdf (accessed November 12, 2007).

26. Maurer, *Pious Property*, 13.

27. Grewal, *Transnational America*, 16.

28. Four organizations are representative of this period: the American-Arab University Graduates (AAUG), founded in 1967; the National Association of Arab Americans (NAAA), founded in 1972; the Arab-American Anti-Discrimination Committee (ADC), founded in 1980; and the Arab American Institute, founded in 1984. Each of these has been active in the political process, seeking to influence policy and educate Arab Americans on

the U.S. political system, and has been modeled after Jewish or pro-Israel organizations. See Haddad, "Muslims in U.S. Politics," 94.

29. Ibid., 92.

30. Producer of the controversial PBS documentary "Jihad in America," Emerson claims that Muslims use mosques for terrorist training. He was among the first pundits to attribute the Oklahoma City bombing to Muslim terrorists, and testified in 1995 in congressional hearings regarding the proposed counterterrorism legislation that "radical Islamic networks now constitute the primary domestic, as well as international, national security threat facing the FBI and other law enforcement agencies." See U.S. House of Representatives, Committee on International Relations, Subcommittee on Africa, *Testimony of Steve Emerson*, 104th Cong, 1st sess., April 6, 1995.

31. See http://www.danielpipes.org/ (accessed November 28, 2008).

32. Ihsan Bagby, Paul M. Pearl, and Bryan T. Froehle, *The Mosque in America: A National Portrait* (Washington, D.C.: Council on American-Islamic Relations, 2001), http://www/cairnet/org/mosquereport/Msjid_Study_Project_2000_Report.pdf (accessed September 21, 2006).

33. Pew Research Center, "Muslim Americans: Middle Class and Mostly Mainstream."

34. See An-Na'im, *Islam and the Secular State* and *Toward an Islamic Reformation: Civil Liberties, Human Rights, and International Law* (Syracuse, N.Y.: Syracuse University Press, 1990). See also Maher Hathout, *In Pursuit of Justice: The Jurisprudence of Human Rights in Islam* (Los Angeles: Muslim Public Affairs Council, 2006).

35. Sulayman S. Nyang, "Seeking the Religious Roots of Pluralism in the United States of America: An American Muslim Perspective," *Journal of Ecumenical Studies* 34 (1997): 402–18.

36. Ibid., 404–6.

37. Ibid., 406.

38. Ibid., 410.

39. Jane I. Smith, "Does Islam Encourage Pluralism? American Muslims Engage the Debate," in *Muslims in the United States: Identity, Influence, Innovation*, ed. Philippa Strum (Washington, D.C.: Woodrow Wilson Center), 170.

40. See Amina Wadud, "Alternative Qur'anic Interpretation and the Status of Muslim Women," in *Windows of Faith: Muslim Women Scholar-Activists in North America*, ed. Gisela Webb (Syracuse, N.Y.: Syracuse University Press, 2000), 3–21. For a fuller discussion of Muslim women's voices see Yvonne Y. Haddad, Jane I. Smith, and Kathleen M. Moore, *Muslim Women in America: The Challenge of Islamic Identity Today* (New York: Oxford University Press, 2006).

41. Eboo Patel, conversation with the author, February 27, 2006, Chicago, Illinois. See also Eboo Patel and Patrice Brodeur, eds., *Building the Interfaith Youth Movement: Beyond Dialogue to Action* (Lanham, Md.: Rowman and Littlefield, 2006), and Eboo Patel, *Acts of Faith: The Story of An American Muslim, the Struggle for a Soul of a Generation* (Boston: Beacon, 2007).

CHAPTER 2

1. Michael Fischer and Mehdi Abedi, *Debating Muslims: Cultural Dialogues in Postmodernity and Tradition* (Madison: University of Wisconsin Press, 1990).

2. Notions of authenticity and identity are not settled but are hotly contested. For instance, the search for authenticity has been criticized by authors in the literature on postcoloniality, mainly because of its association with ethnic nationalism. Debates about authenticity privilege certain perceptions of boundaries and insiderhood. R. Radhakrishnan writes that the typical question this boils down to is this: "Who has got it right, the insider or the outsider?" Attempts to establish authenticity in hybridized spaces, to produce the credentials to speak, on behalf of a certain historicized culture, have "verged dangerously toward blood-and-guts fundamentalism, mystical and primordial essentialism, or forms of divine separatism." R. Radhakrishnan, *Diasporic Mediations: Between Home and Location* (Minneapolis: University of Minnesota Press, 1996), 162–71.

3. Fischer and Abedi, *Debating Muslims*, 255.

4. See Ramadan, *Western Muslims*, and Yilmaz, *Muslim Laws*.

5. See Akhil Gupta, "The Song of the Nonaligned World: Transnational Identities and the Reinscription of Space in Late Capitalism," *Current Anthropology* 7 (1992): 63–77; Inderpal Grewal and Caren Kaplan, eds., *Scattered Hegemonies: Postmodernity and Transnational Feminist Practices* (Minneapolis: University of Minneapolis Press, 1994); Inderpal Grewal, "The Postcolonial, Ethnic Studies and the Diaspora: The Contexts of Immigrant/Migrant Cultural Studies in the US," *Socialist Review* 24 (1994): 45–74; Gayatri Gopinath, "Bombay, U.K., Yuba City: Bhangra Music and the Engineering of Diaspora," *Diaspora* 4 (1995): 303–21.

6. From the Deuteronomy to the Psalms, *diaspora* is used to refer to God's wrathful scattering of his people as threat or punishment. See further discussion of the Biblical roots of *diaspora* in Khachig Tololyan, "Rethinking Diaspora(s): Stateless Power in the Transnational Moment," *Diaspora* 5 (1996): 3–36.

7. Stefan Helmreich, "Kinship, Nation and Paul Gilroy's Concept of Diaspora," *Diaspora* 2 (1992): 245.

8. See, for instance, Werbner, who writes about the ways in which the Pakistani diasporic public sphere in Manchester has shifted from a male-dominated space to a gendered public sphere in which women participate and share in the construction of a "transnational consciousness, the very real and immediate awareness of the global predicaments of Muslims" through philanthropic donations to such places as Bosnia, Kosovo, Chechenia, and Kashmir. She writes of Al Masoom, a women's organization in Manchester that "has been in the forefront of this shift in diasporic consciousness, the reconstruction of identity and space which has followed the settlement in Britain." Pnina Werbner, "Public Spaces, Political Voices: Gender, Feminism and Aspects of British Muslim Participation in the Public Sphere," in *Political Participation and Identities of Muslims in Non-Muslim States*, ed. W. A. R. Shadid and P. S. Van Koningsveld (Kampen, the Netherlands: Kok Pharos Publishing House, 1996), 53–70. See also Grewal, *Transnational America*; and Chandra Talpade Mohanty, *Feminism without Borders: Decolonizing Theory, Practicing Solidarity* (Durham, N.C.: Duke University Press, 2003).

9. According to one scholar, "the Diaspora [has] had a very specific meaning: the exile of the Jews from their historic homeland and their dispersion throughout many lands, signifying as well the oppression and moral degradation implied by that dispersion." William Safran, "Diasporas in Modern Societies: Myths of Homeland and Return," *Diaspora* 1 (1991): 83–84.

10. Tololyan, "Rethinking Diaspora(s)," 13–14, and Steven Vertovec, "Three Meanings of 'Diaspora' Exemplified among South Asian Religions," *Diaspora* 6 (1997): 278–79.

11. Tololyan, "Rethinking Diaspora(s)," 13.

12. See, for example, Tweed, *Our Lady of Exile*; Homi K. Bhabha, "Anxiety in the Midst of Difference," *PoLAR* 21 (1998): 123–37; and Kibria, "The 'New Islam.'"

13. See Homi K. Bhabha, *The Location of Culture* (London: Routledge, 1994), and Dipesh Chackrabarty, "Reconstructing Liberalism? Notes toward a Conversation between Area Studies and Diasporic Studies," *Public Culture* 10 (1998): 457–81.

14. Vertovec, "Three Meanings of 'Diaspora,'" 279.

15. Werbner, "The Place Which Is Diaspora: Citizenship, Religion and Gender in the Making of Chaordic Transnationalism," *Journal of Ethnic and Migration Studies* 28 (2002): 119–33.

16. Elizabeth Mavroudi, "Diaspora as Process: (De)constructing Boundaries," *Geography Compass* 1 (2007): 468.

17. Gilroy, *The Black Atlantic*, 135.

18. Ibid.., 120.

19. See Lewis, *Islamic Britain*, 180–81. See also Gopinath, "Bombay," and Rahinder Dudrah, "Drum'n'dhol: British Bhangra Music and Diasporic South Asian Identity Formation," *European Journal of Cultural Studies* 5 (2002): 363–83.

20. Vertovec, "Three Meanings of 'Diaspora,'" 281.

21. Smadar Lavie and Ted Swedenburg, eds., *Displacement, Diaspora and Geographies of Identity* (Durham, N.C.: Duke University Press, 1996), 17.

22. Roger Ballard, "Introduction," in *Desh Pardesh: The South Asian Presence in Britain*, ed. Roger Ballard (London: Hurst & Co., 1994), 5.

23. See Stuart Hall, "When Was the 'Post-Colonial'? Thinking at the Limit," in *The Post-Colonial Question*, ed. Iain Chambers and Lidia Curti (New York: Routledge, 1996), 242–60.

24. Aihwa Ong, *Flexible Citizenship: The Cultural Logics of Transnationality* (Durham, N.C.: Duke University Press, 1999).

25. See, for example, Saskia Sassen, *Globalization and Its Discontents: The New Mobility of Money and People* (New York: New Press, 1999).

26. Tololyan, "Rethinking Diaspora(s)," 7.

27. Elizabeth McAlister, *Rara: Vodou, Power and Performance in Haiti and Its Diaspora* (Berkeley: University of California Press, 2002).

28. McAlister describes "religioscapes" as the subjective religious maps, with their attendant theologies that Appadurai identifies as another site in the flow and flux of diasporic activity.

29. McAlister, *Rara*. Stuart Hall, "Cultural Identity and Diaspora," in *Colonial Discourse and Post-Colonial Theory: A Reader*, ed. P. Williams and L. Chrisman (New York: Columbia University Press, 1994), 395.

30. Valerie Kerruish, *Jurisprudence as Ideology* (London: Routledge, 1991), 196.

31. Peter Fitzpatrick, "Introduction," in *Dangerous Supplements: Resistance and Renewal in Jurisprudence*, ed. Peter Fitzpatrick (Durham, N.C.: Duke University Press, 1991), 1.

32. See Fitzpatrick's discussion of the provenance of law in *The Mythology of Modern Law* (London: Routledge, 1992), 13–19.

33. See Jacques Derrida, *Of Grammatology*, trans. Gayatri Chakravorty Spivak (Baltimore: Johns Hopkins University Press, 1998; orig. pub. 1976), and Jacques Derrida, *Dissemination*, trans. Barbara Johnson (Chicago: University of Chicago Press, 1981).

34. Ofelia Schutte, "Cultural Alterity: Cross-Cultural Communication and Feminist Theory in North-South Contexts," *Hypatia* 13 (1998): 66.

35. For a similar point on the new plurality of regulatory practices in local contexts in Hawaii, see Christine Harrington and Barbara Yngvesson, "Diaspora Jurisprudence: The Politics of Native Entitlement" (unpublished paper distributed to "Tourist Productions," New York University Seminar, October 16, 2001; on file with author).

36. Peter Goodrich and Yifat Hachamovitch, "Time Out of Mind: An Introduction to the Semiotics of Common Law," in *Dangerous Supplements: Resistance and Renewal in Jurisprudence*, ed. Peter Fitzpatrick (Durham, N.C.: Duke University Press, 1991), 162.

37. Stuart Hall, "Cultural Identity," 402.

38. Ramadan, *Western Muslims*, 68.

39. The prohibition of *bida* in Islam is rooted in the belief that the Sunnah (the Way) will be corrupted by innovations and that the innovation would become the norm, moving worshipers away from "pure" religion. Innovations include changes in the manner of worship, or anything adding to the prescribed prayers found in revelation and the *ahadith* (sayings of the Prophet Muhammad).

40. For instance, see the various reports on anti-Islamic reactions in the European Union following the 9/11 terrorist attacks in the United States, issued by the EU Agency for Fundamental Rights (formerly the European Monitoring Centre on Racism and Xenophobia) (http://eumc.europa.eu/fra/index.php) and by the EU Monitoring and Advocacy Program (http://www.eumap.org/topics/minority/reports/eumuslims) (accessed March 2, 2007).

41. Aziz al-Azmeh, "Afterword," in *Islam in Europe: Diversity, Identity, and Influence*, ed. Aziz al-Azmeh and Effie Fokas (Cambridge, U.K.: Cambridge University Press, 2007), 209.

42. Appadurai, *Fear of Small Numbers*, 5.

43. Inclusion of the religion question in the National Census has permitted researchers to collect large-scale data on Muslims and other religious groups in the United Kingdom. See, for instance, Serena Hussain, *Muslims on the Map: A National Survey of Social Trends in Britain* (London: I. B. Tauris, 2008).

44. See "'Remove Full Veils' Urges Straw," *BBC News*, October 6, 2006, http://news.bbc.co.uk/2/hi/uk_news/politics/5411954.stm (accessed September 2, 2008).

45. The term *majoritarian* refers to countries in which the majority of the population is Muslim. This does not necessarily mean that the government is Islamic.

46. See M. Ali Kettani, *Muslim Minorities in the World Today* (London: Mansell Publishing, 1986); Omar Khalidi, "Muslim Minorities: Theory and Experience of Muslim Interaction in Non-Muslim Societies," *Journal Institute of Muslim Minority Affairs* 10 (1989): 425–37; Ramadan, *Western Muslims*; and Yilmaz, *Muslim Laws*.

47. Yvonne Y. Haddad, "The Challenge of Muslim Minorityness: The American Experience," in *The Integration of Islam and Hinduism in Western Europe*, ed. W. A. R. Shadid and P. S. van Koningsveld (Kampen, the Netherlands: Kok Publishing, 1991), 134.

48. There are four schools that are considered the "major" schools of jurisprudence in Sunni Islamic thought—Hanbali, Hanafi, Shafii, and Maliki—and four in Shi'a Islamic thought—Ja'afari, Zaydi, Ibadi, and Zahiri.

49. Khaled Abou al-Fadl, "Islamic Law and Muslim Minorities: The Juristic Discourse on Muslim Minorities from the Second/Eighth to the Eleventh/Seventeenth Centuries," *Islamic Law and Society* 1 (1994): 154.

50. Ibid., 158–69.

51. Haddad, "The Challenge," 139. This return is known as the Medinan model, referring to the instance in the life of the Prophet Muhammad when the community of believers emigrated from Mecca to Medina long enough to regroup and empower themselves for their return to Mecca.

52. The Muslim College became a postgraduate institution for training imams in the West. In July 2005, after the London bombings, Dr. Badawi was denied entry into the United States, even though he had been issued a visa when he was scheduled to speak at a conference in the United States.

53. Tariq Ramadan, *To Be a European Muslim: A Study of Islamic Sources in the European Context* (Leicester, U.K.: Islamic Foundation, 1999). Ramadan believes that there is a European Islam. Regularly called Islam's "Martin Luther," because his views challenge mainstream Islamic beliefs, Ramadan currently teaches at St. Anthony's College at the University of Oxford. In 2004 Ramadan accepted a position at Notre Dame University in Indiana, Unites States, but was forced to resign before taking up the position when the U.S. State Department revoked his visa, based on Ramadan's prior contributions to organizations with connections to Hamas.

54. Ramadan, *Western Muslims*, 70.

55. See conference booklet at http://www.islamonline.net/English/EuropeanMuslims/Figh/2005/12/07.shtml (accessed July 25, 2008).

56. Dr. Tamimi earned a Ph.D. in political theory at Westminster University in 1998. Since 1999 he has headed the Institute of Islamic Political Thought in London.

57. The text of the speech (in Arabic) is on file with the author.

58. Azzam al-Tamimi, "Nahwa Muntalaqat Insanivva Ii al-Ta'amull rna' al-Mujtama' al Gharbi," *Al-Mujtama'* 26, no. 1182 (January 2–8, 1996), 44ff. (Text of speech on file with the author.) My translation.

59. Arjun Appadurai, "Patriotism and Its Futures," *Public Culture* 5 (1993): 417.

60. Vertovec and Peach, *Islam and Europe*, 40.

61. Yilmaz, *Muslim Laws*.

62. See the Group's announcement at http://womensphere.wordpress.com/2008/02/18/the-national-muslim-womens-advisory-group-nmwag-formally-launched-by-the-prime-minister/ (accessed December 1, 2008).

63. Azzam al-Tamimi, interview with the author, London, October 31, 1998. During the interview, Dr. Tamimi stated that the most important task facing Muslims in Britain today is the "normalization" of Muslim life in Britain. He clarified his statement adding that this normalization needed to be done within Muslim communities rather than vis-à-vis the dominant institutions of British society. This work entails providing norms and justifications within an Islamic idiom.

64. Azzam al-Tamimi, interview by Grace Halsell, *Washington Report on Middle East Affairs*, December 1998, 23–24.

65. Sally Engle Merry persuasively argues a similar point vis-à-vis our understanding of culture. She writes, "Cultural forms and practices are locally expressed but connected to global systems of economic exchange, power relations, and systems of meaning. They are constructed and transformed over historical time through the activities of individuals as well as through larger social processes. . . . Culture is continuously produced and reproduced at particular historical times in specific places situated within global movements of people and capital." Sally Engle Merry, "Law, Culture and Cultural Appropriation," 577–78. The same can be said of religion.

66. Derrida, *Dissemination*, 314–15.

67. Ibid., 316.

68. Rodolphe Gasche, *The Tain of the Mirror: Derrida and the Philosophy of Reflection* (Cambridge, Mass.: Harvard University Press, 1986), 238.

69. Azzam al-Tamimi, "Nahwa Muntalaqat Insanivva," 44.

70. Chackrabarty, "Reconstructing Liberalism?" 457–81.

CHAPTER 3

1. The congressional oath of office reads, "I, Loyal Citizen of the Republic, do solemnly swear (or affirm) that I will support and defend the Constitution of the United States against all enemies, *foreign and domestic*; that I will bear true faith and allegiance to the same; that I take this obligation freely, without any mental reservation or purpose of evasion; and that I will well and faithfully discharge the duties of the office on which I am about to enter. So help me God" (emphasis added).

2. Clarence Page, "No 'American' Holy Book," *Chicago Tribune*, December 11, 2006, Commentary Section, 21.

3. The U.S. Constitution prohibits religious tests of those who are elected to public office. Thus, official ceremonies of oath of office are devoid of religious content (although the inauguration ceremony features the president placing his hand on the Bible).

4. See Dennis Prager, "America, Not Keith Ellison, Decides What Book a Congressman Takes His Oath On," *Townhall*, November 28, 2006, http://www.townhall.com/columnists/DennisPrager/2006/11/28/america,_not_keith_ellison,_decides_what_book_a_congressman_takes_his_oath_on (accessed July 13, 2007).

5. Ibid. Prager argues that Ellison should "not be allowed" to take the oath on the Qur'an even in a photo-op. Prager drew attention to Ellison's decision when he published his column on the Web site townhall.com, criticizing Congressman-elect Ellison for his decision to forego the use of the Bible in favor of the Qur'an in his voluntary photo-op oath. In an interview with the National Public Radio, Prager said that "[the Bible] is a symbol since George Washington did it. It is something that we do, that Americans do to affirm their American-ness" ("Religious Texts and the Swearing-in Tradition," *Day to Day*, NPR, December 5, 2006, http://web.lexis-nexis.com.proxy.library.ucsb.edu:2048/universe/document?_m=37c3f3dada4eda9ccc9412d35d55d1a3&_docnum=1&wchp=dGLbVzW-zSkVb&_md5=5419bc00cad2166f4f9bc6d0d31cb35e [accessed July 16, 2007]).

6. See Erika Howsare, "Goode Makes Complete Ass of Self: Anti-Muslim Letter Goes Out to Hundreds—Not All Are Amused," *C-Ville—Charlottesville's News and Arts Weekly*, no. 18.51 (December 19–25, 2006), http://www.c-ville.com/index.php?cat=141404064431134&ShowArticle_ID=11041812060944420 (accessed July 13, 2007). Goode's December 7 letter to constituents was first posted in this *C-Ville* newsweekly Web site on December 19 and was later reprinted in "A Muslim Goes to Congress—Members Disagree about Threat to Traditional U.S. Values and Beliefs," *Charlotte Observer*, December 28, 2006, 14A. The story and content of the letter were widely circulated by the Associated Press and were picked up by numerous Web sites and news and policy organizations.

7. "Jefferson's Koran," *Chicago Tribune*, January 4, 2007, Editorial Section, 18. Keith Ellison converted to Islam in college.

8. Goode cited at "Group Wants Congressman Virgil Goode to Explain Comments about Muslims," *Fox News*, February 19, 2007, http://www.foxnews.com/story/0,2933,252843,00.html (accessed July 13, 2007).

9. Bratton used this logic to justify the intensive militarization of metropolitan policing, with the training by United States military of about 70 LAPD officers in Iraq. This initiative was meant to help the LAPD to prepare for the "eventuality" of suicide bombers and IEDs in Los Angeles. Cited in Sohail Daulatzai, "Protect Ya Neck: Muslims and the Carceral Imagination in the Age of Guantanamo," *Souls* 9 (2007): 143, 147. See also Pamela Hess, "Analysis: Police Take Military Counsel," http://lapd.com/article.apsx?a=4150 (accessed May 2, 2008).

10. For an incisive analysis of this trend, see Grewal, *Transnational America*. For discussion of historical deference to prison administrators in the maintenance of racialized security in prisons, specifically as it has affected Muslims in prison, see Moore, *Al-Mughtaribun*. Racialized security is now being revived.

11. For instance, see "Fear and Bigotry in Congress," *New York Times*, December 23, 2006, Editorial Desk, 18; "Our Nation's Values—Threat Comes from Virginia Congressman, Not Muslims," *Charlotte Observer*, December 28, 2006, 14A; "Taking an Oath on Qur'an Should Be OK; Keith Ellison, the first Muslim elected to Congress, plans to place his hand on Islam's holy book when he takes the oath of office," *Denver Post*, December 31, 2006, Editorial Section, E-4.

12. See, for instance, Dan Miller, "Loyalty Should Be to the Constitution: Spiritual Reflections," *Savage Pacer*, February 3, 2007, 20.

13. See note 1, this chapter, for the full congressional oath of office.

14. Much of the debate on blogs in the weeks following Ellison's announcement and Dennis Prager's editorial reflects this idea. For instance, see postings on *townhall.com*, beginning November 28, 2006, in response to Prager's "America, Not Keith Ellison, Decides What Book a Congressman Takes His Oath On." See also Robert Spencer, *The Politically Incorrect Guide to Islam (and the Crusades)* (Washington, D.C.: Regnery Publishing, 2005); and Robert Spencer, *Islam Unveiled: Disturbing Questions about the World's Fastest-Growing Faith* (San Francisco: Encounter Books, 2002).

15. See Razack, *Casting Out*.

16. See Alice Crary, "The Happy Truth: J. L. Austin's How to Do Things with Words," *Inquiry* 45 (2002): 59–80, and Peter Brooks, *Troubling Confessions: Speaking Guilt in Law and Literature* (Chicago: University of Chicago, 2000), 30.

17. In many courtrooms, witnesses may choose to give an affirmation instead of an oath, promising to tell the truth without reference to a deity. Similarly, elected officials may choose to use a law book (as did John Adams in his inaugural), or nothing at all.

18. For a discussion of iconic texts see James W. Watts, "Ten Commandments Monuments and the Rivalry of Iconic Texts," *Journal of Religion and Society* 6 (2004), 1–12. See also Noah Feldman, *Divided by God: America's Church-State Problem—and What We Should Do About It* (New York: Farrar, Straus and Giroux, 2005).

19. Brooks, *Troubling Confessions*, 102.

20. Cited in ibid., 99.

21. Alan Cooperman, "Muslim Candidate Plays Defense: Lead Shrinks as Minnesota Democrat Repudiates Association with Farrakhan," *Washington Post*, September 11, 2006, A-03.

22. Rob Hotakainen and Brady Averill, "Newcomers Prepare for the 110th Congress," *Star Tribune*, November 13, 2006, 8A.

23. Keith Ellison, "What Should Be Done with Iran? First Muslim Congressman Speaks Out," interview by Glenn Beck, CNN *Headline News*, November 14, 2006, 19:00:00 ET. Transcript available at http://transcripts.cnn.com/TRANSCRIPTS/0611/14/gb.01.html (accessed June 10, 2008).

24. David Kronke, "King Holds Court at TV Critics Convention," *Daily News of Los Angeles*, January 10, 2007.

25. Howsare, "Goode Makes Complete Ass of Self."

26. Rachel L. Swarnes, "Congressman Criticizes Election of Muslim," *New York Times*, December 21, 2006, 31; Zachary A. Goldfarb, "Va. Lawmaker's Remarks on Muslims Criticized," *Washington Post*, December 21, 2006, A-11.

27. Cited in "Thomas Jefferson's Qur'an," *MuslimBridges.org*, http://www.muslimbridges.org/content/view/453/ (accessed October 12, 2008).

28. Rochelle Riley, "Be America and End Religious Hypocrisy," *Detroit Free Press*, January 5, 2007, 9A.

29. "Qur'an Once Owned by Jefferson Located with the Help of LOC," *All Things Considered*, NPR, January 3, 2007, http://web.lexis-nexis.com.proxy.library.ucsb.edu:2048/universe/document?_m=5d33280445725a0ead519f3def299c9f&_docnum=1&wchp=dGLbVzW-zSkVb&_md5=e6e133f4ddace1eac49983966d69d9cb (accessed July 16, 2007).

30. Thomas Jefferson, cited in Denise A. Spellberg, "Could a Muslim Be President? An Eighteenth Century Constitutional Debate," *Eighteenth Century Studies* 39, no. 4 (2006): 490.

31. Thomas Kidd, "Is It Worse to Follow Mahomet Than the Devil? Early American Uses of Islam," *American Society of Church History* 72 (2003): 766.

32. This book had been translated into English in 1792 and had already been through two editions in the United States by 1792. Robert J. Allison, "The United States and the Specter of Islam: Early Nineteenth Century," http://research.yale.edu/ycias/database/files/MESV3-1.pdf (accessed July 12, 2007).

33. Kidd, "Is It Worse to Follow Mahomet?" 771.

34. Ibid., 767.

35. Ibid., 777.

36. Cited in Spellberg, "Could a Muslim Be President?" 485.

37. Allison, "The United States and the Specter of Islam," 486.

38. Spellberg, "Could a Muslim Be President?" 487.

39. Ibid.

40. Cited in Spellberg, "Could a Muslim Be President?" 493.

41. Ibid., 494.

42. Ibid.

43. Ibid.

44. Nadine Farid, "The Faculty Edition: Commemorating Forty Years of Legal Scholarship: Oath and Affirmation in the Court: Thoughts on the Power of a Sworn Promise," *New England Law Review* 40 (2006): 556.

45. Eric Collins, "Judge Throws Out Quran Lawsuit," *Greensboro News and Record*, December 9, 2005, A1.

46. Cited in Farid, "The Faculty Edition," 558.

47. *American Civil Liberties Union of North Carolina, Inc., and Syidah Mateen, Declaratory Judgment vs. State of North Carolina* (181 N.C. App. 430; 639 S.E.2d 136; 2007 N.C. App. LEXIS 153; September 18, 2006, Heard in the Court of Appeals, January 16, 2007, filed).

48. Citations in court opinion accessible at http://www.aclu.org/images/asset_upload_file287_29873.pdf.

49. American Family News Network, http://www.onenewsnow.com/2007/06/no_carolina_courtroom_oaths_ex.php (accessed July 12, 2007).

50. See Steve Noble, Chairman, Called2Action, cited in CNN Newsroom programs such as *Missions in Iraq*; *War and Politics*; *The Qur'an in Court*; *Driving v. Flying*, May 25, 2007, 10:00 ET, http://transcripts.cnn.com/TRANSCRIPTS/0705/25/cnr.01.html (accessed July 12, 2007).

51. See, for instance, Bill O'Reilly's interview with Evangelist Franklin Graham, *Fox News Network*, Fox News Channel, July 28, 2005. During the interview, O'Reilly states that our "primary enemy is centered around Allah." See also O'Reilly's interview with Franklin Graham in *The O'Reilly Factor*, http://www.lexisnexis.com.proxy.library.ucsb.edu:2048/us/lnacademic/results/docview/docview.do?docLinkInd=true&risb=21_T3958749023&format=GNBFI&sort=RELEVANCE&startDocNo=1&resultsUrlKey=29_T3958747693&cisb=22_T3958749025&treeMax=true&treeWidth=0&csi=174179&docNo=3 (accessed July 12, 2007).

52. David Garland, *The Culture of Control: Crime and Social Control in a Contemporary Society* (Chicago: University of Chicago Press, 2001).

53. Jonathan Simon, Governing through Crime: How the War on Crime Transformed American Democracy and Created a Culture of Fear (New York: Oxford University Press, 2007).

54. Aside from this naming skirmish, another barrier was raised after the election against Obama's qualifications for the office of president. On December 8, 2008, the U.S. Supreme Court rejected an emergency appeal filed by a New Jersey voter, who said that the

president-elect was ineligible for office because he was not a "natural-born" citizen, since Obama's father, a Kenyan, was at the time of Obama's birth a British subject. Others tried to prove that Obama's Hawaiian birth certificate was a forgery. These efforts to "cast out" Obama as an American citizen illustrate the racial ordering of citizenship. See http://www.scotusblog.com/wp/us-views-sought-on-misspent-federal-funds/ (accessed December 8, 2008).

55. See, for example, the *Los Angeles Times* editorial on Obama's inaugural oath, published on November 30, 2008, http://www.latimes.com/news/opinion/editorials/la-ed-oath30–2008nov30,0,7859834.story (accessed December 1, 2008).

56. American Civil Liberties Union of North Carolina, Inc., and Syidah Mateen, Declaratory Judgment vs. State of North Carolina (181 N.C. App. 430; 639 S.E.2d 136; 2007 N.C. App. LEXIS 153; September 18, 2006, Heard in the Court of Appeals, January 16, 2007, filed).

CHAPTER 4

1. Modood, *Multicultural Politics*, 145.

2. Ibid., 134.

3. Text of the speech is reproduced in *Ecclesiastical Law Society* 10 (2008): 262–75.

4. Siddiqi is a commercial law barrister and head of the Hijaz College Islamic University in Warwickshire (the Midlands). The Web site for the Muslim Arbitration Tribunal is http://www.matribunal.com/ (accessed December 1, 2008).

5. Abul Taher, "Revealed: UK's First Official Sharia Courts," *Sunday Times* [London], September 14, 2008, 2, http://www.timesonline.co.uk/tol/news/uk/crime/article4749183.ece (accessed September 18, 2008). See also "First UK Sharia Court Up and Running in Warwickshire," *Coventry Telegraph*, September 9, 2008, http://www.coventrytelegraph.net/news/north-warwickshire-news/2008/09/09/first-uk-sharia-court-up-and-running-in-warwickshire-92746–21708478/ (accessed December 7, 2008).

6. See http://www.dailymail.co.uk/news/article-1080509/Islamic-courts-cleared-deal-family-divorce-disputes-Government-endorses-sharia.html (accessed December 9, 2008).

7. Werner Menski, "Rethinking Legal Theory in the Light of South-North Migration," in *Migration, Diasporas and Legal Systems in Europe*, ed. Shah and Menski, 18.

8. David Pearl and Werner Menski, *Muslim Family Law*, 3rd ed. (London: Sweet and Maxwell, 1998), 51–83.

9. The mufti of Egypt and president of al-Azhar University issued a fatwa on February 25, 1982, to this effect, and the Islamic World League in Jeddah, Saudi Arabia issued a separate fatwa in 1989.

10. For a discussion of the formulation of *angrezi shari'a* with regard to marriage and divorce, see Ihsan Yilmaz, *Muslim Laws*, 67–81.

11. Menski, "Rethinking Legal Theory," 21.

12. See report at http://www.eukn.org/eukn/themes/Urban_Policy/Security_and_crime_prevention/Anti_crime_policy/Extremism/living-apart-together_1002.html (accessed December 9, 2008).

13. See Yahya Birt, "The Trouble with Shari'a," *Emel Magazine* 42 (2008), where he points to particular concerns about Muslim women's rights voiced by such scholars as

Maleiha Malik, a leading specialist on discrimination law at King's College, University of London, who has written extensively on issues related to minority protection. Malik argues that the state should apply all human rights and antidiscrimination laws rigorously to avoid the structural discrimination within shari'a councils as alternative dispute resolution models. See, for instance, Maleiha Malik, "Speech Control," *Index on Censorship* 36 (2007): 18–21. Further objections are raised by various Muslim umbrella organizations. For instance, the Muslim Council of Britain supports "engagement not endorsement," working for the "common good" and not just the good of the Muslim community, and working toward equitable treatment under existing liberal legal mechanisms.

14. See British Muslims for Secular Democracy Web site at http://www.bmsd.org.uk/articles.asp?id=18 (accessed December 1, 2008).

15. Ali Mazrui, "*Shariacracy* and Federal Models in the Era of Globalization: Nigeria in Comparative Perspective," in *Democratic Institution Performance: Research and Policy Perspectives*, ed. Edward R. McMahon and Thomas Sinclair (Westport, Conn.: Greenwood Publishing, 2002), 63–76.

16. Johannes Harnischfeger, *Democratization and Islamic Law: The Shari'a Conflict in Nigeria* (Frankfurt, Germany: Campus Verlag, 2008), 15. Taking effect in 2000, the Zamfara Law inaugurated the extension of shari'a from personal law to criminal law, and following the example of Zamfara, 11 other Muslim-dominated states followed suit. In Kaduna, the attempt to pass a shari'a bill in the legislature provoked demonstrations, in particular a large demonstration on February 21, 2000, which led to confrontation between Christians and Muslims, massive killings, and the destruction of religious buildings.

17. Mazrui, "*Shariacracy*," 68.

18. See Amir Ali, "Evolution of Public Sphere in India," *Economic and Political Weekly* 36 (2001): 2419–25.

19. Tahir Abbas, "British Muslim Minorities Today: Challenges and Opportunities to Europeanism, Multiculturalism, and Islamism," *Sociology Compass* 1 (2007): 724.

20. Jonathan Birt, "Good Imam, Bad Imam: Civic Religion and National Integration in Britain Post-9/11," *Muslim World* 96 (2006): 692.

21. Ibid., 689.

22. David Rose, "Muslim fanatic prisoners to be 'deprogrammed' using controversial techniques to 'cure' them of beliefs," *Daily Mail*, October 18, 2008, http://www.dailymail.co.uk/news/article-1077861/Muslim-fanatic-prisoners-programmed-using-controversial-techniques-cure-beliefs.html (accessed November 29, 2008).

23. Philip Lewis, *Islamic Britain*, 56.

24. Mohamed Keshavjee, "Alternative Dispute Resolution in a Diasporic Muslim Community in Britain," in Shah, *Law and Ethnic Plurality*, 148–49.

25. Ibid. See also Ballard, "Introduction," in *Desh Pardesh*, ed. Ballard, 1–34.

26. Katy Gardner and Abus Shukur, "I'm Bengali, I'm Asian, and I'm Living Here: The Changing Identity of British Bengalis," in *Desh Pardesh*, ed. Ballard, 150–51.

27. See Philip Lewis, *Islamic Britain*; Ihsan Yilmaz, *Muslim Laws*; and Samia Bano, "Islamic Family Arbitration, Justice, and Human Rights in Britain," *Law, Social Justice, and Global Development Journal* 1 (2007), http://www.go.warwick.ac.uk/elj/lgd/2007_1/bano (accessed December 8, 2008).

28. Bano, "In Pursuit of Religious and Legal Diversity," 295.

29. Cited in ibid., 293.

30. Bano, "Islamic Family Arbitration," 12.

31. Ibid.

32. This matter was mentioned by Dr. Zaki Badawi, the former chief imam of the London Central Mosque, Regents Park, and chair of the Imams and Mosques Council in Britain, in an interview with the author, November 17, 1997.

33. A panel of religious scholars convened at the Central Mosque in Birmingham in 1982, deciding to establish the Islamic Shari'a Council as a "quasi court" to decide disputes according to Islamic law. Council members represent all major schools of Islamic thought. Web site accessible at http://www.islamic-sharia.org/ (accessed December 7, 2008).

34. Bano, "Islamic Family Arbitration," 14; for discussion of *talaq* divorce and British law, see also Yilmaz, *Muslim Laws*, 77–80.

35. Cited in Bano, "In Pursuit of Religious and Legal Diversity," 297.

36. Ibid., 286, 288.

37. I discuss the *mahr* in American case law in the next chapter.

38. Sonia Nurin Shah-Kazemi, *Untying the Knot: Muslim Women, Divorce and Shariah* (London: Nuffield Foundation, 2001), 48.

39. See, for instance, Mohamed Keshavjee, "Alternative Dispute Resolution in a Diasporic Muslim Community in Britain," in Shah, *Law and Ethnic Plurality*, 145–75. Keshavjee finds that women do not seek external interventions in the personal problems, and they do not want their fathers and husbands to discover that they have talked of trouble to a person outside of the immediate family.

40. Keshavjee, "Alternative Dispute Resolution," 164.

41. Bano, "In Pursuit of Religious and Legal Diversity," 300.

42. Susan F. Hirsch, *Pronouncing and Persevering: Gender and the Discourses of Disputing in an African Islamic Court* (Chicago: University of Chicago Press, 1998), 59. Hirsch studies another Muslim minority community, the Swahili Muslims of Mombasa, coastal Kenya, where, she argues, some Swahili people stand behind the Islamic courts as a symbol of an embattled Muslim autonomy in an officially secular Kenyan state.

43. Bano, "Islamic Family Arbitration," 20.

44. Bano, "In Pursuit of Religious and Legal Diversity," 302.

45. Ibid.

46. Ibid., 303.

47. Ibid., 304.

48. Ibid.

49. Cited in Razack, *Casting Out*, 144.

50. Bano, "Islamic Family Arbitration," 15.

51. See, for instance, Hussain, *Muslims on the Map*.

52. See Hirsch, *Pronouncing and Persevering*, 83; and, for example, Erin P. Moore, *Gender, Law and Resistance in India* (Tucson: University of Arizona Press, 1998); Amira el-Azhary Sonbol, ed., *Women, the Family and Divorce Laws in Islamic History* (Syracuse, N.Y.: Syracuse University Press, 1996); and Baudouin Dupret, Barbara

Drieskens, and Annelies Moors, eds., *Narratives of Truth in Islamic Law* (London: I. B. Tauris, 2008).

53. Hirsch, *Pronouncing and Persevering*, 115.

CHAPTER 5

1. See http://usinfo.state.gov/products/pubs/muslimlife (posted October 2002; accessed September 27, 2005).

2. For a related story, see Jane Perlez, "Muslim-as-Apple-Pie Videos Are Greeted with Skepticism," *New York Times*, October 30, 2002, Foreign Desk Section, 1.

3. Edward Said writes about how a particular kind of discourse, which differentiates and devalues the Muslim Other in relation to Europeans, is produced in western centers of intellectual production, including universities, the media, and social, religious, and legal institutions. See *Orientalism* (New York: Vintage Books, 1979).

4. Moore, *Al-Mughtaribun*, 97.

5. Ann Elizabeth Mayer, "Universal versus Islamic Human Rights: A Clash of Cultures or a Clash with a Construct?" *Michigan Journal of International Law* 15 (1994): 307–98

6. See, for example, Sally Engle Merry and Neal Milner, eds., *The Possibility of Popular Justice: A Case Study of Community Mediation in the United States* (Ann Arbor: University of Michigan, 1993).

7. *Jabri v. Quaddura*, 108 S.W. 3d. 404 (Tex. App. 2003), discussed below.

8. John P. Bartkowski and Jen'nan Ghazal Read, "Veiled Submission: Gender, Power and Identity among Evangelical and Muslim Women in the United States," *Qualitative Sociology* 26, no. 1 (Spring 2003): 71–92.

9. The report is available at http://www.fbi.gov/ucr/01hate.pdf.

10. For information about the EEOC guidelines, visit http://www.eeoc.gov/facts/backlash-employee.html to read "Questions and Answers about the Workplace Rights of Muslims, Arabs, South Asians, and Sikhs under the Equal Employment Opportunity Laws"; see also report by Human Rights Watch, "'We are Not the Enemy': Hate Crimes against Arabs, Muslims, and Those Perceived to Be Arab or Muslim after September 11," *Human Rights Watch Monitor* 14 (2002), http://www.hrw.org/en/reports/2002/11/14/we-are-not-enemy (accessed September 10, 2009).

11. See Bartkowski and Read, "Veiled Submission."

12. The full covering, including the face veil.

13. *Sultaana Lakiana Myke Freeman, Plaintiff, v. State of Florida, Department of Highway Safety and Motor Vehicles, Defendant*, No. 2002-CA-2828, June 6, 2003, Circuit Court of the 9th Judicial Circuit in and for Orange County, Fl (Judge Thorpe) at *17.

14. *Sultaana Lakiana Myke Freeman, Appellant, v. Department of Highway Safety and Motor Vehicles, Appellee*, No. 5D03-2296, 2005 Fla. Dist. Ct. App. LEXIS 13904, at *22 (Court of Appeal of Florida, Fifth District, September 2, 2005).

15. *Maysa Mounla-Sakkal, M.D. v. Western Reserve Care System, et al.*, NO. 4: 98CV2251 2000 U.S District Court LEXIS22203 (Northern District of Ohio, May 18, 2000) (subsequent history, aff'd, *Maysa Mounla-Sakkal, M.D., Plaintiff-Appellant, v. Youngstown*

Hospital Association, Inc., et al., Defendants-Appellees, No. 00-3805, 2002 U.S. App. LEXIS 2080 (6th Cir. Feb. 4, 2002).

16. The White House, Office of the Press Secretary, "Guidelines on Religious Exercise and Religious Expression in the Federal Workplace," August 14, 1997, Washington, D.C., http://clinton2.nara.gov/WH/New/html/199708193275.html (accessed November 23, 2006).

17. *Venters v. City of Delphi*, No. 96-1355, 1997, U.S. App LEXIS 22360 (7th Cir., Aug 19, 1997).

18. *Sheveka Gibson v. The Finish Line, Inc., of Delaware*, 261 F.Supp.2d 785 (W.D.Ky 2003).

19. *Firoozeh H. Butler, Plaintiff-Appellant, v. MBNA Technology, INC., Defendant-Appellee*, No. 04-10058, 2004, U.S. App LEXIS 20132 (5th Cir., Sept. 24, 2004) at *9.

20. *Eyvine Hearn, et al., United States of America, Plaintiffs, v. Muskogee Public School District 020, et al., Defendants*, C.A. No. CIV 03-598-S, 2004, U.S. District Court (Eastern District Oklahoma), and U.S. Senate, Committee on the Judiciary, the Subcommittee on the Constitution, Civil Rights, and Property Rights, *Testimony of Nashala Hearn*, 108th Cong., 2nd sess., June 8, 2004.

21. The 1895 Pennsylvania statute states that "no teacher in any public school shall wear in said school or while engaged in the performance of his duty as such teacher any dress, mark, emblem or insignia indicating the fact that such teacher is a member or adherent of any religious order, sect or denomination" (Pennsylvania Religious Garb Statute, 24 Pa. Cons. Stat. Ann. 11–1112 (b)(2009).

22. The case is cited as *United States v. Bd. of Educ.*, 911 F.2d 882, 889, 894 (3d Cir. 1990) (holding that the Pennsylvania religious garb statute does not violate the religious discrimination provisions of Title VII of the federal Civil Rights Act of 1964); see also *Cooper v. Eugene Sch. Dist. No. 4J*, 723 P.2d 298, 310 (Or. 1986) (upholding the Oregon religious garb statute as a mechanism for "contributing to the child's right to the free exercise and enjoyment of its religious opinions or heritage, untroubled by being out of step with those of the teacher").

23. The only decision that strikes down a religious garb statute in the United States also involves the Pennsylvania statute. See *Nichol v. ARIN Intermediate Unit 28*, 268 F. Supp. 2d 536, 541 (W.D. Pa. 2003). In Nichol, a federal district court held that the Pennsylvania religious garb statute was unconstitutional as applied to a woman who was suspended for one year for refusing to remove or tuck in a small cross necklace while working as an instructional assistant at a public elementary school. Ibid. The court held that the school's implementation of the state religious garb statute violated the woman's free exercise right because it was "openly and overtly averse to religion because it singled out and punished only symbolic speech by its employees having religious content or viewpoint, while permitting its employees to wear jewelry containing secular messages or no messages at all." Ibid. at 548. The court concluded that the policy also violated the free speech provision of the First Amendment because it was "a content driven regulation which violated plaintiff's right to free (symbolic or expressive) speech on a matter of public concern." Ibid. The court rejected the school board's Establishment Clause concerns, largely because of the inconspicuous nature of the employee's necklace. Ibid. at 553–54.

24. In the United States, several organizations sponsor or support the exploration of Islamic jurisprudence, including but not limited to the Fiqh Council of North America (FCNA), the Council of Shia Muslim Scholars of North America, and Karamah: Muslim Women Lawyers for Human Rights (which touts gender-equitable Islamic jurisprudence).

25. Azizah Y. Al-Hibri, "An Introduction to Muslim Women's Rights," in *Windows of Faith: Muslim Women Scholar-Activists in North America*, ed. Gisela Webb (Syracuse, N.Y.: Syracuse University Press, 2000).

26. Models of a Muslim marriage contract that would serve these purposes can be found on the Web site of Karamah, a Muslim women's human rights organization in the United States: http://www.karamah.org. See also the Muslim Women's League, at http://www.mwlusa.org.

27. *Odatalla v. Odatalla*, 355 N.J. Super. Ct. 305, 810 A.2d 93 (Ch. Div. 2002).

28. *Habibi-Fahnrich v. Fahnrich*, No. 46186/93, 1995 WL 507388 at *1–3 (N.Y. Sup. Ct., July 10, 1995).

29. *In Re. Marriage of Shaban*, 105 Cal. Rptr. 2d 863 (Cal. Ct. App. 2001).

30. *Jabri v. Quaddura*, 108 S.W. 3d. 404 (Tex. Ct. App. 2003).

31. *Chaudry v. Chaudry*, 388 A.2d 1000 (N.J. Super.Ct. App. Div. 1978).

32. The term *womanist* was developed by women of color, specifically by African American women, as an alternative to the word *feminist*, which some felt had focused specifically on oppression experienced by white, middle-class women. A womanist theology has developed out of the history of black theology in the United States, seeking to make sense out of the black female experience in the United States. Some Muslim thinkers explore the racial dimensions of their position.

33. Asma Barlas, "Qur'anic Hermeneutics and Sexual Politics," *Cardozo Law Review* 28 (2006): 143–51.

34. Qudsia Mirza, "Islamic Feminism and Gender Equality," *ISIM Review (International Institute for the Study of Islam in the Modern World)* 21 (2008): 30.

35. See Hassan's article titled "Are Human Rights Compatible with Islam?" http://www.religiousconsultation.org/hassan2.htm (accessed November 3, 2008).

36. Citations from *Zakiyyah Muhammad, Plaintiff and Respondent, v. Islamic Society of Orange County et al., Defendants and Appellants*, No, G036534, G036986, and G037172, 2008 Cal.Ct. App. LEXIS 2693, at *44–47 (Cal. App. March 28, 2008).

37. Ibid., 49.

38. Cited in ibid., 51.

39. Ibid., 31–32.

EPILOGUE

1. Ihsan Yilmaz, *Muslim Laws*, and Mona Siddiqi, "When Politics Fails: Global Politics and the Study of Religion," *Journal of the American Academy of Religion* 73 (2005): 1141–53.

2. Ramadan, *Western Muslims*, 35.

3. Ihsan Yilmaz, *Muslim Laws*, 43.

4. Ramadan, *Western Muslims*, 48.

5. See Muhammad Khalid Masud, "Muslim Jurists' Quest for the Normative Basis of Shari'a" (inaugural lecture, International Institute for the Study of Islam in the Modern World, Leiden University, Leiden, the Netherlands, 2001).

6. Razack, *Casting Out*, 160.

7. The U.S. Supreme Court recently rejected appeals from Muslim men arrested in the aftermath of the 9/11 attacks in a massive sweep. The lawsuit named Attorney General John Ashcroft and FBI director Robert Mueller as codefendants, charging them with ordering the arrest of Muslim men as a category and their confinement under harsh conditions. According to David Savage, the Court refused to hear the appeal on the basis that, according to Justice Stephen Breyer, "if they were looking for suspects from 9/11 . . . it is not surprising that they might look for people who looked like Arabs. That isn't surprising to me because that's what the suspects looked like." Cited in David G. Savage, "Supreme Court Is Asked to Dismiss Top Officials from Lawsuit," *Los Angeles Times*, December 11, 2008, A16.

Bibliography

COURT CASES AND CONGRESSIONAL TESTIMONY

American Civil Liberties Union of North Carolina, Inc., and Syidah Matteen, Plaintifs, v. State of North Carolina, 181 N.C. Ct. App. 430; 639 S.E.2d 136 (N.C. App. 2007).

U.S. House of Representatives. Committee on International Relations. Subcommittee on Africa. *Testimony of Steve Emerson.* 104th Cong, 1st sess., April 6, 1995.

BOOKS AND ARTICLES

Abbas, Tahir. "British Muslim Minorities Today: Challenges and Opportunities to Europeanism, Multiculturalism, and Islamism." *Sociology Compass* 1 (2007): 724.

Abou al-Fadl, Khaled. "Islamic Law and Muslim Minorities: The Juristic Discourse on Muslim Minorities from the Second/Eighth to the Eleventh/Seventeenth Centuries." *Islamic Law and Society* 1 (1994): 141–87.

———. "Legal Debates on Muslim Minorities: Between Rejection and Accommodation." *Journal of Religious Ethics* 22 (1994): 127–62.

———. "Muslim Minorities and Self-Restraint in Liberal Democracies." *Loyola Law Review* 26 (1996): 1525–42.

———. *The Place of Tolerance in Islam.* Edited by Joshua Cohen and Ian Lague. Boston: Beacon Press, 2002.

———. *The Great Theft: Wresting Islam from the Extremists.* New York: HarperSanFrancisco, 2005.

Ahmed, Akbar S., and Donnan Hastings, eds. *Islam, Globalization and Postmodernity.* London: Routledge, 1994.

Ahsan, Manazi. "The Muslim Family in Britain." In *God's Law versus State Law: The Construction of an Islamic Identity in Western Europe*. Edited by Michael King, 21–30. London: Grey Seal, 1995.

Albright, Madeleine. *The Mighty and the Almighty: Reflections on America, God, and Global Affairs*. With the assistance of Bill Woodward. New York: Harper Collins, 2006.

Ali, Amir. "Evolution of Public Sphere in India." *Economic and Political Weekly* 36 (2001): 2419–25.

Allison, Robert J. *The Crescent Obscured: The United States and the Muslim World, 1776–1815*. New York: Oxford University Press, 1995.

An-Na'im, Abdullahi Ahmed. *Toward an Islamic Reformation: Civil Liberties, Human Rights, and International Law*. Syracuse, N.Y.: Syracuse University Press, 1990.

———. *Islam and the Secular State: Negotiating the Future of Shari'a*. Cambridge, Mass.: Harvard University Press, 2008.

Appadurai, Arjun. "Disjuncture and Difference in the Global Cultural Economy." *Public Culture* 2 (1990): 1–24.

———. "Patriotism and Its Futures." Public Culture 5 (1993): 411–29.

———. *Modernity at Large: Cultural Dimensions of Globalization*. Minneapolis: University of Minnesota Press, 1996.

———. *Fear of Small Numbers: An Essay on the Geography of Anger*. Durham, N.C.: Duke University Press, 2006.

Axel, Brian Keith. *The Nation's Tortured Body: Violence, Representation and the Formation of a Sikh "Diaspora."* Durham, N.C.: Duke University Press, 2001.

Azmeh, Aziz al-. *Islams and Modernities*. 2nd ed. London: Verso, 1996.

———. "Afterword." In *Islam in Europe: Diversity, Identity, and Influence*. Edited by Aziz al-Azmeh and Effie Fokas, 208–15. Cambridge, U.K.: Cambridge University Press, 2007.

Bagby, Ihsan. "Imams and Mosque Organizations in the United States: A Study of Mosque Leadership and Organizational Structure in American Mosques." In *Muslims in the United States: Identity, Influence, Innovation*. Edited by Philippa Strum, 19–36. Washington, D.C.: Woodrow Wilson Center, 2006.

Bagby, Ihsan, Paul M. Pearl, and Bryan T. Froehle. *The Mosque in America: A National Portrait*. Washington, D.C.: Council on American-Islamic Relations, 2001. http://www/cairnet/org/mosquereport/Msjid_Study_Project_2000_Report.pdf (accessed September 21, 2006).

Balkin, J. M. *Cultural Software: A Theory of Ideology*. New Haven, C.T.: Yale University Press, 1998.

Ballard, Roger, ed. *Desh Pardesh: The South Asian Presence in Britain*. London: Hurst, 1994.

———. "The Political Economy of Migration: Pakistan, Britain, and the Middle East." In *Migrants, Workers, and the Social Order*. Edited by J. Eades, 17–43. New York: Tavistock, 1997.

Bano, Samia. "Islamic Family Arbitration, Justice, and Human Rights in Britain." *Law, Social Justice, and Global Development Journal* 1 (2007). http://www.go.warwick.ac.uk/elj/lgd/2007_1/bano (accessed December 8, 2008).

———. "In Pursuit of Religious and Legal Diversity: A Response to the Archbishop of Canterbury and the 'Shari'a Debate' in Britain." *Ecclesiastical Law Society* 10 (2008): 283–309.

Barlas, Asma. "Qur'anic Hermeneutics and Sexual Politics." *Cardozo Law Review* 28 (2006): 143–51.

Bartkowski, John P., and Jen'nan Ghazal Read. "Veiled Submission: Gender, Power and Identity among Evangelical and Muslim Women in the United States." *Qualitative Sociology* 26, no. 1 (Spring 2003): 71–92.

Basch, Linda, Nina Glick Schiller, and Cristina Szanton Blanc. *Nations Unbound: Transnational Projects, Postcolonial Predicaments, and Deterritorialized Nation-States.* Langhorne, Pa.: Gordon and Breach, 1994.

Berger, Peter L. *Facing Up to Modernity: Excursions in Society, Politics, and Religion.* New York: Basic Books, 1977.

Berger, Peter L., and Samuel P. Huntington. *Many Globalizations: Cultural Diversity in the Contemporary World.* New York: Oxford University Press, 2002.

Berger, Peter L., and Thomas Luckmann. *The Social Construction of Reality: A Treatise on the Sociology of Knowledge.* New York: Doubleday Anchor Books, 1966.

Bhabha, Homi K. "Cultures In Between." *Artforum* 32 (1993): 167–68.

———. *The Location of Culture.* London: Routledge, 1994.

———. "Anxiety in the Midst of Difference." *PoLAR* 21 (1998): 123–37.

Bhalla, A. S., ed. *Globalization, Growth and Marginalization.* New York: St. Martin's, 1998.

Birt, Jonathan. "Good Imam, Bad Imam: Civic Religion and National Integration in Britain Post-9/11." *Muslim World* 96 (2006): 687–705.

Birt, Yahya. "The Trouble with Shari'a." *Emel Magazine* 42 (2008). http://www.yahyabirt. com/?p=139 (accessed July 23, 2008).

Bowen, John. *Why the French Don't Like Headscarves: Islam, the State and Public Space.* Princeton: Princeton University Press, 2007.

Brigham, John. *The Cult of the Court.* Philadelphia: Temple University Press, 1987.

———. "Right, Rage, and Remedy: Forms of Law in Political Discourse." *Studies in American Political Development* 2 (1988): 303–16.

———. *The Constitution of Interests.* New York: NYU Press, 1996.

Brigham, John, and Kathleen M. Moore. "Domestic Introduction." *Legal Studies Forum* 21 (1997): 403–6.

Brooks, Peter. *Troubling Confessions: Speaking Guilt in Law and Literature.* Chicago: University of Chicago Press, 2000.

Brubaker, R. "The 'Diaspora' Diaspora." *Ethnic and Racial Studies* 28 (2005): 1–19.

Burbach, Roger, Orlando Nunez, and Boris Kagarlitsky. *Globalization and Its Discontents: The Rise of Postmodern Socialisms.* London: Pluto Press, 1997.

Butler, Jon. "Theory and God in Gotham." *History and Theory* 45 (2006): 47–61.

Cainkar, Louise. "The Impact of the September 11th Attacks and Their Aftermath on Arab and Muslim Communities in the United States." *Global Security and Cooperation Quarterly* 13 (2004): 1–21. http://www.ssrc.org/programs/gsc/publications/quarterly13/ cainkar.pdf (accessed September 21, 2006).

Carter, Jimmy. *Our Endangered Values: America's Moral Crisis.* New York: Simon and Schuster, 2005.

Chackrabarty, Dipesh. "Reconstructing Liberalism? Notes toward a Conversation between Area Studies and Diasporic Studies." *Public Culture* 10 (1998): 457–81.

Collins, Eric. "Judge Throws Out Quran Lawsuit."*Greensboro News and Record*, December 9, 2005, A1.

Connolly, William E. *Pluralism*. Durham, N.C.: Duke University Press, 2005.

Council on American Islamic Relations. *A Rush to Judgment: A Special Report on Anti-Muslim Stereotyping, Harassment and Hate Crimes Following the Bombing of Oklahoma City's Murrah Federal Building*. Washington, D.C.: Council on American Islamic Relations, 1995.

———. *The Search for Convenient Scapegoats: The Crash of TWA Flight 800 in the Media*. Washington, D.C.: Council on American Islamic Relations, 1996.

Crary, Alice. "The Happy Truth: J. L. Austin's How to Do Things with Words."*Inquiry* 45 (2002): 59–80.

Daulatzai, Sohail. "Protect Ya Neck: Muslims and the Carceral Imagination in the Age of Guantanamo."*Souls* 9 (2007): 132–47.

De la Campa, Roman. "The Latino Diaspora in the United States: Sojourns from a Cuban Past."*Public Culture* 6 (1994): 293–317.

Derrida, Jacques. *Dissemination*. Translated by Barbara Johnson. Chicago: University of Chicago Press, 1981.

———. *Of Grammatology*. Translated by Gayatri Chakravorty Spivak. Baltimore: Johns Hopkins University Press, 1998. (Orig. pub. 1976.)

Dudrah, Rahinder. "Drum'n'dhol: British Bhangra Music and Diasporic South Asian Identity Formation."*European Journal of Cultural Studies* 5 (2002): 363–83.

Dupret, Baudouin, Barbara Drieskens, and Annelies Moors, eds. *Narratives of Truth in Islamic Law*. London: I. B. Tauris, 2008.

Esposito, John L. *The Islamic Threat: Myth or Reality?* 2nd ed. New York: Oxford University Press, 1995.

Ewick, Patricia, and Susan Silbey. *The Common Place of Law: Stories from Everyday Life*. Chicago: University of Chicago Press, 1998.

Farid, Nadine. "The Faculty Edition: Commemorating Forty Years of Legal Scholarship: Oath and Affirmation in the Court: Thoughts on the Power of a Sworn Promise."*New England Law Review* 40 (2006): 555–62.

Feldman, Noah. *Divided by God: America's Church-State Problem—and What We Should Do about It*. New York: Farrar, Straus and Giroux, 2005.

Fischer, Michael, and Mehdi Abedi. *Debating Muslims: Cultural Dialogues in Postmodernity and Tradition*. Madison: University of Wisconsin Press, 1990.

Fisher, Linda E. "Guilt by Expressive Association: Political Profiling, Surveillance, and the Privacy of Groups."*Arizona Law Review* 46 (2004): 621.

Fitzpatrick, Peter, ed. *Dangerous Supplements: Resistance and Renewal in Jurisprudence*. Durham, N.C.: Duke University Press, 1991.

———. *The Mythology of Modem Law*. London: Routledge, 1992.

Garland, David. *The Culture of Control: Crime and Social Control in a Contemporary Society*. Chicago: University of Chicago Press, 2001.

Gasche, Rodolphe. *The Tain of the Mirror: Derrida and the Philosophy of Reflection*. Cambridge, Mass.: Harvard University Press, 1986.

Ghosh, Amitav. "The Diaspora in Indian Culture."*Public Culture* 2 (1989): 73–78.

Gilbert, Geoff. "The Burgeoning Minority Rights Jurisprudence of the European Court on Human Rights." *Human Rights Quarterly* 24 (2002): 736–80.

Gillespie, Marie. *Ethnicity and Cultural Change*. New York: Routledge, 1995.

Gilroy, Paul. *The Black Atlantic: Modernity and Double Consciousness*. Cambridge, Mass.: Harvard University Press, 1993.

Goldberg, David Theo. "Racial Europeanization." *Ethnic and Racial Studies* 29 (2006): 331–64.

Goldfarb, Zachary A. "Va. Lawmaker's Remarks on Muslims Criticized." *Washington Post*, December 21, 2006, A-11.

Goodrich, Peter, and Yifat Hachamovitch. "Time Out of Mind: An Introduction to the Semiotics of Common Law." In *Dangerous Supplements: Resistance and Renewal in Jurisprudence*. Edited by Peter Fitzpatrick, 159–81. Durham, N.C.: Duke University Press, 1991.

Gopinath, Gayatri. "Bombay, U.K., Yuba City: Bhangra Music and the Engineering of Diaspora." *Diaspora* 4 (1995): 303–21.

Grewal, Inderpal. "The Postcolonial, Ethnic Studies and the Diaspora: The Contexts of Immigrant/Migrant Cultural Studies in the US." *Socialist Review* 24 (1994): 45–74.

———. *Transnational America: Feminisms, Diaspora, Neoliberalisms*. Durham, N.C.: Duke University Press, 2005.

Grewal, Inderpal, and Caren Kaplan, eds. *Scattered Hegemonies: Postmodernity and Transnational Feminist Practices*. Minneapolis: University of Minnesota Press, 1994.

Gupta, Akhil. "The Song of the Nonaligned World: Transnational Identities and the Reinscription of Space in Late Capitalism." *Current Anthropology* 7 (1992): 63–77.

Haddad, Yvonne Yazbeck. "The Challenge of Muslim Minorityness: The American Experience." In *The Integration of Islam and Hinduism in Western Europe*. Edited by W. A. R. Shadid and P. S. van Koningsveld. Kampen, the Netherlands: Kok Publishing, 1991.

———, ed. *The Muslims in America*. New York: Oxford University Press, 1991.

———. "Muslims in U.S. Politics: Recognized and Integrated, or Seduced and Abandoned?" *SAIS Review* 21 (2001): 91–102.

Haddad, Yvonne Yazbeck, and Adair T. Lummis. *Islamic Values in the United States: A Comparative Study*. New York: Oxford University Press, 1987.

Haddad, Yvonne Yazbeck, and Jane Idleman Smith. *Muslim Communities in North America*. Albany: State University of New York Press, 1994.

———. "Adjusting the Tie That Binds: Challenges Facing Muslim Women in America." In *Muslim Women in the United Kingdom and Beyond*. Edited by Tansin Benn and H. A. Jawad, 39–64. Boston: Brill, 2002.

Haddad, Yvonne Yazbeck, Jane Idleman Smith, and Kathleen M. Moore. *Muslim Women in America: The Challenge of Islamic Identity Today*. New York: Oxford University Press, 2006.

Hall, Stuart. "Cultural Identity and Diaspora." In *Colonial Discourse and Post-Colonial Theory: A Reader*. Edited by P. Williams and L. Chrisman, 392–403. New York: Columbia University Press, 1994.

———. "When Was the 'Post-Colonial'? Thinking at the Limit." In *The Post-Colonial Question*. Edited by Iain Chambers and Lidia Curti, 242–60. New York: Routledge, 1996.

Hall, Stuart, Charles Critchter, Tony Jefferson, John Clarke, and Brian Robert. *Policing the Crisis: Mugging, the State, and Law and Order*. New York: Holmes and Meier, 1978.

Halliday, Fred. *Arabs in Exile: Yemeni Migrants in Urban Britain*. London: I. B. Tauris, 1992.

Harnischfeger, Johannes. *Democratization and Islamic Law: The Shari'a Conflict in Nigeria*. Frankfurt, Germany: Campus Verlag, 2008.

Harrington, Christine B., and Barbara Yngvesson. "Diaspora Jurisprudence: The Politics of Native Entitlement." Paper distributed to "Tourist Productions," New York University Seminar, New York, N.Y., October 16, 2001 (on file with author).

Hathout, Maher. *In Pursuit of Justice: The Jurisprudence of Human Rights in Islam*. Los Angeles: Muslim Public Affairs Council, 2006.

Hedges, Chris. "Democrats Won, but Arabs in America Still Suffer from Bush's War on Terror." *AlterNet*, December 6, 2006. http://www.alternet.org/rights/45100/ (accessed December 6, 2006).

Helmreich, Stefan. "Kinship, Nation and Paul Gilroy's Concept of Diaspora." *Diaspora* 2 (1992): 243–49.

Hess, Pamela. "Analysis: Police Take Military Counsel." Los Angeles Police Protective League. http://lapd.com/article.apsx?a=4150 (accessed May 2, 2008).

Hibri, al-, Azizah Y. "An Introduction to Muslim Women's Rights." In *Windows of Faith: Muslim Women Scholar-Activists in North America*. Edited by Gisela Webb. Syracuse, N.Y.: Syracuse University Press, 2000.

Hirsch, Susan F. *Pronouncing and Persevering: Gender and the Discourses of Disputing in an African Islamic Court*. Chicago: University of Chicago Press, 1998.

Hoogvelt, Ankie M. M. *Globalization and the Postcolonial World: The New Political Economy of Development*. Baltimore: Johns Hopkins University Press, 1997.

Hotakainen, Rob, and Brady Averill. "Newcomers Prepare for the 110th Congress." *Star Tribune*, November 13, 2006, 8A.

Human Rights Watch. "'We Are Not the Enemy': Hate Crimes against Arabs, Muslims, and Those Perceived to Be Arab or Muslim after September 11." *Human Rights Watch Monitor* 14 (2002). http://www.hrw.org/en/reports/2002/11/14/we-are-not-enemy (accessed September 10, 2009).

Hunt, Alan. *Explorations in Law and Society: Toward a Constitutive Theory of Law*. London: Routledge, 1993.

Hussain, Serena. *Muslims on the Map: A National Survey of Social Trends in Britain*. London: I. B. Tauris, 2008.

Isin, Engin F., and Myer Siemiatycki. "Making Space for Mosques: Struggles for Urban Citizenship in Diasporic Toronto." In *Race, Space, and the Law: Unmapping a White Settler Society*. Edited by Sherene H. Razack, 185–210. Toronto: Between the Lines, 2002.

Kamali, Mohammed Hassan. "Fiqh and Adaptation to Social Reality." *Muslim World* 86 (1996): 62–84.

Kasim, Husain. *Legitimizing Modernity in Islam: Muslim Modus Vivendi and Western Modernity*. London: Edwin Mellen Press, 2005.

Kerruish, Valerie. *Jurisprudence as Ideology*. London: Routledge, 1991.

Keshavjee, Mohamed. "Alternative Dispute Resolution in a Diasporic Muslim Community in Britain." In *Law and Ethnic Plurality: Socio-Legal Perspectives*. Edited by Prakash Shah, 145–75. Leiden: Martinus Nijhoff, 2007.

Kettani, M. Ali. *Muslim Minorities in the World Today*. London: Mansell Publishing, 1986.

Khalidi, Omar. "Muslim Minorities: Theory and Experience of Muslim Interaction in Non-Muslim Societies." *Journal Institute of Muslim Minority Affairs* 10 (1989): 425–37.

Kibria, Nazli. "The 'New Islam' and Bangladeshi Youth in Britain and the US." *Ethnic and Racial Studies* 31 (2008): 243–66.

Kidd, Thomas S. "Is It Worse to Follow Mahomet Than the Devil? Early American Uses of Islam." *American Society of Church History* 72 (2003): 766–90.

Killian, Caitlin. *North African Women in France: Gender, Culture, and Identity*. Stanford: Stanford University Press, 2006.

King, Michael, ed. *God's Law versus State Law: The Construction of an Islamic Identity in Western Europe*. London: Grey Seal, 1995.

Klausen, Jytte. *The Islamic Challenge: Politics and Religion in Western Europe*. Oxford: Oxford University Press, 2005.

Lavie, Smadar, and Ted Swedenburg, eds. *Displacement, Diaspora and Geographies of Identity*. Durham, N.C.: Duke University Press, 1996.

Layton-Henry, Zig. *The Politics of Immigration: Immigration, 'Race' and 'Race' Relations in Post-War Britain*. Oxford: Blackwell, 1992.

Lewis, Bernard, and Dominique Schnapper, eds. *Muslims in Europe*. London: Pinter, 1994.

Lewis, Philip. *Islamic Britain: Religion. Politics, and Identity among British Muslims*. London: I. B. Tauris, 1994.

———. *Young, British and Muslim*. London: Continuum International, 2007.

Maitra, Priyatosh. *The Globalization of Capitalism in Third World Countries*. Westport, Conn.: Praeger, 1996.

Malik, Maleiha. "Accommodating Muslims in Europe: Opportunities for Minority Fiqh." *ISIM Newsletter* 13 (2003): 10–11.

———. "Speech Control." *Index on Censorship* 36 (2007): 18–21.

Masud, Muhammad Khalid, ed. *Travellers in Faith: Studies of the Tablighi Jama'at as a Transnational Islamic Movement for Faith Renewal*. Leiden: Brill, 2000.

———. "Muslim Jurists' Quest for the Normative Basis of Shari'a." Inaugural lecture, International Institute for the Study of Islam in the Modern World, Leiden University, Leiden, the Netherlands, 2001.

Masud, Muhammad Khalid, Brinkley Messick, and David Powers, eds. *Islamic Legal Interpretation: Muftis and Their Fatwas*. Cambridge, Mass.: Harvard University Press, 1996.

Maurer, Bill. *Pious Property: Islamic Mortgages in the United States*. New York: Russell Sage Foundation, 2006.

Mavroudi, Elizabeth. "Diaspora as Process: (De)constructing boundaries." *Geography Compass* 1 (2007): 467–79.

Mayer, Ann Elizabeth. "Universal versus Islamic Human Rights: A Clash of Cultures or a Clash with a Construct?" *Michigan Journal of International Law* 15 (1994): 307–98.

Mazrui, Ali. "*Shariacracy* and Federal Models in the Era of Globalization: Nigeria in Comparative Perspective." In *Democratic Institution Performance: Research and Policy*

Perspectives. Edited by Edward R. McMahon and Thomas Sinclair, 63–76. Westport, Conn.: Greenwood Publishing, 2002.

McAlister, Elizabeth. *Rara: Vodou, Power and Performance in Haiti and Its Diaspora*. Berkeley: University of California Press, 2002.

———. "Globalization and the Religious Production of Space." *Journal for the Scientific Study of Religion* 44 (2005): 249–55.

McCann, Michael. *Rights at Work: Pay Equity and the Politics of Legal Mobilization*. Chicago: University of Chicago Press, 1994.

Meer, Nasar, and Tehseen Noorani. "A Sociological Comparison of Anti-Semitism and Anti-Muslim Sentiment in Britain." *Sociological Review* 56 (2008): 195–219.

Menski, Werner. *Comparative Law in a Global Context: The Legal Systems of Asia and Africa*. 2nd ed. Cambridge: Cambridge University Press, 2006.

———. "Rethinking Legal Theory in the Light of South-North Migration." In *Migration, Diasporas and Legal Systems in Europe*. Edited by Prakash Shah and Werner Menski, 13–28. London: Routledge-Cavendish, 2006.

Merry, Sally Engle. "Legal Pluralism: Review Essay." *Law and Society Review* 22 (1988): 869–96.

———. *Getting Justice and Getting Even: Legal Consciousness among Working-Class Americans*. Chicago: University of Chicago Press, 1990.

———. "Law, Culture and Cultural Appropriation." *Yale Journal of Law and the Humanities* 10 (1998): 575–603.

Merry, Sally Engle, and Neal Milner, eds. *The Possibility of Popular Justice: A Case Study of Community Mediation in the United States*. Ann Arbor: University of Michigan, 1993.

Mirza, Qudsia. "Islamic Feminism and Gender Equality." *ISIM Review (International Institute for the Study of Islam in the Modern World)* 21 (2008): 30–31.

Mittelman, James H., ed. *Globalization: Critical Reflections*. Boulder, Colo.: Lynne Rienner, 1997.

Modood, Tariq. Multicultural Politics: Racism, Ethnicity, and Muslims in Britain. Minneapolis: University of Minnesota Press, 2005.

Mohanty, Chandra Talpade. *Feminism without Borders: Decolonizing Theory, Practicing Solidarity*. Durham, N.C.: Duke University Press, 2003.

Moore, Erin P. *Gender, Law and Resistance in India*. Tucson, Ariz.: University of Arizona Press, 1998.

Moore, Kathleen M. *Al-Mughtaribun: American Law and the Transformation of Muslim Life in the United States*. Albany, N.Y.: State University of New York Press, 1995.

———. "The Hijab and Religious Liberty: U.S. Anti-Discrimination Law and Muslim Women in the United States." In *Muslims on the Americanization Path?* Edited by Yvonne Y. Haddad and John L. Esposito, 129–58. Atlanta: Scholars Press, 1998.

———. "Legal Pluralism in Britain: The Rights of Muslims after the Rushdie Affair." In *Europe's Other: European Union Law between Modernity and Postmodernity*. Edited by Peter Fitzpatrick and James Henry Bergeron. London and Aldershot, U.K.: Dartmouth/Ashgate Publishing, 1998.

———. "Representations of Islam in the Language of the Law: Some Recent U.S. Cases." In *Muslims in the West: From Sojourners to Citizens*. Edited by Yvonne Yazbeck Haddad, 187–204. New York: Oxford University Press, 2002.

———. "United We Stand: American Attitudes toward (Muslim) Immigration Post-9/11." *Muslim World* 92 (2002): 39–58.

———. "Anti-Muslim Discrimination and Violence." In *Social Issues in America: An Encyclopedia*. Edited by James Ciment, 140–51. New York: M. E. Sharpe, 2006.

———. "Muslims in the United States: Pluralism under Exceptional Circumstances." *Annals of the American Academy of Political and Social Sciences* 612 (2007): 116–32.

Moore, Kathleen M., and Stephen R. Pelletier. "Weaving New Fabric: The Challenge of Immigration for Muslim-Christian Relations." *Islam and Christian-Muslim Relations* 10 (1999): 177–96.

Narayan, Vma. "Essence of Culture and a Sense of History: A Feminist Critique of Cultural Essentialism." *Hypatia* 13 (1998): 86–106.

Nielsen, Jorgen. *Muslims in Western Europe*. 2nd ed. Edinburgh: University of Edinburgh Press, 1995.

Nielsen, Laura Beth. *License to Harass: Law, Hierarchy, and Offensive Public Speech*. Princeton: Princeton University Press, 2004.

Nimer, Mohamed. "The Muslim Experience of Discrimination in the United States." *Journal of Islamic Law* 2 (1997): 21–44.

———. "American Muslim Organizations: Before and After 9/11." In *Muslims in the United States: Identity, Influence, Innovation*. Edited by Philippa Strum, 5–18. Washington, D.C.: Woodrow Wilson Center, 2006.

Nisbet, Erik C., and James Shanahan. *MSRG Special Report: Restrictions on Civil Liberties, Views of Islam, and Muslim Americans*. Ithaca, N.Y.: Cornell University, Media and Society Research Group, 2004. http://www.comm.cornell.edu/msrg/report1a.pdf (accessed March 12, 2006).

Nomani, Asra. *Standing Alone in Mecca: An American Woman's Struggle for the Soul of Islam*. San Francisco: HarperSanFrancisco, 2005.

Nyang, Sulayman S. "Seeking the Religious Roots of Pluralism in the United States of America: An American Muslim Perspective." *Journal of Ecumenical Studies* 34 (1997): 402–18.

———. *Islam in the United States of America*. Chicago: ABC International Group, Inc., 1999.

Ong, Aihwa. *Flexible Citizenship: The Cultural Logics of Transnationality*. Durham, N.C.: Duke University Press, 1999.

———. *The Buddha Is Hiding: Refugees, Citizenship, and the New America*. Berkeley: University of California Press, 2003.

Page, Clarence. "No 'American' Holy Book." *Chicago Tribune*, December 11, 2006, Commentary Section, 21.

Parrott, Stuart. "Europe: Britain's Muslim Leader Opposes Joining a Federal Europe." *Radio Free Europe/Radio Liberty*, January 20, 1998. http://rferl.org/nca/features/1998/F. RU.980120141016.html (accessed December 11, 2008).

Patel, Eboo. *Acts of Faith: The Story of an American Muslim, the Struggle for a Soul of a Generation*. Boston: Beacon, 2007.

Patel, Eboo, and Patrice Brodeur, eds. *Building the Interfaith Youth Movement: Beyond Dialogue to Action*. Lanham, Md.: Rowman and Littlefield, 2006.

Pearl, David, and Werner Menski. *Muslim Family Law*. 3rd ed. London: Sweet and Maxwell, 1998.

Peek, Lori. "Becoming Muslim: The Development of a Religious Identity." *Sociology of Religion* 66 (2005): 215–42.

Pew Forum on Religion and Public Life. "Muslim Americans: Middle Class and Mostly Mainstream." Washington, D.C.: Pew Research Center, May 22, 2007. http://pewresearch.org/assets/pdf/muslim-americans.pdf (accessed June 10, 2007).

Prager, Dennis. "America, Not Keith Ellison, Decides What Book a Congressman Takes His Oath On." *Townhall*, November 28, 2006. http://www.townhall.com/columnists/ DennisPrager/2006/11/28/america,_not_keith_ellison,_decides_what_book_a_ congressman_takes_his_oath_on (accessed July 13, 2007).

Radhakrishnan, R. *Diasporic Mediations: Between Home and Location*. Minneapolis: University of Minnesota Press, 1996.

Ramadan, Tariq. *To Be a European Muslim: A Study of Islamic Sources in the European Context*. Leicester, U.K.: Islamic Foundation, 1999.

———. *Western Muslims and the Future of Islam*. Oxford: Oxford University Press, 2004.

Razack, Sherene H. *Casting Out: The Eviction of Muslims from Western Law and Politics*. Toronto, Canada: University of Toronto Press, 2008.

Reis, Michele. "Theorizing Diaspora: Perspectives on "Classical" and "Contemporary" Diaspora." *International Migration* 42 (2004): 41–60.

Rex, John. "Integration in Urban Britain." *Dialogue* (April 2001): 6.

Riley, Rochelle. "Be America and End Religious Hypocrisy." *Detroit Free Press*, January 5, 2007, 9-A.

Roof, Wade Clark. "Pluralism as a Culture: Religion and Civility in Southern California." *Annals of the American Academy of Political and Social Sciences* 612 (2007): 82–101.

Safran, William. "Diasporas in Modern Societies: Myths of Homeland and Return," *Diaspora* 1 (1991): 83–84.

Said, Edward. *Orientalism*. London: Vintage Books, 1979.

Santos, Bonaventura de Sousa. *Toward a New Common Sense: Law, Science, and Politics in Paradigmatic Transition*. London: Routledge, 1997.

Sassen, Saskia. *Globalization and Its Discontents: The New Mobility of Money and People*. New York: New Press, 1999.

Savage, David G. "Supreme Court Is Asked to Dismiss Top Officials from Lawsuit." *Los Angeles Times*, December 11, 2008, A16.

Schmidt, Garbi. *Islam in Urban America: Sunni Muslims in Chicago*. Philadelphia: Temple University Press, 2004.

Schutte, Ofelia. "Cultural Alterity: Cross-Cultural Communication and Feminist Theory in North-South Contexts." *Hypatia* 13 (1998): 53–72.

Shah, Prakash. *Legal Pluralism in Conflict: Coping with Cultural Diversity in Law*. London: Glass House (Cavendish), 2005.

———, ed. *Law and Ethnic Plurality: Socio-Legal Perspectives*. Leiden: Martinus Nijhoff, 2007.

Shah, Prakash, and Werner Menski, eds. *Migration, Diasporas, and Legal Systems in Europe*. New York: Routledge-Cavendish, 2006.

Shah-Kazemi, Sonia Nurin. *Untying the Knot: Muslim Women, Divorce and Shariah.* London: Nuffield Foundation, 2001.

Shahidian, Hammed. "Saving the Savior."*Sociological Inquiry* 69 (1999): 303–27.

Siddiqi, Mona. "When Politics Fails: Global Politics and the Study of Religion."*Journal of the American Academy of Religion* 73 (2005): 1141–53.

Siddiqui, Ataullah. "Ethics in Islam: Key Concepts and Contemporary Challenges."*Journal of Moral Education* 26 (1997): 423–31.

Silbey, Susan S. "Let Them Eat Cake: Globalization, Postmodern Colonialism, and the Possibility of Justice."*Law and Society Review* 21 (1997): 207–36.

Simon, Jonathan, Governing through Crime: How the War on Crime Transformed American Democracy and Created a Culture of Fear. New York: Oxford University Press, 2007.

Smith, Jane I. *Islam in America.* New York: Columbia University Press, 1999.

———. "Does Islam Encourage Pluralism? American Muslims Engage the Debate." In *Muslims in the United States: Identity, Influence, Innovation.* Edited by Philippa Strum, 165–79. Washington, D.C.: Woodrow Wilson Center, 2006.

Smith, Neil. "The Satanic Geographies of Globalization: Uneven Development in the 1990s."*Public Culture* 10 (1997): 169–89.

Smith, Tom W. "Estimating the Muslim Population in the United States." American Jewish Committee, Global Jewish Advocacy 2001. http://www.ajc.org/site/apps/nl/content3.asp?c=ijITI2PHKoG&b=843637&ct=1044159 (accessed September 2, 2009).

———. "The Muslim Population of the United States: The Methodology of Estimates."*Public Opinion Quarterly* 66 (2002): 404–17.

Sonbol, Amira el-Azhary, ed. *Women, the Family and Divorce Laws in Islamic History.* Syracuse, N.Y.: Syracuse University Press, 1996.

Spellberg, Denise A. "Could a Muslim Be President? An Eighteenth Century Constitutional Debate."*Eighteenth Century Studies* 39, no. 4 (2006): 485–506.

Spencer, Robert. *Islam Unveiled: Disturbing Questions about the World's Fastest-Growing Faith.* San Francisco: Encounter Books, 2002.

———. *The Politically Incorrect Guide to Islam (and the Crusades).* Washington, D.C.: Regnery Publishing, 2005.

Spencer, Sarah. *Migrants, Refugees, and the Boundaries of Citizenship.* Swansea, U.K.: Institute for Public Policy Research and the University of Wales, Swansea, 1955.

Spivak, Gayatri Chakravorty. "Subaltern Studies: Deconstructing Historiography." In *Selected Subaltern Studies.* Edited by Ranajit Guha and Gayatri Chakravorty Spivak, 193–227. New York: Oxford University Press, 1988.

Strum, Philippa, and Danielle Tarantolo, eds. *Muslims in the United States.* Washington, D.C.: Woodrow Wilson International Center for Scholars, 2003.

Swarnes, Rachel L. "Congressman Criticizes Election of Muslim."*New York Times,* December 21, 2006, 31.

Swirko, Cindy. "Middle School Suspends Muslim Student."*Gainesville Sun,* October 1, 1998, A-8.

Tamimi, Azzam al-. "Nahwa Muntalaqat Insanivva Ii al-Ta'amull rna' al-Mujtama' al Gharbi."*Al-Mujtama'* 26, no. 1182 (January 2–8, 1996): 44–48. (Text of speech also on file with the author.)

———. Interview by Grace Halsell. *Washington Report on Middle East Affairs*, December 1998, 23–24.

Taylor, Charles. *Multiculturalism and "The Politics of Recognition": An Essay*. With a commentary by Amy Gutmann. Princeton: Princeton University Press, 1992.

Thomas, Ed. "No. Carolina Courtroom Oaths Expanded beyond Bible."*OneNewsNow*, June 8, 2007.

Tololyan, Khachig. "Rethinking Diaspora(s): Stateless Power in the Transnational Moment."*Diaspora* 5 (1996): 3–36.

Tweed, Thomas A. Our Lady of Exile: Diasporic Religion at a Cuban Catholic Shrine in Miami. New York: Oxford University Press, 1997.

Vertovec, Steven. "Three Meanings of 'Diaspora,' Exemplified among South Asian Religions."*Diaspora* 6, no. 3 (1997): 277–99.

Vertovec, Steven, and Ceri Peach, eds. *Islam in Europe: The Politics of Religion and Community*. London: Macmillan, 1997.

Vertovec, Steven, and Alisdair Rogers, eds. *Muslim European Youth: Reproducing Ethnicity, Religion and Culture*. Aldershot, U.K.: Ashgate, 1998.

Visweswaran, Kamala. "Diaspora by Design: Flexible Citizenship and South Asians in U.S. Racial Formations."*Diaspora* 6 (1977): 5–30.

Wadud, Amina. "Alternative Qur'anic Interpretation and the Status of Muslim Women." In *Windows of Faith: Muslim Women Scholar-Activists in North America*. Edited by Gisela Webb, 3–21. Syracuse, N.Y.: Syracuse University Press, 2000.

Waldinger, Roger, and David Fitzgerald. "Transnationalism in Question."*American Journal of Sociology* 109, no. 5 (March 2004): 1177–95.

Warner, Stephen R., and Judith G. Wittner, eds. *Gatherings in Diaspora: Religious Communities and the New Immigration*. Philadelphia: Temple University Press, 1998.

Watts, James W. "Ten Commandments Monuments and the Rivalry of Iconic Texts."*Journal of Religion and Society* 6 (2004): 1–12.

Werbner, Pnina. "Public Spaces, Political Voices: Gender, Feminism and Aspects of British Muslim Participation in the Public Sphere." In *Political Participation and Identities of Muslims in Non-Muslim States*. Edited by W. A. R. Shadid and P. S. Van Koningsveld, 53–70. Kampen, the Netherlands: Kok Pharos, 1996.

———. "The Place Which Is Diaspora: Citizenship, Religion and Gender in the Making of Chaordic Transnationalism."*Journal of Ethnic and Migration Studies* 28 (2002): 119–33.

———. "Islamophobia: Incitement to Religious Hatred—Legitimizing a New Fear?"*Anthropology Today* 21, no. 1 (2005): 5–9.

Werbner, Pnina, and Tariq Modood, eds. *Debating Cultural Hybridity: Multi-Cultural Identities and the Politics of Anti-Racism*. London: Zed Books, 1997.

Williams, Rowan. "Civil and Religious Law in England: A Religious Perspective."*Ecclesiastical Law Society* 10 (2008): 262–75.

Yilmaz, Ihsan. *Muslim Laws, Politics and Society in Modern Nation States: Dynamic Legal Pluralisms in England, Turkey and Pakistan*. Aldershot, U.K.: Ashgate, 2005.

Yngvesson, Barbara. *Virtuous Citizens, Disruptive Subjects: Order and Complaint in a New England Court*. New York: Routledge, 1993.

Index